Joseph Priestley

An History of Early Opinions Concerning Jesus Christ

Vol. 3

Joseph Priestley

An History of Early Opinions Concerning Jesus Christ
Vol. 3

ISBN/EAN: 9783337766863

Printed in Europe, USA, Canada, Australia, Japan

Cover: Foto ©Lupo / pixelio.de

More available books at **www.hansebooks.com**

AN
HISTORY
OF
EARLY OPINIONS
CONCERNING
JESUS CHRIST,

COMPILED FROM

ORIGINAL WRITERS;

PROVING THAT THE CHRISTIAN CHURCH WAS
AT FIRST UNITARIAN.

By JOSEPH PRIESTLEY, LL.D. F.R.S

AC. IMP. PETROP. R. PARIS. HOLM. TAURIN. AUREL. MED.
PARIS. CANTAB. AMERIC. ET PHILAD. SOCIUS.

VOL. III.

Id verum quodcunque primum, id adulterum quodcunque posterius. TERTULLIAN.

Ει μεν εβυλουίο παυίες, εφ' ας το ονομα τυ θευ και σωίηρος ημων Ιησυ χριτυ επικεκλησαι, μηδεν τη αληθεια τυ ευαγγελιυ παρεγχωρειν, τη δε παραδοσει των αποτολων, και τη απλοίηίι της πιςεως εξαρκεισθαι, υδεν αν ημιν εδει λογων εν τω παρουίι. BASIL.

BIRMINGHAM,
PRINTED FOR THE AUTHOR, BY PEARSON AND ROLLASON;
AND SOLD BY J. JOHNSON, NO. 72, ST. PAUL'S
CHURCH-YARD, LONDON.
MDCCLXXXVI.

CONTENTS

OF THE THIRD VOLUME.

BOOK III.

THE History of the Unitarian Doctrine. Page 1

Introduction. ibid

CHAPTER I.

That the Jews in all Ages were Believers in the Divine Unity. 7

SECTION I.

The Fact acknowledged by the Christian Fathers. 9

SECTION II.

Of the Reasons why, according to the Christian Fathers, the Doctrine of the Trinity was not discovered to the Jews. 18

SECTION III.

The Sentiments of the Jews, as expressed by themselves, on the Subject. 26

SECTION IV.

Of the Jewish Angel METATRON, *&c.* 40

CHAPTER II.

General Considerations relating to the supposed Conduct of Christ and the Apostles, with Respect to the Doctrines of his Pre-existence and Divinity. 50

CHAPTER III.

Of the Conduct of our Saviour himself with respect to his own supposed Pre-existence and Divinity. 64

CHAPTER IV.

Of the Testimony of Athanasius to the Caution with which the Apostles divulged the Doctrines of the Pre-existence and Divinity of Christ. 86

CHAPTER V.

Of the concurrent Testimony of other Fathers to the Caution of the Apostles, in teaching the Doctrines of the Pre-existence and Divinity of Christ. 101

CONTENTS.

CHAPTER VI.

Of the Caution observed by the Apostles in teaching the Doctrines of the Pre-existence and Divinity of Christ to the Gentile Converts. 113

CHAPTER VII.

Of John being thought to have been the first who clearly and boldly taught the Doctrines of the Pre-existence and Divinity of Christ. 123

SECTION I.

The Acknowledgments of the Christian Fathers that John was the first who taught the Doctrines above-mentioned. 125

SECTION II.

Reflections on the Subject 148

CHAPTER VIII.

Of the Nazarenes and the Ebionites; shewing that they were the same People, and that none of them believed the Divinity or Pre-existence of Christ. 158

CHAPTER IX.

Of the supposed Church of Orthodox Jews at Jerusalem, subsequent to the Time of Adrian. 190

CHAPTER X.

Of the supposed Heresy of the Ebionites and Nazarenes, and other Particulars relating to them. Page 201

CHAPTER XI.

Of the sacred Books of the Ebionites. 212

CHAPTER XII.

Of Men of Eminence among the Jewish Christians. 219

CHAPTER XIII.

Unitarianism was the Doctrine of the primitive Gentile Churches. 233

SECTION I.

Presumptive Evidence that the Majority of the Gentile Christians in the early Ages were Unitarians. 235

SECTION II.

Direct evidence in Favour of the Gentile Christians having been generally Unitarians. 258

CHAPTER XIV.

An Argument for the Novelty of the Doctrine of the Trinity, from the Manner in which it was taught and received in early Times. 272

CONTENTS.

CHAPTER XV.

Objections to the preceding State of Things considered. Page 295

SECTION I.

Of the Testimony of Eusebius to the Novelty of the Unitarian Doctrine. ibid

SECTION II.

Of the Excommunication of Theodotus by Victor. 303

SECTION III.

Of the Part taken by the Laity in the Excommunication of the early Unitarians, and other Considerations relating to the Subject. 308

CHAPTER XVI.

Of the State of the Unitarian Doctrine after the Council of Nice. 318

SECTION I.

Of the State of the Unitarians from the Time of the Council of Nice, to the sixth Century. 322

SECTION II.

Of the State of the Unitarians after the sixth Century. 364

CHAPTER XVII.

Of Philosophical Unitarianism   Page 376

CHAPTER XVIII.

Of the Principles and Arguments of the ancient Unitarians.   399

SECTION I.

Their Zeal for the Divine Unity, and their Sense of the Word Logos.   ibid.

SECTION II.

Arguments of the ancient Unitarians from Reason.   415

SECTION III.

Arguments of the ancient Unitarians from the Scriptures.   423

CHAPTER XIX.

Of the Practice of the Unitarians with respect to Baptism.   439

ERRATA.

N. B. (*b*) signifies *from the bottom of the page.*

Page 20. line 4. for in some places, read, to some persons
—— ibid. line 5. for in, read to
—— 136. line 1. for himself, read him
—— 154. line 15. for with, read of
—— 264. line 5. for logos, read the logos
—— 277. line 9. (*b*) for which, read in which
—— 292. line 11. for it, read them
—— 295. line 4. (*b*) for by, read that
—— 347. line 6. for his, read their
—— 422. line 1. (*b*) for unto, read into

REFERENCES.

Page 140. line 3. for κοφορειται, read κυφορειται
—— 207. line 3. for πιευματα, read πνευμα
—— 261. note * line 4. read αιτελευθιον αυτω

THE HISTORY OF OPINIONS

CONCERNING

CHRIST.

BOOK III.

THE HISTORY OF THE UNITARIAN DOCTRINE.

INTRODUCTION.

AFTER the view that has been given of the rife and progrefs of the doctrine of the *trinity*, which fprung from the abfurdity and myftery of Platonifm, and terminated in a myftery ftill more unintelligible and abfurd, in which every thing that is fimple and excellent in chriftianity was wholly fwallowed up and loft, and a polytheifm little better than that of the heathens took its place (for the worship of Chrift led to that of the virgin Mary, and a thoufand other perfons, called *faints*) it is with peculiar fatisfaction that I proceed to give an account of the doctrine of the *divine unity,* or *the Hiftory of Unitarianifm.*

If I had not given what I imagine will appear to be a fatisfactory account of the rife of *chriftian idolatry,* it might have appeared a very extraordinary and unaccountable thing; confidering that the Jews, from whom the chriftians fprung, were all zealous unitarians in the time of our Saviour, and that they have continued fuch to this day. It even appears to have been the great object of the Jewifh religion, as contained in the books of Mofes, to preferve in the world the knowledge and worfhip of the one true God, notwithftanding the univerfal tendency to polytheifm among all nations, in the early ages.

The doctrine of one great omniprefent being, the maker, and the immediate governor of all things, was too great and fublime, I do not only fay, to have been *difcovered*

covered by mankind, but even to be *retained* by any of them, after it was revealed, without particular provisions for that purpose. Though, I have no doubt, but that the first parents of the human race were instructed in the knowledge of the divine unity, their posterity soon adopted the notion of different gods, to whom they imagined the government of the world was delegated; and their attention to these inferior deities, on whom they thought that they more immediately depended, withdrew their attention, as it naturally would, from the supreme God, under whom they at first supposed that these lesser gods had acted. Then, being left to their own imaginations with respect to the *characters* of these gods, and having no models by which to frame them besides beings like themselves, they presently conceived them to be of very different dispositions, some of them cruel and base, and others lewd; and of course delighting in cruel, base, and lewd actions. To procure the favour, or to avert the displeasure, of these gods, they would,

would, therefore, practice many abominable, horrid, and atrocious rites.

The religious ceremonies, and the general character and practice of the heathen world, abundantly prove, that idolatry was not a mere speculative mistake, a thing only foolish and absurd, but of a very serious and alarming nature; and that it was therefore nothing that could be called *jealousy* in the true God, to take such extraordinary measures as the history of revelation represents him to have taken, in order to cure mankind of their proneness to idolatrous worship. It was a part which it became the supreme God, the benevolent parent of all his offspring, to take, and what a regard to their own happiness required. The mischief was of so alarming a nature, that the greatest severities were necessary, and therefore *proper*, to be employed for this purpose; and they must know nothing of the nature and tendency of the ancient idolatry, who find any thing to censure in the severity with which the Israelites were ordered to act, with a view to the extirpation of of it from among themselves, or the nations inhabiting the diftrict that was deftined for them.

It is not poffible to imagine any inftructions, or regulations, more proper to effect the extirpation of idolatry, and to guard the people from it, than the laws of Mofes, interpreted by his repeated and earneft remonftrances on the fubject with refpect to the Ifraelites. Let the reader only perufe the book of Deuteronomy, and then form his judgment. And yet, fo feducing were the idolatrous cuftoms of thofe times, that their whole hiftory fhews how prone the Jews always were to abandon their own purer religion, and more fimple rites, though, to appearance, fufficiently fplendid, and having little of aufterity in them. For they had only one faft day in the whole year, and three great feftivals.

But the intention of the Divine Being, was equally anfwered by the obedience or the difobedience of that people; and after a feries of difcipline, they returned from the captivity of Babylon, with *a new heart and a new spirit,* in this respect. For they never discovered the least proneness to idolatry afterwards; but, on the contrary, always shewed the most scrupulous dread and jealousy on this subject. Nay, to a neglect of their religion, there succeeded the most superstitious attention to the smallest punctilios relating to it.

CHAPTER I.

That the Jews in all Ages were Believers in the Divine Unity..

IT is impossible to read the sacred books of the Jews (with minds freed from the strongest prejudices) without perceiving that the doctrine of the *divine unity* is most rigorously inculcated in them. It is the uniform language of those books, that one God, without any assistant, either equal or subordinate to himself, made the world, and all things in it, and that this one God continues to direct all the affairs of men.

This is so evident from the bare inspection of the books, and the well known principles of the Jews in our Saviour's time, that even the christian Fathers, desirous as they were to find advocates for their doctrine of the trinity, and pressing even Platonism into the service, could not but allow it. They ransacked every part of the Old Testament,

Testament, as we have seen, for proofs, or intimations, of the doctrine of the trinity, or of the divinity of Christ; but, though they imagined they found many such, yet they always acknowledged that the doctrines were delivered so obscurely, that the bulk of the Jewish nation had not perceived them.

They thought, indeed, that Moses himself, and the prophets, were acquainted with these doctrines; but that there were good reasons why they did not endeavour to make them intelligible to the rest of their countrymen; partly, lest it should have hindered the operation of their religion to divert them from idolatry, and partly, because the doctrines were too sublime to be communicated at so early a period, and before men's minds were properly prepared for them.

SECTION I.

The Fact acknowledged by the Christian Fathers.

AS these concessions are of considerable consequence to my argument, I shall produce a number of them, from the earliest christian writers to a pretty late period, to shew that it was the uniform persuasion of all those who were the greatest friends to the doctrine of the trinity.

I shall begin with Justin Martyr, the first who advanced the doctrine of the personification of the logos. What the Jews thought of their Messiah in his time, appears very clearly from a passage in his dialogue with Trypho, which will be produced hereafter. In the mean time, I shall give his opinion with respect to the doctrine of the Jews in general on the subject. " The Jews," he says, " thinking it was " the Father of all who spake to Moses, " when it was the Son of God, who is " also

" also called an angel, and an apostle, are
" justly censured by the Spirit of God, and
" by Christ, as not knowing either him or
" his Father *."

Clemens Alexandrinus considered the doctrine of the œconomy (or that of the incarnation of the logos) to be the doctrine of the *perfect,* alluded to by Paul in his epistle to the Colossians, where he speaks of their being *filled with the knowledge of his will,* and of the *mystery which was hid from ages and generations, but now made manifest to the saints,* " so that there are other mys-
" teries," he says, " which were hid till
" the times of the apostles, and delivered
" by them as they received them from the
" Lord†." In another passage he speaks

---

* Ιϰδαιοι ϰν ηγησαμενοι αει τον πατερα των ολων λελαληκεναι τω Μωσει, τϰ λαλησαντ۞ αυτω οντ۞ υιε τϰ θεϰ, ος ϰ) αγγελ۞ ϰ) αποστολ۞ κεκληται, δικαιως ελεγχονται ϰ) δια τϰ προφητικϰ πνευματ۞, ϰ) δι αυτϰ τϰ χριϛϰ, ως ϰτε τον πατερα, ϰτε τον υιον εγνωσαν. Apol. 1. p. 94.

† Το μυϛηριον το αποκεκρυμμενον απο των αιωνων ϰ) απο των γενεων, ο νυν εφανερωθη τοις αγιοις αυτϰ. οις ηθελησεν ο θεος γνωρισαι, τι το πλϰτ۞ της δοξης τϰ μυϛηριϰ τϰτϰ εν τοις εθνεσιν. ωϛε αλλα μεν τα μυϛηρια τα αποκεκρυμμενα αχρι των αποϛολων, ϰ) υπ αυτων παραδοϑεντα ως απο τϰ κυριϰ παρειληφασιν. Strom. lib. 5. p. 576.

of this œconomy as what chriſtians only were acquainted with*.

Tertullian had the ſame ideas. "I adore," ſays he, "the fulneſs of the ſcriptures," meaning thoſe of the Old Teſtament, "which manifeſt the maker and the things made; but in the goſpel I find the miniſter, or the perſon by whom it was made, and the judge, viz. the word of the maker †." "It is the faith of the Jews ſo to believe in one God, as not to acknowledge the Son, or the Spirit.— What is the difference between us and them, but this? What need is there of the goſpel, which is the ſubſtance of the New Teſtament (ſaying, that *the law and the prophets were until John*) if from that period the Father, Son, and Spirit, being three, are not believed to make one God.

---

* Ημεις εσμεν —— οι την οικονομιαν τȣ Θεȣ κατανενοηκοτες. Ad Gentes, Opera, p. 40.

† Igitur in principio deus fecit cœlum et terram. Adoro ſcripturæ plenitudinem, quæ mihi et factorem manifeſtat et facta. In evangelio vero amplius et miniſtrum atque arbitrum rectoris invenio ſermonem. Ad Herm. ſect. 22. Opera, p. 241.

"So

"So God would renew his covenant, that,
"in a new manner, he should be believed
"in, together with the Son, and his Spirit;
"that God may be known in his proper
"names and persons *."

"The Jews," says Hippolytus, "ho-
"noured the Father, but they did not give
"thanks; for they knew not the Son †."

Origen also says, "the Jews were not
"acquainted with the incarnation of the
"only begotten Son of God ‡."

Eusebius speaks of the christians as differing from the Hebrews, in that the latter

---

* Judaicæ fidei ista res, sic unum deum credere, ut filium adnumerare ei nolis, et post filium spiritum. Quid enim erit inter nos et illos, nisi differentia ista? Quod opus evangelii, quæ est substantia novi testamenti, statuens legem et prophetas usque ad Joannem, si non exinde pater et filius et spiritus, tres crediti, unum deum sistunt? Sic deus voluit novare sacramentum, ut nove unus crederetur per filium et spiritum, ut coram jam deus in suis propriis nominibus et personis cognosceretur, qui et retro per filium et spiritum prædicatus non intelligebatur. Ad Praxeam, sect. 30. Opera, p. 518.

† Ιουδαιοι μεν γαρ εδοξασαν πατερα αλλ' ουκ ηυχαριστησαν υιον γαρ ουκ επεγνωσαν. In Noetum, sect. 14. Opera, p. 16.

‡ Deerat enim illis in trinitate etiam de unigeniti incarnatione cognoscere. Opera, vol. 1. p. 290.

did not acknowledge the divinity of Christ*. He considered the doctrine of the divinity of Christ as peculiar to christians, and distinguishing them from Jews. " If any " Jew," says he, " be asked, whether God " has a *logos*, he will say, certainly. Every " Jew will say, that he has one, or more of " them; but if he be asked whether he has " *a Son*, he will not acknowledge it †."

Cyril of Jerusalem says, " In this respect " our doctrine is more sublime than that of " the Jews, in that they acknowledge one " God the Father, but do not admit that he " is the Father of our Lord Jesus Christ, " in which they contradict their own pro- " phets, who say, in the scriptures, *The* " *Lord said unto me, thou art my Son, this* " *day have I begotten thee* ‡." Cyril of

---

* Μηΐε την θεοίηία συνορωνίες αυΐα. Demonstratio, lib. 4. cap. 1. p. 144.

† Ει γεν τις Ιεδαιων εροιΐο τινα, ει λογον εχοι ο θεος; παντως πε φησει· επει κ) λογον, κ) λογες πλειες εχειν αυΐον, ομολογησειεν, αν, Ιεδαιος ων, απας. ει δε κ) υιον εχει· εκ ει αν ομολογησειεν, ερωΐηθεις. Contra Marcellam, lib. 1. p. 4.

‡ Ταυΐη γαρ αν των Ιεδαιων ανωΐερα φρονεμεν. οι μεν γαρ ειναι ενα θεον παΐερα καΐαδεχονΐαι τοις δογμασι— το δε κ) παΐερα ειναι τε κυριε ημων Ιησε χριςε, τείον ε παραδεχονΐαι, τοις οικειοις προφηΐαις εναγΐια

Alexandria also says, " the Jews believed
" that there was a God who was before all
" things, and after him the creatures, but
" nothing intermediate between them *."

Basil ranks the unitarians with Jews.
" If any one," says he, " suppose the Father,
" Son, and Holy Spirit to be one, one Being
" under different names, and that they are
" but one hypostasis, under three denomina-
" tions, we rank him with the Jews †."

" The Hebrews," says Leontius, " have
" only one hypostasis, or person, and one
" nature of God; plainly admitting no tri-
" nity, nor saying that God is Father, Son,
" or Spirit, except that they call God Father,
" as the father of all men. They prove this
" one hypostasis from the words of Moses:

εναντια φρονουντες, οι φασι, εν ταις θειαις γραφαις, κυριος ειπε προς με, υιος μου ει συ. εγω σημερον γεγεννηκα σε. Cat. 7. p. 102.

* Intellexerunt enim in his quæ credita sunt, deum qui-dem esse ante omnia, et post illum creaturam. interme-dium autem aliud omnino nihil. De Trinitate, lib. 3. Opera, vol. 2. p. 398.

† Εἰς τον αυτον πατερα λεγει, ᾱ υιον, ᾱ αγιον πνευμα· ᾱ εν πραγμα πολυωνυμον υποτιθεσθαι, ᾱ μιαν υποστασιν υπο των τριων προσηγοριων εκφωνουμενην· τον τοιουτον ημεις εν τη μεριδι των Ιουδαιων τασσομεν. Epist. 73. vol. 3. p. 123.

" Hear,

" Hear, O Israel, the Lord thy God is one
" Lord*."

Lastly, Theophylact says, " in the Old
" Testament God was known to the Jews
" only, but not as Father; he was after-
" wards revealed by the gospel to all the
" world with the Son †."

This is a series of testimony, sufficiently extensive for my purpose, as it clearly shows what was the general opinion among christians concerning the ancient faith of the Jews; and it is uncontradicted by any other evidence whatever. Some writers of yesterday have maintained, that the Jews always believed in a trinity, and that they

---

* Igitur Hebræi unam dicunt hypostasin (sive personam) unamque naturam dei; nullam plane trinitatem admittentes, ac neque patrem, neque filium, neque spiritum sanctum dicentes: nisi forte sic deum, inquiunt, adpellemus patrem; ut qui omnium sit hominum pater. Unam ex eo probant esse hypostasin dei, quia Moses dixerit: audi Israelitica natio, dominus deus tuus, dominus unus est. De Sectis. Bib. Pat. App. p. 1849.

† Ει γαρ και εν τη παλαια εγνωστο, αλλ' Ιυδαιοις μονοις · και εδε τελοις, ως πατηρ · υςερονδε, δια τε ευαγγελιε εξεκαλυφθη τη οικεμενη πασῃ, μετα τε υιε. In Rom. Opera, vol. 2. p. 4.

expected that their Messiah would be the second person in that trinity; but the christian Fathers, who say just the contrary, were as much interested as any men could be, in finding that doctrine among the Jews, and they were nearer the source of information.

It was, indeed, imagined, as I have observed, that Moses and the prophets were themselves acquainted with the mystery of the trinity; but that they thought it was not a proper time to make a full discovery of that doctrine for the satisfaction of the body of the Jews. Eusebius says, that "Isaiah knew that there was a God in "God*" "The prophets," says Chrysostom, "who foretold concerning Christ, "concealed their treasure in obscure "words†;" which implies that, in his opinion, they knew it themselves. "Adam," says Epiphanius, "being a prophet, knew

---

* Ησαιας προφητων μεγιϛ@ σαφως οιδε θεον εν θεω ειναι. Demonstratio, lib. 5. cap. 4. p. 225.

† Ουτως κ) οι προφηται χριϛον κηρυξαντες τη ασαφεια των λεξεων εκρυψαν τον θησαυρον. De Sigillis, Opera, vol. 6. p. 169.

CHAP. I.   *in the Divine Unity.*   17

" the Father, Son, and Spirit, and knew
" that the Father spake to the Son, when he
" said, *Let us make man* *."

Pope Gregory likewise represents the people of the Jews as ignorant of the trinity, though the prophets might teach it †.

* Και ηδει πατερα θεον κ᾽ υιον κ᾽ αγιον πνευμα, προφητης γαρ ην. Lib. 1. p. 6.

† Ipsa enim dei cognitio quæ apud illam in spiritalibus patribus fuit, nota omni Hæbræorum populo non fuit. Nam omnipotentem deum, sanctam videlicet trinitatem cum prophetæ prædicarent, populus ignorabat: solum decalogum tenebat in fide, legem trinitatis nesciens. Super Ezekiel, Hom. 16. Opera, vol. 2. p. 83.

SECTION II.

Of the Reasons why, according to the Christian Fathers, the Doctrine of the Trinity was not discovered to the Jews.

AS the ignorance of the Jews, concerning the doctrine of the trinity, was an objection to the truth of it, which the christian Fathers, who defended it, could not be quite easy under, and they were often urged with it, as we shall see, by the unitarians; it may be amusing to know more particularly in what manner they accounted for the fact.

That there should be a *gradual revelation* of so great a mystery as that of the trinity, the Fathers thought to be an argument of great wisdom on the divine dispensations, as they were by this means better adapted to the different states of the world.

Chrysostom represents Moses as saying, " that the world was made by God, and not " by Christ, as accommodating himself to " the stupidity of his hearers. Paul him-" self," he says, " was contented to teach " the same doctrine at Athens. But he af-
" terwards

"terwards held a different language in the
"epistle to the Colossians; and says, that
"*God in Christ created all things that are in
"heaven and in earth.* And John, the son
"of Thunder, cried, saying, *All things were
"made by him, and without him was not
"any thing made that was made.* But not so
"Moses; and justly, because it would not
"have been proper to give those meat who
"had need to be fed with milk *."

"As Moses," says Cyril of Alexandria,
"was slow of speech, so the law of Moses
"was slow to explain the reason of it, and
"to open the theology of the holy trinity†."

* Και μη ξηνισθης αγαπηίε, ει Μωυσης ταυίην ειρεχε την οδον, εν αρχη κ) προοιμιοις τοις παχυίεροις Ιεδαιοις διαλεγομεν۞, οπε γε κ) ο Παυλ۞, εν τη χαρίῃ, ηνικα τοσαυίη η επιδοσις γεγονε τε κηρυγμαί۞, μελλων τοις εν Αθηναις διαλεγεσθαι απο των ορωμενων ποιείίαι προς αυίες την διδασκαλιαν, εδω λεγων· ο θεος ο ποιησας τον κοσμον κ) παντα τα εν αυίω. Ηνικα προς Κολοσσαις επεςελλε, μηκείιταυίην ερχομενε την οδον, αλλ' είερως αυίοις διαλεγομενου κ) λεγονί۞, οίι εν αυίω εκίισθη τα παντα τα εν τοις ερανοις, κ) τα επι της γης, τα οραία κ) τα αοραία, είίε θρονοι, είίε κυριοίηίες, είίε αρχαι, είίε εξεσιαι, τα παντα δι αυίον κ) εις αυίον εκίισθη· κ) Ιωαννης δε ο της βρονίης υιος, εβοα λεγων· παντα δι αυίου εγενείο, κ) χωρις αυτε εγενετο ουδε εν. αλλ' εχ ο Μωυσης ετως· εικοτως. εδε γαρ ην ευλογον τοις ετι γαλακτοτροφεισθαι δεομενοις ιερεας μεταδεναι τροφης. In Gal. 1. Opera, vol. 2. p. 13.

† Sicut Moses erat tardioris linguæ, ita etiam lex Mosaica est tardioris linguæ ad explicandam ejus quod est rationem, et aperiendam sanctæ trinitatis theologiam. Collectania. Opera, vol. 1. p. 1036.

"Observe,"

"Observe," says Job the monk, "the wisdom of divine providence, that to the ancients the Father appeared superior; in the new, the Son appeared in some places to be inferior to the Father, but in many equal to him; the holy spirit in many inferior, but in some equal; that what is unequal in human apprehension, might be brought to a perfect equality*." According to this writer therefore, the doctrine of the divinity of the spirit was not fully revealed even in the time of the apostles, but was reserved for a later period.— However, Epiphanius thought that the divinity of Christ was taught by the prophets, though not that of the Spirit. "One God," says he, "was chiefly preached by Moses, a duality by the prophets, and a trinity by the evangelists; this being suited to a more advanced state of know-

‡ Και σκοπει της θεuργου προνοιας τον πανσοφον τε κ̓ αρρεπη ζυγον. ο πατηρ εδοκει τοις παλαι το μειζον εχειν: ο υιος δε παλιν κατα την νεαν ενιοις μεν το ελατίον, τοις πολλοις δε το ισον· το δε αγιον πνευμα τοις πολλοις μεν το ελατίον, ολιγοις δε το ισον. ινα ȣν το ανισον το απο της των ανθρωπων υπολη̄ψεως εις ισοτητα επαναχθη. Phot. Bib. S. 222. p. 623.

"ledge."

" ledge *." He says the same thing in his Ancoratus, Sect. 73. Opera, vol. 2. p. 78.

The reason that is generally given by the Fathers why the Jews were not instructed in the doctrine of the trinity is, lest it should afford them a pretence for relapsing into polytheism; and certainly there was great danger of its operating in that manner. "The multitude of the Jews," says Eusebius, "were in ignorance of this hid-
" den mystery, when they were taught to
" believe in one God only, on account of
" their being frequently drawn into idola-
" try; they did not know that he was the
" Father of the only begotten Son. This
" mystery was reserved for the Gentile
" church, out of special favour to them †."

---

* Θεοτης δε μια εν Μωυση μαλιςα καταγγελλεται, δυας δε εν Προφηταις σφοδρα κηρυσσεται. Τριας δε εν ευαεγγελιοις φανερυται, πλειον κατα καιρυς και γενεας αρμοζυσα τω δικαιω, εις γνωσιν και πιςιν. H. 74. Opera, vol. 1. p. 899.

† Το δε πληθος τυ Ιυδαιων εθνους εν αγνοια ετυγχανε τυ κεκρυμμενου τυτυ μυςηριου, οθεν θεον μεν εδιδασκετο ενα ειδεναι, δια το τη πολυθεω πλανη συνεχως υποσυρεσθαι. πατερα δε οντα τον θεον υιου τυ μονογενους ηγνοει· τυτο γαρ εφυλατ]ετο τη εξ εθνων εκκλησια το μυςηριον, κα]α την αξαιρετον χαριν αυτη δεδωρημενον. Contra Marcel. lib. 1. cap. 20. p. 99.

Gregory Nazianzen, therefore, representing the propriety of judaism being abolished by degrees, says, " the Father was preached " in the Old Testament, and the Son ob- " scurely; in the New, the Son clearly, and " the spirit obscurely, he revealing himself " more clearly to us. For it was not safe " to preach the divinity of the Son clearly, " while that of the Father was not under- " stood, nor that of the Spirit, while that " of the Son was not received, lest too great " a burden should be laid upon us, or lest " we should be dazzled with too much " light, &c*." And Chrysostom farther observes, that " the precept, *Hear, O Israel,* " *the Lord thy God is one Lord*, was not " given till after the sin of the golden calf†;"

* Εχει γαρ ϋτως, εκηρυσσε φανερως η παλαια τον πατερα, τον υιον αμυδροτερον. εφανερωσεν η καινη τον υιον, υπεδειξε τϋ πνευματος την θεοτητα, εμπολιτευεται νυν το πνευμα, Cαφεϛεραν ημιν παρεχον την εαυτϋ δηλωσιν. ϋ γαρ ην ασφαλες, μηπω της τϋ πατρος θεοτητος ομολογηθεισης, τον υιον εκδηλως κηρυτ7εσθαι· μηδε της τϋ υιου παραδεχθεισης, Το πνευμα το αγιον, ιν ειπω τι κ) τολμηρο7εριν επιφορ7ιζεσθαι. μη καθαπερ τροφη τη υπερ δυναμιν βαρηθεν7ες, και ηλιακω φω7ι σαθρο7ερον ε7ι προσβαλον7ες τη οψιν, και εις το κα7α δυναμιν κινδυνευσωσι. Or. 37. Opera, p. 608, 609.

† Ο7ε γουν εποιησαν τον μοσχον, κ) το γλυπ7ον προσεκυνησαν, 7ο7ε ηκουσαν· κυριος ο θεος σε κυριος εις εϛιν Scr. 24. Opera, vol. 5. p. 350.

as if it had not been the intention of providence to give them any such precept, if they had not previously shewn a disposition to abuse more perfect instruction.

Job the monk, of whose writings we have a particular account in Photius, comparing the great revolutions in the state of religion to *earthquakes,* says, " As the first earth-
" quake had cured the world of idolatry,
" by contrary remedies, but concealed the
" difference of hypostases; so in the last
" times, the Jewish opinion of one person
" having gained strength in time, and by
" the law, and having destroyed idolatry;
" the Son then, in a manner worthy of
" God, and friendly to man, took flesh, and
" revealed the mystery of the trinity by de-
" grees." He likewise says, " the Saviour
" very wisely spake lowly of himself, and
" withheld the beams of his divinity, and
" prepared to let it shine forth in works *."

---

* Και καθαπερ ο πρωτος σεισμος δια των εναντιων ιασατο το πολυθεον επικυψαμενος των υποστασεων το διαφορον. ετω χ̣ εν εσχατοις καιροις, της Ιεδαικης δοξης εις εν προσωπω νομω χ̣ χρονω κρατυνθεισης, χ̣ περιελεσης το πολυθεον, ο υιος τηνικαυτα θεοπρεπως τε χ̣ φιλανθρωπως και σαρκα λαμ-
βανει, και το της τριαδος κατα μικρον ανακαλυπτει μυστηριον.

επαγει

It was customary, as we shall see, to represent the doctrine of the trinity as something *sublime*, and of difficult apprehension; and therefore fit for persons of ripe understanding, and deep reflection; of which on that account, even the christians of the first ages were allowed to be ignorant, and the common people in general, till a much later period. It was natural, therefore, to alledge this, also, as another reason why the Jews, living in the infant age of the world, should not have this sublime and difficult lesson taught them. "The Jews," says Eusebius, "were not taught the doc-
"trine of the trinity, on account of their
"infant state*." Basil gives the same account†. Cyril of Alexandria, says, "The

επαγει δε τυ]οις, ως πανσοφως ο σωτηρ τοις μεν ρημασιν εταπεινολογειτε, και την της θεοτητος συνεςελλεν αυγην, τοις εργοις δε ταυτης παρεσκευαζεν ασπα]ειν, και δι αυταν εδοκει κηρυττεσθαι της παντοκρατορικης δυναμεως το αξιωμα. Photii. Bib. sect. 222. p. 619.

* Και τα νηπιαζοντι των Ιυδαιων λαω. Ec. Theol. lib. 2. cap. 18, p. 130.

† Ην γαρ τι, ως εοικεν, χ προ τε κοσμυ τυ]υ, ο τη μεν διανοια ημων εςι θεωρη]ον, ανιςορη]ον δε κα]ελειφθη, δια το τοις εισαγομενοις ετι χ νηπιοις κατα την γνωσιν ανεπιτηδειον. Basil, vol. 1. p. 6.

"doctrine

"doctrine of the trinity was taught in
"types only, and not clearly. For what
"reason? Because the light of divine
"vision is not easily accessible to those who
"are but lately called to the knowledge
"of the truth, and have not their minds
"exercised to those speculations*."

Our Saviour said that divorces had been allowed to the Jews on account of the *hardness of their hearts.* This also is given as a reason by Eusebius, why the Jews were not taught the doctrine of the trinity †.

* Ος εν τυποις ἐΊι μονον, εχι δε κ̣ αισθηΊως, εδιδασκεΊο· δια ποιαν αιΊιαν; οτι τοις αρΊι κεκλημενοις εις επιγνωσιν αληθειας κ̣ εκ ευΊριϐη τοις επ αυΊη θεωρημασι την διανοιαν εχεσιν, απροσιΊον πως ειναι δοκει κ̣ εςιν αληθως, το φως της θεοπΊιας. Contra Jul. lib. 1. Juliani, Opera, vol. 2. p. 19.

† Οτι προς την σκληροκαρδιαν τε ΙεδαιωΥ λαε. Ec. Theol. lib. 2. cap. 20. p. 134.

SECTION III.

The Sentiments of the Jews, as expressed by themselves, on the Subject.

HAVING seen what the christian Fathers say in general of the ignorance of the Jews concerning the doctrine of the trinity, let us see what the Jews themselves have said on the subject, as far as we are able to collect it, either from the writings of the christian Fathers, or their own.

As the christian Fathers found the doctrine of the trinity obscurely hinted at in the Old Testament, and particularly in the account of the creation, in which God is represented as saying, *Let us make man*, we may wish to know what the Jews replied, when they were urged with this argument; and it is remarkable, that their answer was in general the same with that of the unitarian in the *Clementines*, in reply to Simon, who had urged that very circumstance, as a proof that there were more gods than one. However, there is a variety in the answers given by the Jews to this question, but all of them sufficiently

ficiently natural, and not improper. Theodoret says, "the Jews say that when God "said *let us make man*, he used the kingly "style*;" and this seems to be the most natural interpretation. But according to Tertullian, the Jews said that God addressed himself to the angels. "Did he speak to "angels, when he said, *let us make man*, as "the Jews say, who do not acknowledge "the Son; or, as if he himself was Father, "Son, and Spirit, did he, say they, make "himself more than one, and speak in the "plural number †." This also is the answer which Basil reports. "The Jews say "God spake to the angels, when he said, "*let us make man*," addressing himself to an unitarian, who he said was "a Jew pre- "tending to be a christian‡." Cyril of

---

* In Gen. xix. Opera, vol. 1. p. 15.

† Aut numquid angelis loquebatur, ut Judæi interpretantur, quia nec ipsi filium agnoscunt; an quia ipse erat pater, filius et spiritus, ideo pluralem se præstans, pluraliter sibi loquebatur. Ad Praxeam, sect. 12. p. 506.

‡ Ακυε κỳ συ ο εκ της νεας καταλομης, ο τον Ιυδαισμον πρεσβευων εν χριστιανισμω προσποιησει. τινι λεγει κατ' εικονα ημετεραν. Hom. 8. Opera, vol. 1. p. 105.

Jerusalem

Jerusalem says, that the Jews acknowledged only one God the Father *.

We may form a very good judgment of the sentiments of the Jews on this subject, from the account of a solemn conference between Gregentius, a christian bishop, and Herbanus, a learned Jew, in the presence of an Arabian prince, in the fifth century. As it is the only work of the kind that remains of so early an age, I shall quote several extracts from it, to shew how the Jews of that age felt and reasoned.

The Jew expresses his dread of idolatry in very strong terms. " The prophet " Moses," he says, " if you read the penta-" teuch, pronounces a dreadful curse upon " the children of Israel, from God, the an-" gels, and saints, calling in all the ele-" ments under heaven, if we should ever " receive any other god beside the God of " our Fathers. Why then should you make " any words on the subject; for God him-" self by the prophets strictly orders us,

* Οἱ τε μεν ειναι ενα θεον πατερα καταδεχονται τοις δογμασι. Cat. 7. p. 102.

" saying,

" saying, there shall be no other god in
" thee, nor shalt thou worship a strange
" god; I am the Lord thy God, who
" brought thee out of the land of Egypt.
" What think you of this *?"

" It is grievous to me to desert the God
" of the law, whom you acknowledge to
" be a true god, and to worship a younger
" god, not knowing whence he sprung †."

" Whence do you derive your faith in
" the Father, Son, and Spirit, and intro-
" duce three strange gods ‡." " Where
" did any prophet foretel that Christ was
" to be *God man,* as you say ||." " Why

---

* Μωυσης ο προφητης, ει την πεν]α]ευχον αναγνως, μεγεθη
κιταζων τεθεικεν ημιν τοις υιοις Ισραηλ, απο θεε κ̣ των αγγελων, κ̣ των αγιων, θεις κ̣ παν]α τα στοιχεια τα υπ' ερανον
υπο καιαραν, ει ποτε ετερον θεον υποδεξομεθα παρεξ τε
θεε των πα]ερων. Τι εν λοιπον πολυπραγμονεις; κ̣ γαρ κ̣
αυ]ος ο θεος δια τε προφητε παρεγγυα ημιν λεγων· εκ εσαι
εν σοι θεος προσφαιος, εδε προσκυνησεις θεω αλλοτριω. εγω
γαρ ειμι κυριος ο θεος σε, ο αναγαγων σε εκ της γης Αιγυπ-
τε· Τι εν δοκει σοι προς ταυτα. P. 36.

† Ουκεν βαρυ μοι εσι καταλιπειν τον θεον τε νομε, ον κ̣
συ μαρτυρεις, οτι εσι θεος αληθειας, κ̣ προσκυνησαι θεω
νεωτερω, ποθεν επεισαχθεντι εκ ειδως. Ibid. p. 115.

‡ Ποθεν εν εξελαβεσθε πατερα κ̣ υιον κ̣ πνευμα πιστευειν,
κ̣ εισφερετε εις το μεσον τρεις θεες αλλοκοτες. Ibid. p. 6.

|| Και πε ηνιξατο τις των προφητων, οτι θεος ανθρωπος εσαι
ο χριστος, ον τροπον λελαληκας. Ibid. p. 112.

" did

"did not God order Moses and the pro-
"phets to believe in the Father, Son, and
"Holy Spirit, but yourselves only, who
"have lately discovered it, as you pre-
"tend*."

"How do you call your Christ God, if
"my God has chosen him, &c. He cannot
"be a god, of whom you acknowledge it
"is said in the prophet, *I have made thee*
"*strong.* How can you call him your God
"and Saviour, who, as the prophet witnes-
"ses, can do nothing without my God†?"

Lastly, having quoted the words of the
prophet, "*I have heard thee in an acceptable*
"*time, I have formed thee,*" he says, "How
"dare you then make him equal to him
"that formed him‡?"

---

* Τω Μωση κỳ τοις προφηταις πως εκ εξεθετο ο θεος πιστευειν εις πατερα κỳ υιον και αγιον πνευμα, αλλ' η μονοις
υμιν νεωςι τυτο εξευρηκοσιν, ως υμεις φατε. Gregent. p. 7.

† Και ει υτως εχει, ποιω δε τροπω τον χριςον συ θεον προ-
σαγορευεις, εφ ω θεος ο εμος εξελεξατο, και ηγαπησε, και τα
εξης; κκυν εκ εςι θεος. ως λεγεις, οτι φασκει περι αυτε δια
τυ προφητυ, οτι εγω γαρ ειμι ο ενισχυσας σε. πως δε και
αποκαλεις αυτον θεον και σωτηρα σε, ος τις καθως η προφη-
τεια μαρτυρει, ανευ τε εμε θεε πραττειν τι ε δυναται; Ibid.
p. 111.

‡ Πως εν συ τολμας ισον τω πλαση αυτε θεον ονομαζων·
Ibid. p. 151.

"The

"The doctrine of the trinity," says the Rabbi Isaac, in his *Munimen Fidei*, "as held by learned christians, rests on the slightest evidence, and is contrary to the doctrine of the prophets, the law, and right reason, and even to the writings of the New Testament. For the divine law gives its sanction to the unity of God, and removes all plurality from him*." This writer shews, in many places, that the doctrine of the trinity is not taught in the New Testament. See p. 397. 403. 418, &c.

The contempt which the author of a Jewish treatise, entitled, *Nizzachon Vetus*, expresses for the christian doctrine of God being confined in the womb of woman, is peculiarly strong†. As to those who said

---

* Accedit his, quod dogma de trinitate falsum est, et a quibusdam eruditis Nazarenorum, rebus levissimis, sine ullo vero prophetico fundamento recens superstructum, quodque legi divinæ, verbis prophetarum, humanæ rationi, dictisque plurimis scriptorum novi testamenti repugnat. Quippe lex divina comprobat dei unitatem, omnemque pluralitatem ab eo segregat. p. 113.

† Quomodo igitur iste deus esse posset, qui fœminam plenum immunditiis ventrem habentem, ingressus est? Et quem

that Mary was not rendered unclean by the birth of Jesus, he says the contrary is evident, from the offering that she brought for her purification*.

Having seen what the christians, both unitarians and trinitarians, and also what the Jews, thought of the doctrine of the Old Testament concerning God, it may be some farther satisfaction to know in what manner the heathens decided in this case. We have the opinion of the emperor Julian on this subject, and it is decisively in favour of the Jews, and the unitarian christians. He says, " Moses not only once, or " twice, or three times, but many times

---

quem toties mater illius, novem graviditatis mensibus, eo detulit, quo satura itabat? Quique tempore nativitatis editus est inquinatus, et sordens, involutus secundinis, et abominabilis sanguine partus ac profluvii. Nizzachon. Vetus, p. 7.

* Quod si dicat adversarius: non inquinatus fuit intra viscera ejus. Nam, cum in Maria muliebris consuetudo defecisset, intravit eam spiritus, exivitque sine dolore, et sine sanguinis sorditie. Ad hæc respondere licet: annon vos fatemini eam obtulisse sacrificium puerperarum, cujus immundities causa erat? Idem enim sacrificium offerebant leprosus, hæmorrhousa, et puerpera, par turturum, aut duos pullos columbarum. Ibid.

" commands

"commands to worship only one God,
"who, he says, is over all. He mentions
"no other God, but only angels, and lords,
"and many gods," that is, the heathen
gods. "This great Being he made to be
"the first, but he made no second, like him,
"or unlike him, as you have done. If you
"can produce a single expression in Moses
"to this purpose, do it. That saying of
"his, *A prophet shall the Lord your God
"raise up unto you, of your brethren, like
"unto me, hear him,* is not said of the son
"of Mary. But if this be granted to you,
"he says that he shall be like to himself,
"and not to God, a prophet like himself,
"of man, and not of God*."

* Ο τοινυν Μωσης εκ απαξ, εδε δις, εδε τρις, αλλα πλεισακις ενα Θεον μονον αξιοι τιμαν, ον δη κ; επι πασιν ονομαζει, Θεον δε ετερον εδαμε, αγγελες δε ονομαζει, κ; κυριες, κ; μεντοι κ; Θεες πλειονας. εξαιρετον κ; τον πρωτον, αλλον δε εχ υπειληφε δευτερον, ετε ομοιον, ετε ανομοιον, καθαπερ υμεις απεξειργασθε. ει δε εστι τις παρ υμιν υπερ τεων μια Μωσεως ρησις, ταυτην εστε δικαιοι προφερειν. Το γαρ, προφητην υμιν αναστησει κυριος ο Θεος υμων, εκ των αδελφων υμων, ως εμε· αυτε ακεσεσθε· μαλιστα μεν εν εκ ειρηται περ. τε γεννηθεντ@ εκ Μαριας. ει δε τις υμων ενεκα συγχωρησειεν, εαυτω φησιν αυτον ομοιον γεννησεσθαι, κ; ε τω Θεω· προφητην ωσπερ εαυτον, ἐξ ανθρωπων, αλλ' εκ εκ Θεε. Cyril Contra Jul. lib. 8. Juliani, Opera, vol. 2. p. 253.

It has been seen that Philo personified the logos as much as the christian Fathers, and that they probably learnt of him the doctrine of a divine logos being the medium of all the communications of God to the patriarchs, and of this principle occasionally assuming a visible form. But Philo had no idea that this doctrine had any connexion with that of the Messiah, as he gives no hint that this was a character to be assumed by the logos; nor does it appear that the Jews in any age had such an expectation; though this has been pretended by some modern christians.

It is unquestionable that, in our Saviour's time, the Jews expected no other than a man in the character of their Messiah. Mary, the mother of Jesus, evidently expected that the Messiah was to be born in the usual way, of two human parents. For when the angel informed her that she should *conceive and bear a son*, who should be called *the son of the highest*, and to whom God would *give the throne of his father David*, she replied, Luke i. 34. *How shall this*

this be, seeing I know not a man. Our Saviour could not possibly have puzzled the Jewish doctors as he did, by asking them how David could call the Messiah his lord, when he was his son, or descendant, on any other principle. For if they had themselves been fully persuaded that the Messiah, though descended from David, was the maker and God of David, a satisfactory answer to his question was very obvious. Origen reproaches Celsus for his ignorance, in not knowing that the Jews never believed that the Messiah would be God, or the Son of God *. Facundus very properly says, that " Martha and Mary would never have " said to Christ, *if thou hadst been here*, had " they thought him to be God omnipresent." This writer also says, that the Jews always had expected, and that, in his time, they did expect, a mere man for their Messiah. " They did not know," he says, " that " Christ, the Son of God, was God; but " they thought that Christ would be a mere

---

* Ουκ οιδε μεντοιγε, ὁτι 𐐪 πανυ τι Ιυδαιοι λεγυσι θεον οντα τον χρισον καταβησεσθαι, η θευ υιον. Con. Celsum, lib. 4. p. 162.

" man,

" man, which any one may perceive that
" the Jews at this time alſo think *."

Many chriſtians imagine, that the child called *Immanuel* by Iſaiah (chap. vii. 8.) muſt be God, becauſe the word ſignifies, *God with us*. But the Jews underſtood their ſcriptures, and their own ideas with reſpect to giving names, too well to draw any ſuch inference from this circumſtance. Euſebius ſays, that they aſſerted it was not even the Meſſiah that was intended by Immanuel, but only ſome common child †.

Baſnage, who ſtudied the hiſtory and opinions of the Jews more carefully, perhaps, than any other modern writer, and who has written largely on this very ſubject, though a trinitarian himſelf, has exploded all the pretences of Cudworth, and others, to find the doctrine of the trinity,

---

* Sed non propterea Chriſtum dei filium, deum ſciebant; hominem autem purum arbitrati ſunt Chriſtum.— Quod etiam nunc putantes Judæos quilibet videbit. Lib. 9. cap. iii. p. 139.

† Ταυτα δε παντα περι τυ τυχοντος παιδιυ λεγεσθαι, υκ οιδα πως συνησαιεν οι εκ περιτομης. In Eſ. cap. 9. Montfaucon's Collectio, vol. 2. p. 391.

either

either among the ancient or the modern Jews. " The chriſtians and the Jews," he ſays, " ſeparate at the ſecond ſtep in " religion. For after having adored toge- " ther one God, abſolutely perfect, they " find immediately after the abyſs of the " trinity, which entirely ſeparates them. " The Jew conſiders three perſons as three " Gods, and this tritheiſm ſhocks him. " The chriſtian who believes the unity of " one God, thinks that the Father, the Son, " and the Holy Spirit, ſhould all be called " God, and have the ſame worſhip. It is " impoſſible to reconcile opinions ſo con- " trary*."

* " Les chretiens s'ecartent des Juifs des le ſecond pas
" qu'ils font dans la religion. Car apres avoir adoré en-
" ſemble un dieu, ſouverainement parfait, ils trouvent un
" moment apres l'abime de la trinité, qui les ſepare, et les
" eloigne ſouverainement. Le Juif regarde trois perſon-
" nes comme trois dieux, et ce tritheiſme lui fait horreur.
" Le chretien, qui croit l'unité d'un Dieu, veut a meme
" tems q'on donne ce titre au pere, au fils, au Saint Eſprit,
" et q'on les adore. Il eſt impoſſible de concilier des opi-
" nions ſi contraires; cependant il y a des theologiens
" hardis, qui ont tenté de le faire." Hiſt. des Juifs, lib. 4. cap. 3. ſect. 1.

This writer alfo fays, that " the Jews " confider themfelves as bearing their tefti- " mony to the unity of God among all the " nations of the world*." How far the Jews of late years are from admitting the divinity of the Meſſiah, we may judge from what Orobio faid in his controverfy with Limborch, viz. that, admitting what is im- poffible, that the Meſſiah whom they ex- pect fhould teach that doctrine, he ought to be ftoned as a falfe prophet †.

It has, however, been imagined by fome, that the Jews had a knowledge of the doc- trine of the trinity, that it fpread from them among the Gentiles, and that traces of it may be perceived in the myfteries of hea- then religions. But if this be the cafe, it is obvious to afk, why are no traces of this doctrine to be found in the Jewifh fcrip- tures, and the Jewifh worfhip? Or, if the

---

* " Les temoins de l'unité de dieu dans toutes les na- " tions du monde." Hift. des Juifs, lib. 7. cap. 33. fect. 15.

† Dato impoffibili quod Meffias, quem expectamus, eam doctrinam [v. g. fe equalem effe deo] Ifraelem edo- ceret, jure foret, ut pfeudopropheta, lapidandus. Lim- berch's Amica Collatio, p. 111.

Jews

Jews had once been in poffeffion of this knowledge, but had loft it in the time of our Saviour, why did not he, who rectified other abufes, rectify this, the moft important of them all.

If an expectation of a Meffiah had been prevalent among the Gentiles, we fhould certainly perceive fome traces of it in their writings. It might have been expected, both on account of the interefting nature, and the obfcurity of the fubject, that there would have been different opinions about it. that it would have been a common topic in their philofophical fchools, and that their hiftorians would have given fome account of the origin of fuch an expectation.

The fixth eclogue of Virgil may be alledged as a proof of fuch an expectation. But I do not imagine that any perfon now thinks that Virgil himfelf ever expected fuch a perfonage as he defcribes. The ufe that a poet might make of a vague report of a prophecy (brought probably from the eaft, and ultimately from the Jewifh fcriptures) but ferioufly believed by no perfon that

that we know of, merely to embellish a poem, is one thing; but the actual and universal expectation of such a person, is another

---

SECTION IV.

Of the Jewish Angel METATRON, *&c.*

IN the third of Ben Mordecai's Letters, written by the late Rev. Mr. Taylor of Portsmouth, p. 72. I find the following extraordinary paragraph: " Among the no-
" tions of the more modern Jews, we must
" also observe, that the Cabbalists believed
" *El Shaddai* to be the same person as the
" angel *Metatron*, whom they supposed to
" be the instructor of Moses, and the Mes-
" siah, i. e. as Dr. Allix expresses it, He
" was, according to the christian phrase,
" the logos before his incarnation, or, ac-
" cording to the jewish phrase, the soul of
" the Messiah, whom they look upon as
" something between God and the angels,
" whom

"whom nothing separates from God." Allix, p. 456*.

"Bishop Pearson, in proving, by several "arguments, that Christ is called Jehovah, "says, the Jews themselves acknowledge "that Jehovah shall be clearly known in the "days of the Messiah, and not only so, but "that it is the name which doth properly "belong to him, for the proof of which he "quotes the book *Sepher Ikkarim*, ii. 8. "*The scripture calleth the name of the Messias* "*Jehovah our righteousness,* and Midrash "Tillim, on Pf. xxi. *God calleth the Messias*

---

* Here Mr. Taylor inserts the following note in French, but I shall give it in English: Calmet, on the word *Metatron*, says, "The Hebrews give this name to the first of "the angels, him who conducted them in the wilderness, "and of whom it is said, in Moses, *I shall send my angel to* "*go before you.* He acted towards the Israelites the part "of the officer whom the Romans called *Metator*. He "marked out the encampments, traced the form of them, "the dimensions, extent, &c. He is thought to be the "archangel Michael, who was at the head of the people "in the wilderness, that it was he who wrestled with Ja- "cob, who is called *the face of God*, in Exod. xxxiv. 14. "and who is the mediator between God and man; that "he writes down good actions, and keeps a register of "them."

"by

"by his own name, and his name is Jehovah,
"as it is, Ex. xv. 3. *The Lord is a man of
"war, Jehovah is his name.* And it is writ-
"ten of the Messias, Jer. xxiii. 6. *And this
"is the name which they shall call him, Jeho-
"vah our righteousness.* Thus Echa Rab-
"biti, Lam. i. 6. What is the name of the
"Messias? Rabba said, Jehovah is his
"name, as it is said, Jer. xxiii. 6. The
"same he reports of Rabbi Levi; and the
"Bishop concludes, that the Rabbins then
"did acknowledge, that the name Jehovah
"did belong to the Messias."

Consulting Dr. Allix's own work on the subject, I find the following reference to authorities for what he advances: " See "Reuchlin, L. i. De Cabala, p. 651. where "he proves Metatron to be the Messiah "from their writings; or, in short, take "the confession of Manasseh Ben Israel, "Q. 6. In Gen. f. 2." The former of these authors I have not, and in the latter I find no such passage as Dr. Allix quotes. But as there is abundant evidence that the Jews in general, and

in

CHAP. I.   *in the Divine Unity.*   43

in all ages, from the time of our Saviour to the present, considered their Messiah as a *mere man*, and a proper descendant of David, I own that I am disposed to examine, with some rigour, any pretended evidence to the contrary; though the speculative opinions of some of the Cabbalists among them is a thing of little consequence, when they can be proved to be different from those that were entertained by the nation in general.

What Calmet says concerning the angel Metatron in Ben Mordecai's note, has no relation to the Messiah; so that the most that I should be disposed to infer from what the Jewish Cabbalists may have said on the subject would be, that this *Metraton* was something similar to what Philo represents the *logos* as being, namely an *efflux of the divinity*, but no *being*, or *person*, permanently distinguished from him. And it is highly improbable, that any Jew should have supposed that their Messiah, a man descended from David, would have no proper human soul, besides this *Metatron*, or *logos*, supplying the place of it; though they might suppose the

Messiah

Messiah to be distinguished by the presence and influence of this divine efflux.

The Jewish Cabbalists might easily admit even that the Messiah might be called *Jehovah*, without supposing that he was any thing more than a man, who had no existence before his birth. That it must have been the mere *name*, and not the *nature* of God, that the Jews supposed their Messiah to partake of, is all that can be admitted in the case. Several things in the scriptures are called by the name of Jehovah, as Jerusalem, in the passage above quoted, is called *Jehovah our righteousness*; but this never led the Jews to suppose, that there were two Jehovahs, a greater and a less. Nothing can be more expressly declared, than that there is but one Jehovah; and in the passages quoted by Bishop Pearson, there is no intimation of there being two Jehovahs; so that if the Messiah be Jehovah, there must have been no other Being above him, which Mr. Taylor would not suppose.

From reading the above quoted passage from Mr. Taylor, the reader would conclude, that it was the universal opinion of the

the Jewish Cabbalists, if not of the Jews in general, that this great angel *Metatron* was the soul of the Messiah. But this would be a mistake; for Beausobre quotes some of them, who said, that the soul of the Messiah was the same that had been the soul of Adam, and likewise that of David. The Cabbalistic proof of this mystery, he says, is the letter A in *Adam*, meaning Adam, the D David, and the M the Messiah. Histoire de Manicheisme, vol. 2. p. 492. So little dependence is there on the whimsical and uncertain notions of these Jewish Cabbalists. However, when they are quoted, they ought to be quoted fairly. Mr. Taylor probably saw nothing of them, but what he found in Dr. Allix.

Basnage gives a large account of the Jewish angel *Metatron*, shewing that he is the same with the angel Michael, concerning whom the Jews had many absurd fancies. He particularly shews, that the name of God being in this angel, means nothing more than that the letters of the words *Metatron*, מטטרון, and those of *Shadai*, שדי, considered as numerals express the same number

ber, viz. 314. lib. 4. cap. 19. vol. 3. p. 137.

Many mistakes on this subject have been occasioned by its being taken for granted, that what is said of the *logos* may be applied to the *Messiah*, because the generality of christians have supposed them to be synonymous. But this was not the case with the Jews; and there is a passage quoted by Basnage, in his History of the Jews, L. IV. c. xxiv. s. 9. which shews, that some of their writers considered them as quite distinct from each other. " Jonathan says, that the Messiah " and Moses will appear at the end of the " world, the one in the desart, and the other " at Rome, and that the *word*, or the *logos*, " will march between them."

Till I see much more evidence than I have yet met with (and I have not spared any pains to come at it) I cannot admit that any Jew ever supposed that their Messiah either pre-existed, or was, properly speaking, God.

With respect to all these pretences to make the Jews favourable to the doctrine of the trinity, Mr. Basnage says, " They
" cannot

" cannot be advanced without the authors
" of them deceiving themselves. The
" Jews will never," he says, " be con-
" vinced by endeavouring to persuade them
" that they believe what they do not believe,
" and that they do not oppose the doctrine
" of the trinity, which is the principal ob-
" ject of their blasphemies."

He mentions a Jewish writer, Jacob, the son of Amram, who laughs at the pretensions of christians to bring proofs of the trinity from the cabbala. " The cabbalists," says he, " under several of the letters conceal
" mysteries which the vulgar cannot dis-
" cover, they only meant to teach the unity
" of God, and to explain his attributes, and
" they were very ignorant who looked into
" their writings for the trinity*."

---

* Mais peut-on avancer, cela sans vouloir se tromper, puis que l'unité d'un dieu le dogme capital de Juifs, et que la pluralité des personnes fait le plus grand obstacle à leur conversion.——On ne convaincra jamais les Juifs, lors qu'on s'entêtera de leur persuader qu'ls ont cru ce qu'ils ne croient pas, et qu'ils ne s'opposent point au dogme de la trinité, qui est le principal object de leurs blasphemes.——Jacob, fils d'Amram, dans un ouvrage manuscrit qu'il intitule la porte de la verité, se mocque des chretiens qui tirent de la cabbale des preuves pour la trinitaté. Car, dit

How far Manasseh Ben Israel was from supposing that there was any trinity in the divine nature, appears from the very section that Dr. Allix has quoted, which contains his interpretation of Gen. i. 26. And God said, *Let us make man.* After reciting a variety of interpretations, he concludes as follows, " Or shall we say that, what seems
" to be of greater consequence, we gene-
" rally undertake with more study and de-
" liberation, and therefore that the scrip-
" ture, in describing the creation of man,
" makes use of the plural number, *Let us*
" *make*, which is the language of a person
" commanding and exciting himself to un-
" dertake and do any thing; so that God
" would shew that all other creatures were
" made for the use of man. But whether
" God be supposed to speak to all second
" causes, or to intelligencies only, or to the
" elements, or to souls, or to use the stile
" of a king, or lastly, whether he be sup-

dit il, les cabbalistes enferment sous l'ecorce de la lettre des mysteres que le vulgaire ne decouvre pas. Les theologiens n'ont dessein que d' enseigner, l'unité de dieu, et d'expliquer ses attributes ; et il faut être ignorant pour chercher chez eux la trinité. L.7. c.31. vol. 4. p.2159. &c.

" posed

"posed to excite or command himself, all
"ground of controversy is removed. For
"it does not follow, that there is any mul-
"tiplication of the first cause, which is
"most simple, and one, because the phrase,
"*let us make*, is used. For Moses might
"very safely make use of this language,
"since he every where most clearly teaches,
"that there is but one God; and, there-
"fore, he only will defend his error by
"these words, who knowingly and wil-
"ingly errs *."

* Aut dicemus, plerumque id, quod majoris momenti videtur, majori quoque studio et deliberatione nos aggredi: ideoque scripturam in creatione hominis peculiari modo loqui in plurali, *faciamus*: quod verbum videtur imperantis sibi ipsi, et ad suscipiendum ac faciendum aliquid incitantis: eaque re ostendere dominus vult, omnes reliquas creaturas suo beneficio creatas. Sed sive cum omnibus secundis causis loquatur deus, sive cum intelligentiis tantum, sive cum elementis, sive cum animis, sive regio more haec dicat, seu denique incitet semetipsum, sibique imperet, conciliatione ejusmodi tota tollitur controversia. Etenim non quia *faciamus* dicitur, inde sequitur multiplicatio aliqua primae causae, quae simplissima est et unica. Moses vero causam cur ita scriberet, justam habuit, quia clarissime passim docet unicum numen esse; eoque solus is, qui sciens volens errat, his verbis errorem suam defensurus est. Conciliator, p. 12.

CHAPTER II.

General Considerations relating to the supposed Conduct of Christ and the Apostles, with Respect to the Doctrines of his Pre-existence and Divinity.

THE whole nation of the Jews having been so well grounded in the great doctrine of the *divine unity*, ever since their return from the Babylonish captivity, and their attachment to it having strengthened continually, as the whole of their history shews, especially in consequence of their persecution by Antiochus Epiphanes, and during their subjection to the Romans (in which their utter abhorrence of every thing that had the appearance of *idolatry*, is seen upon all occasions) and this being well-known to, and allowed by all the christian Fathers; it could not but, even in their idea, require the greatest caution and address to teach them any doctrine that could be construed into an infringement of it.

That

That the doctrine of the divinity of Christ *had* this appearance, those Fathers acknowledged; when they supposed that Moses and the prophets could not teach it, lest it should have given the Jews a pretence for relapsing into the worship of many Gods.

They could not imagine that this difficulty would be at all removed by the christian doctrine of Jesus being the Messiah. Because it was well known to them that the Jews expected nothing more than a man for their Messiah; and even a man born in the usual way, a proper descendant of David. Their highest expectation concerning the Messiah was, that he would be a great prince, a conqueror, and a legislator, and perhaps that he would not die. The probability is, that they imagined that the race of their kings descended from David would be revived in him, and continue to the end of time. But all this is far short of the *deification* of the Messiah, or the idea of his being a great pre-existent spirit, the maker of the world under God, and who, in the name of God, had intercourse with the patriarchs. Such notions as these do not appear ever to have entered into the head of any Jew, extravagant as their expectations were concerning the dignity and power of their Messiah.

Here then was a great dilemma in which the christian Fathers, advocates for the doctrines of the pre-existence and divinity of Christ, found themselves. They were under the necessity of maintaining that they were doctrines taught either by Christ or the apostles, or they must have abandoned them themselves. Doctrines of this great extent and magnitude, and so revolting to the minds of all Jews, they could not but suppose would alarm them very much; and therefore, that it was necessary to introduce them with the greatest caution. Still, however, they must have been taught them fully and explicitly at one time or other.

Accordingly, we find, in their accounts of the preaching of our Saviour and his apostles, that they did suppose that the greatest possible caution was used, and that this cautious proceeding was continued even till after the death of most of the apostles; so that the doctrines of the pre-existence and divinity

divinity of Christ were not fully discovered till the publication of the gospel of John, which was one of the last of all the books of the New Testament. But at that time they thought it to be absolutely necessary; as otherwise there would hardly have been any besides unitarians in the church; the knowledge of those great doctrines having, in their opinion, been confined to the apostles and the leading christians only.

A more improbable hypothesis was perhaps never formed by man, to account for any fact whatever; and yet I do not know that the christian Fathers could have done any better. Let their successors, who are equally interested in the solution of the problem, do better if they can. But certainly they who were nearer to the times of the apostles, were in a situation to form a better judgment in this case than any persons at this day can pretend to be; and therefore, I cannot help concluding, that they were well aware, that the supposition of this discovery having been made at an earlier period in the gospel history would have been liable to still greater objections than the hypothesis hypothefis which they did adopt. It is moft probable that the ftate of opinions in their own time made it abfolutely neceffary for them to have recourfe to this hypothefis, lame and wretched as it is.

The primitive Fathers were not prevented by the fuppofition above-mentioned, from attempting to prove the pre-exiftence and divinity of Chrift from thofe books of the New Teftament which were publifhed before the gofpel of John; but neither were they prevented from attempting to prove the fame doctrines, as we have feen, from the books of the Old Teftament, though they acknowledged that the body of the Jewifh nation never learned them from thofe books. In like manner though they fuppofed that the apoftles left fufficient traces of thefe fublime doctrines in their writings, they thought that the common chriftians, for whofe ufe they were written, did not perceive them, or make the proper inferences from them. That they fhould not have done this will not be thought extraordinary, if we confider the extreme *caution* with which, according to the account of
thefe

these Fathers themselves, those doctrines were taught in these books.

Such a revolution has time made in our apprehensions of things, that the doctrines of the pre-existence and divinity of Christ are now taught to children, as some of the first elements of christianity; but formerly the case was very different. They were considered as most sublime and difficult doctrines, and therefore, not to be taught till after every thing else relating to the gospel had been admitted and well understood. That these doctrines were actually considered in this light, appears from a great number of passages in the writings of the Fathers, many of which I shall introduce in other parts of this work, and especially some very striking ones from Origen. But not to advance a thing of this consequence without some evidence, in a place where it will be particularly wanted, I shall produce a few passages of this kind here.

Eusebius, after demonstrating the divine mission of Christ as a prophet, introduces his discourse concerning his pre-existence and divinity

divinity as a " mysterious and recondite doctrine*."

Austin compares the doctrine of the humanity of Christ to milk, and the doctrine of the divinity to strong meat, fit for men †.

"The doctrine of the incarnation," Chrysostom says, "was very difficult to be received ‡;" and then describing the great condescension of the maker of all things in submitting to be carried nine months in the womb of a woman, he says, that on this account the prophets announced it very obscurely. Again, observing that it was necessary to preach the humanity before the divinity of Christ, he says, "this was the order respecting his deity

---

* Καιρος ηδη κ̣ αποῤῥηοτερων εφαψατθαι λογων, των περι της και αυτον μυτικωτερας θεολογιας. Demonstratio, lib. 4. cap. 1. p. 144.

† Ut nutritus atque roboratus perveniat ad manducandum cibum, quod est in principio erat verbum, et verbum erat apud deum, et deus erat verbum. Lac nostrum, Christus humilis est: cibus noster, idem ipse Christus æqualis patri. In 1 John. Opera, vol. 9. p. 594.

‡ Πολυ δυσπαραδεκτος ην ο της Σαρκωσεως λογος. Serm. 8. Opera, vol. 5. p. 131, 132.

"and

"and incarnation, though it is introduced by John in a different manner from the rest, but in perfect agreement with them. But how? I say, that the doctrine not being taught at first, it was proper to dwell upon the incarnation, and to exercise them in the doctrine of the flesh; teaching them, from things grofs and fenfible; but when the doctrine was fixed, and the preaching received, it was then proper to ascend higher *."

Cyril of Alexandria, explaining a paffage in Ifaiah, fays, "here he mixes a great and profound myftery, which required a myftical initiation; for fo it was revealed to the divine Peter †."

* Ουτω δη κ, η ταξις αυτη η περι της θεοτητος κ, περι της οικονομιας, ει κ, απεναντιας τοις αλλοις γεγονε παρα Ιωαννη, αλλ' ομως σφοδρα συμφωνως αυτοις. κ, πως; εγω λεγω· οτι παρα μεν την αρχην ηδεπω τη λογη σπαρεντος, ακολουθον ην τω της οικονομιας ενδιατριβειν λογω, κ, περι της σαρκος γυμναζειν διδασκαλιαν απο των παχυτερων κ, αισθητων προοιμιαζομενους. επειδη δε επαγη τα της γνωσεως, κ, εδεξαντο το κηρυγμα, λοιπον ευκαιρον ην ανωθεν αρχεσθαι. In Pf. 44. Opera, vol. 3. p. 223.

† Immifcet autem hic myfterium profundum et magnum, et quod fuperna quadam myftagogia opus habet. Revelatum eft enim fic divino Petro. In If. cap. 49. Opera, vol. 1. p. 472.

Agobard

Agobard confidered what John taught concerning the divinity of Chrift as being fo difficult to be underftood, that, in order to it, the fame infpiration was neceffary that he himfelf had*.

"Perfection," fays Œcumenious, "is the
"doctrine concerning the divinity of Chrift,
"as far as the human underftanding can
"comprehend it †." Again, he fays, "by
"*firſt elements* the apoftle means the incar-
"nation. For, as with refpect to letters,
"fo in the divine oracles, what relates to
"the incarnation muft be learned in the
"firft place; for thefe were capable of
"being received by unbelievers and chil-
"dren; but to philofophize concerning
"the divinity of Chrift, is left to grown
"men. Do you fee why he refts fo
"long in thefe low things? It is on

* Inde qui hæc dixit accepit Johannes ille, qui difcumbebat fuper pectus domini, et de pectore domini bibebat quod nobis propinaret. Sed propinavit verba. Intellectum autem debes capere unde et ipfe biberat qui tibi propinavit. De Imaginibus, p. 231.

† Τελειοτης δε η αιωνιαιω η περι της θεολογιας χριτα. καθοσον εςιν ανθρωπω δυναιον, ακριβης καταληψις. In Heb. Opera, vol. 2. p. 35ŕ.

"account

"account of the weakness of his hearers, "who were not able to receive the perfect "doctrine. For which reason, having in "the beginning of the epistle philosophized "but a little concerning the divinity of "Christ, he presently changed his dis- "course, and the epistle is full of low "things*." This he gives from Photius. Again, after having observed that the author of the epistle to the Hebrews had spoken of the naked word of God, he says, that "he "returned to the incarnation, lest he should "confound his reader with the sublimity "of his doctrine†."

We see then, that, in the opinion of these Fathers (and some of them who write in

---

* Στοιχεια αρχης, την ενανθρωπησιν λεγει. ωσπερ γαρ επι των γραμμάτων πρωτον τα στοιχεια μανθανομεν. έτως κỳ επι των θειων λογιων εδει πρωτον τα περι της ενανθρωπησεως διδασκεσθαι. ταυτα γαρ ταις απιστοις ετι κỳ νηπιαις ακοαις χωρητα. ως το γε περι της θεότητος τȣ χριστȣ φιλοσοφειν, τελειων ην λοιπον. ορας την αιτιαν δι ην τοις ταπεινοις εμφιλοχωρει; δια την των ακȣοντων ασθενειαν. ȣκ ισχυοντων τα τελεια δεξασθαι· διο κỳ παρα τας αρχας της επιστολης βραχεα φιλοσοφησας περι της θεότητος τȣ χριστȣ. ευθυς κατεπαυσε τον λογον. των μεντοι ταπεινων η επιστολη γεμει. Ibid. p. 352.

† Ερηκως περι γυμνȣ τȣ θεȣ λογȣ, ηλθεν εις την ενανθρωπησιν, ινα μη τω υψει των ειρημενων ιλιγγιασωσι. In Heb. cap. 1. vol. 2. p. 320.

this

this manner lived pretty early, though others of them wrote in a later period) there were very mysterious and difficult doctrines to be revealed, of which no person to whom christianity was preached had the least conception, and to which it was apprehended they must be exceedingly averse. Let us now see in what manner they supposed that our Saviour and the apostles conducted themselves in this nice circumstance, and what period it was that they thought to be the most proper for making the great discovery.

To give some idea of the nature of this question, I would observe, that, if it should appear that a discovery of so great magnitude, as the Fathers represent this to have been, made no noise at all at the time fixed for the discovery, if it excited no particular attention; neither occasioning any doubt or controversy among christians themselves, nor bringing any objection to their doctrine from their enemies, it will afford a strong reason to suppose that no such discovery was made at that particular time. The Jews, to whom the gospel was first preached, as the Fathers admitted, expected nothing

thing more than a man for their Meffiah. They were fully fenfible that no Jew had any idea of his having pre-exifted at all, and much lefs of his having held any office of importance before he came into the world. When was it, then, that the Jews, to whom the gofpel was preached, were taught that Chrift had pre-exifted, that he was the logos of God, the maker of the world under God, or properly God himfelf? Was it in our Saviour's own life-time? Was it at the defcent of the Spirit at Pentecoft? Or was it in a later period of the gofpel hiftory? If no traces can be perceived of any fuch difcovery, in any period of the gofpel hiftory, an argument may be drawn from the confideration of it, highly unfavourable to the doctrine of Chrift having any nature fuperior to that of man; and when this circumftance fhall be fufficiently attended to (as I fufpect it never has been yet) the Arian hypothefis muft be greatly fhaken, but efpecially that of the perfect equality of the Son to the Father.

Confiderations of this kind, if they occur to him, no perfon, who thinks at all, can

abfolutely

absolutely neglect, so as to satisfy himself with having no hypothesis on the subject. We certainly find the apostles, as well as the rest of the Jews, without any knowledge of the divinity of Christ, with whom they lived and conversed as a man; and if they ever became acquainted with it, there must have been a *time* when it was either discovered by them, or made known to them; and the effects of the acquisition, or the communication of extraordinary knowledge, are, in general, proportionably conspicuous.

Had we no written history of our Saviour's life, or of the preaching of the apostles, or only some very concise one; still so very extraordinary an article as this would hardly have been unknown, much less when the history is so full and circumstantial as it is.

Had there been any pretence for imagining, that the Jews, in our Saviour's time, had any knowledge of the doctrine of the trinity, and that they expected the second person in it in the character of their Messiah, the question I propose would have been needless. But nothing can be more evident

evident than that, whatever some may fancy with respect to more ancient times, every notion of a trinity was obliterated from the minds of the Jews in our Saviour's time: It is therefore not only a curious, but a serious and important question, When was it introduced, and by what steps? I have answered it on my hypothesis, of its being an innovation and a corruption of the christian doctrine; let others do the same, on the idea of its being an essential part of it. Let us then see, what it is that the christian Fathers, who themselves believed the preexistence and divinity of Christ, and who were much nearer than we are to the time when the gospel was promulgated, have said on this subject.

CHAPTER III.

Of the Conduct of our Saviour himself, with respect to his own supposed Pre-existence and Divinity.

IF we look into the gospel history, we shall find, that all that our Saviour himself taught, or insinuated, were his divine mission in general, or his being the Messiah in particular; with the doctrine of the resurrection, and that of himself coming again to raise the dead and judge the world. These doctrines, accompanied with moral instructions, and reproofs of the Pharisees, for corrupting the law of God, made up the whole of his preaching. He never told his disciples that he had pre-existed, or that he had had any thing to do before he came into the world; much less that he had made the world, and governed it; and there is abundant

dant evidence that this was admitted by the chriftian Fathers.

Athanafius expreffes his fenfe of the difficulty with which the Jews admitted that Chrift was any thing more than a man very ftrongly in the following paffage: " He calls his humanity *the fon of*
" *man*; for the Jews, always oppofing God,
" held a twofold blafphemy with refpect to
" Chrift; for fome of them being offended
" at his flefh, viz. the fon of man, thought
" him to be a prophet, but not God, and
" called him a glutton and a wine-bibber;
" who were forgiven, for it was then the
" beginning of the preaching, and the world
" could not yet believe him to be God,
" who was made man; wherefore Chrift
" fays, Whofoever fhall fpeak a word againft
" the fon of man, viz. his body, it fhall be
" forgiven him. For I will venture to fay,
" that not even the bleffed difciples them-
" felves were fully perfuaded concerning his
" divinity, till the holy fpirit came upon them
" at the day of Pentecoft. For when they
" faw him after his refurrection, fome wor-
" fhipped

"shipped, but others doubted, yet they
"were not on that account condemned *."

The Fathers say, that whenever our Saviour said any thing that might lead his disciples to think that he was of a nature superior to that of man, they were offended, and that he conciliated their esteem whenever he represented himself as a mere man, such as they expected a prophet, and the Messiah to be. Chrysostom represents John the Baptist likewise as gaining proselytes to Christ, when he spake of him in low terms, but as deterring them when he seemed to speak of him in a higher capacity.

* Την δε ανθρωποτητα αυτε υιον ανθρωπου. νυν γαρ φησιν εδοξασθη ο υιος τε ανθρωπε. οι εν αει τω θεω προσκρεοντες Ιεδαιοι. διπλην προς χριστον την βλασφημιαν εκεκλητο· οι μεν γαρ τη σαρκι αυτε, ηγεν τω υιω τε ανθρωπε προσκοπτοντες, προφητην αυτον, αλλ' ε θεον ειναι ενομιζον, η φαγον αυτον η οικοσιτην εκαλεν, οις η συγγνωμην εδωκεν· αρχη γαρ ην τε κηρυγματος, η επω εχωρει ο κοσμος θεον πιστευειν γενομενον ανθρωπον. διο φησιν ο χριστος οτι, ος αν ειπη λογον κατα τε υιου τε ανθρωπε. ηγουν τε σωματος αυτε, αφεθησεται αυτω· τολμω γαρ λεγειν οτι εδε αυτοι οι μακαριοι μαθηται το τελειον περι της αυτε θεοτητος ειχον φρονημα, εως το πνευμα το αγιον αυτοις τη πεντηκοστη επιφοιτησεν. επει η μετα την αναστασιν ιδοντες αυτον, οι μεν προσεκυνησαν, οι δε εδισασαν· αλλ' εκ εκ τετε κατεκριθησαν. Sermo major de fide, in Montfaucon's Collection, vol. 2. p. 39.

Observe,

CHAP. III.   *his own Divinity*   67

"Obferve," fays he, "how, when he faid,
"He that cometh after me was before me,
"and I am not worthy to loofe his fhoe
"latchet; he took nobody. But when he
"fpake of his humanity, and ufed a lower
"ftyle, then the difciples followed him.
"Nor is this the only cafe of the kind, for
"the multitude were never brought to him
"when any thing high and lofty, as of a God,
"was faid of him, fo much as when they
"heard fomething mild and humble, and
"more adapted to the falvation of men *."

Accordingly Chryfoftom speaks of our Lord's difciples as having regarded him as a man in their intercourfe with him. Nathaniel, he fays, "confeffed Chrift as a man,
"when he addreffed himfelf to him, by the
"title of *Son of God.* John, i. 49. as ap-
"pears by his adding, *thou art the king of*

---

* Θεα δε μοι κακεινο πως οτι μεν ελεγεν, ο οπισω με ερχομενΘ- εμπροσθεν με γεγονε, ϗ οτι εκ ειμι ικανΘ- λυσαι τον ιμανΊα τε υποδηματΘ- αυτε, εδενα ειλεν. οτι δε περι της οικονομιας διελεχθη, ϗ επι το ταπεινοτερον τον λογον ηγαγε, τοτε ηκολεθησαν οι μαθηται. ε τετο δε μονον εςι κατιδειν, αλλ' οτι εκ ετως οι πολλοι προσαγονται οτ αν τι μεγα ϗ υψηλον περι θεε λεγηται, ως οτ αν χρηςον ϗ φιλανθρωπον ϗ εις την των ακεοντων σωτηριαν ηκον. In John i. Hom. 17. Opera, vol. 8. p. 93.

F 2   " *Ifrael*"

" *Israel.*" Ibid. p. 106. He says, that when Nathaniel was introduced to Jesus, his miraculous conception was not known*. As Chrysostom has written the most largely on this subject, I shall quote from him a passage or two of some extent, that we may more clearly perceive how he, and (as he was by no means singular in his ideas) how the christian Fathers in general thought with respect to this question.

"Another reason," he says, "why Christ
" represented himself so much as a man, was
" the weakness of his hearers; and because
" they who first saw and heard him were
" not able to receive more sublime dis-
" courses. And that this is no mere
" conjecture, I will endeavour to shew
" from the scriptures themselves. If he
" delivered any thing great, sublime, and
" worthy of his glory; but why do I
" say, great, sublime, and worthy of his
" glory; if he said any thing above
" human nature" (something is here omitted in the Greek, but supplied in the Latin version) " they were thrown into

---

* Ει δε υιον Ιωσηφ αυτον λεγει, μη θορυβηθης. ετι γαρ ιτετε ωσαις ενομιζετο ειναι. In John, Hom. 18. Op. vol. 8. p. 103.

" tumult

"tumult, and took offence; but if he said
"any thing low, and becoming a man, they
"ran to him, and received his doctrine.
"And where do we see this? In John
"chiefly. For when he said, *Abraham, our
"father rejoiced to see my day, and he saw it,
"and was glad,* they say, *Thou art not yet
"forty years old, and hast thou seen Abra-
"ham.* You see how they were affected to-
"wards him as to a common man. What
"then did he reply? *Before Abraham was
"I am;* and they took up stones to stone
"him. He spake more distinctly, saying,
"*The bread which I shall give for the life of
"the world is my flesh. They said, this is a
"hard saying, who can hear it;* and many of
"his disciples went backward, and walked no
"more with him.

"Tell me, then, what must he do? Must
"he always dwell upon these lofty topics,
"so as to drive away his prey, and deter all
"from his doctrine? But this did not be-
"come his divine philanthropy. Again,
"when he said, *He that heareth my words
"shall never taste of death,* they said, *Do we
"not say well, that thou hast a demon.—
Abraham,

" *Abraham is dead, and the prophets are dead,*
" *and thou sayest, he that heareth my words*
" *shall not taste of death.* And is it to be
" wondered at that the common people
" were thus affected towards him, when
" their rulers had the same opinion." He
then proceeds to instance in Nicodemus.—
" How then must he discourse with persons
" who would hear nothing sublime. Is it
" to be wondered at that he said nothing
" great or sublime concerning himself, to
" men creeping on the ground, and so
" meanly affected. What he said is suffi-
" cient to shew this was the reason, and the
" excuse for such mean discourses.

" On the other hand, as you see men
" scandalized, thrown into confusion, flying
" back from him, railing at him, and de-
" serting him, if he said any thing great
" and lofty; so will I endeavour to shew
" you that they ran to him, and received
" his doctrine, if he said any thing low
" and mean. For the very same persons who
" had fled from him, immediately ran to
" him, when he said, *I can do nothing of my-*
" *self but as the Father has taught me, so I*
" *speak.*

"*speak.* And the evangelists, designing to shew us that they believed on account of the meanness of his discourse, said, *When he spake these things many believed on him.* You will, on many occasions, find the same thing happening. On this account he spake in many things as a man, but sometimes not as a man, but as became a god *." He adds more to the same purpose.

* Ἐστι κὴ ἑτερα μετα ταυτην αιτια, η ασθενια των ἀκουοντων, κὴ το μη δυνασθαι τοτε πρωτον αυτον ιδοντας, κὴ τοτε πρωτον ακουοντας τας ὑψηλοτερας των δογμαων δεξασθαι λογας. κὴ ὁτι ȣ ςοχασμος το λεγομενον, απ αυτων σοι παραςησαι τȣτο πειρασομαι των γραφων, κὴ δειξαι. ειποτε τι μεγα κὴ ὑψηλον κὴ της αὑτȣ δοξης αξιον εφθεγξατο. τι λεγω μεγα κὴ ὑψηλον, κὴ της αὑτȣ δοξης αξιον; ει ποτε τι [ὑπερ] της ανθρωπινης φυσεως ειπε, πλεον εθορυβȣντο κὴ εσκανδαλιζοντο. ει δε ποτε τι ταπεινον κὴ ανθρωπινον, προσειρεχον, κὴ τον λογον εδεχοντο. κὴ τȣτο εςιν ιδειν φησι; παρα τω Ιωαννη μαλιςα. ειποντος γαρ αὑτȣ· Ἀβρααμ ὁ πατηρ ἡμων ηγαλιασατο, ἱνα ιδη την ημεραν την εμην, κὴ ιδε, κὴ εχαρη, λεγȣσι· τεσσαρακοντα ετη ȣπω εχεις, κὴ Ἀβρααμ εωρακας; ορας ὁτι ως περι ανθρωπȣ ψιλȣ διεκειντο; τι ȣν αυτος. προ τȣ τον Ἀβρααμ γινεσθαι φησιν, εγω ειμι. κὴ ηραν λιθȣς, ἱνα βαλλωσιν αυτον. κὴ των μυςηριων μακρȣς επετεινε λογȣς, λεγων. κὴ ὁ αρτος δε ον εγω δωσω ὑπερ της τȣ κοσμȣ ζωης, Σαρξ μȣ εςιν, ελεγον σκληρος εςι ὁ λογος ȣτος, τις δυναται αυτȣ ακȣειν; κὴ πολλοι των μαθητων αυτα απηλθον εις τα οπισω, κὴ ȣκετι μετ αυτȣ περιεπατȣν, τι ȣν εδει ποιειν, ειπε μοι: τοις ὑψηλοτεροις ενδιατριβειν ρημασι διηνεκως, ὡςε αποσοβησαι την θηραν, κὴ παντας αποκρυψασθαι της διδασκαλιας; αλλ' ȣκ ην τȣτο της τȣ θεȣ φιλαν-
θρωπιας

Again, he says, " if they took up stones to stone him, because he said that he was before Abraham, what would they have done if he had told them that he gave the law to Moses. Wherefore, when he said, it *was said to the ancients* he did not say *by whom* it had been said *."

Ἀρωπιας. κ̀ γαρ παλιν επειδη ειπεν ο τον λογον με ακεων, θαναθα μη γευσεθαι εις τον αιωνα ελεγον. ε καλως ελεγομεν οτι δαιμονιον εχεις; Αβρααμ απεθανε, κ̀ οι προφηθαι απεθανον. κ̀ συ λεγεις, οτι ο τον λογον με ακεων ε μη γευσεθαι θαναθε; κ̀ τι θαυμαςον ει το πληθος εἴω διεκειθο, οπε γε ε αυθοι οι αρχονθες ταυθην ειχον την γνωμην. Πως εν τελοις διαλεγεθαι εδει, τοις εδεν των υψηλων φερεσιν; οτι γαρ ολως εκ ειπε τι μεγα κ̀ υψηλον περι εαυθε, ε θαυμαςον ανθρωποις χαμαι συρομενοις, κ̀ ετως ασθηνως εχεσιν. ηρκει μεν εν και τα ειρημενα δειξαι, οτι αυθη η αιθια, και η προφασις ην της των τοθε λεγομενων ευθελειας, εγω δε και απο θαθερε μερες τε το πειρασμαι ποιηθαι φανερον. ωσπερ γαρ αυθες ιδελε σκανδαλιζομενες, θορυβομενες, αποπηδωνθας λοιδορεμενες φευγονθας ειποθε τι μεγα και υψηλον εφθεγξαθο ο χριςος. εἴως υμιν αυθες δειξαι πειρασομαι προςρεχονθας, καθαδεχομενες την διδασκαλιαν, ει ποθε τι ταπεινον και ευθελες ειπεν. αυθοι γαρ αυθοι οι αποπηδωνθες, ειπονθος αυθε παλιν οτι απ εμαυθε ποιω εδεν, αλλα καθως εδιδαξε με ο παθηρ με λαλω, ευθεως προσεδραμον. και βελομενος ημιν ενδειξασθαι ο ευαγγελιςης, οτι δια την ταπεινοθηθα των ρημαθων επιςευσαν, επισημαινεθαι λεγων. ταυθα αυθε λαλησανθος πολλοι επιςευσαν εις αυθον· κ̀ αλλαχε πολλαχε τεθο ευροι τις αν εἴω συμβαινον. δια τεθο πολλα και πολλακις ανθρωπινως εφθεγξεθο, κ̀ παλιν εκ ανθρωπινως. αλλα κ̀ θεοπρεπως. Or. 32. Opera. vol. I. p. 409, 410.

* Ει γαρ, επει ειπε, προ τε Αβρααμ γενεσθαι εγω ειμι, λιθασαι αυθον επεχειρησαν, ει προσεθηκεν οτι κ̀ Μωυσει αυθος τον νομον εδωκε, τι εκ αν εποιησαν. Ser. 51. Opera, vol. 5. p. 696, 697.

" Our

"Our Saviour," he says, "did not always teach his own divinity in express
words, leaving the fuller explication of
it to his disciples. If," says he, "they
(meaning the Jews) were so much offended at the addition of another law
to their former, much more must they
have been with the doctrine of his divinity †."

Chrysostom frequently observes that Christ only intimated his divinity obscurely, and left the full discovery of it to his apostles. Thus he says, that "he himself never said
plainly that he made the heavens and the
earth, and the sea and all things visible
and invisible. And why," says he, "do
you wonder that others should have said
greater things of him than he said of
himself, when he explained many things
by actions, but never clearly in words.
That he made man, he shewed clearly

---

* Δια δε τ8το 8δε περι της θεοτητος της εαυτ8 πανταχ8 φαινεται σαφως παιδευων. Ει γαρ η τ8 νομ8 προσθηκη τοσ8τον αυτ8ς εθορυβει, πολλω μαλλον το θεον εαυτον αποφαινειν. In Matt. v. Hom. 16. vol. 7. p. 154.

"enough,

"enough, as by the blind man; but when
"he was discoursing about the formation of
"the first man, he did not say *I* made
"them, but, *he that* made them, made them
"male and female. And that he made the
"world, he signified by the fishes, by the
"wine, by the loaves, &c. but never clearly
"in words *." He even says, "that the
"high dignity of Christ was more neces-
"sary to be concealed from his disciples,
"because they would immediately have told
"every thing through an excess of joy †."

"Christ," he says, "did not reveal
"his divinity immediately, but was first
"thought to be a prophet, and the Christ,

* Και τι θαυμαζεις ει ετεροι μειζονα περι αυτε ειρηκασιν ων αυτ۞ ειρηκεν. οπε γε πολλα δια ων πραγματων επιδεικνυμεν۞ δια των ρηματων σαφως εκ ελεγεν; οτι γαρ τον ανθρωπον αυτ۞ εποιησεν εδειξε σαφως κ' δια τε τυφλε. ηνικα δε περι της εν αρχη πλασεως ο λογ۞ ην αυτω. εκ ειπεν οτι εγω εποιησα, αλλ' ο ποιησας αρσεν και θηλυ εποιησεν αυτες. Παλιν οτι τον κοσμον εδημιεργησεν και τα εν αυτω δια των ιχθοων δια τε οινε δια των αρτων—— ρημασι εδαμε τετο σαφως; ειπεν. In Matt. v. Opera, vol. 7. p. 154.

† Εδει γαρ τεως λανθανειν, και μαλιςα επι των μαθητων. και γαρ εκ πολλης ηδονης παντα εκηρυξαν. In Matt. cap. 8. Opera, vol. 7. p. 271.

"simply

" simply a man, and it afterwards appeared
" by his works and his sayings what he
" really was *."

Basil of Seleucia says, that " during the
" storm, the disciples of Christ, judging by
" appearances, did not know that the deity
" was concealed in him; for they would not
" have been terrified, if they had known
" that the author of the creation was giving
" orders to the work of his hands." He
adds, that " the apostles themselves were as
" ignorant of his being God as the rest of
" the Jews, when some said that he was
" Elias, or Jeremias, or some of the pro-
" phets;" and that Christ, " knowing the
" ignorance of Peter, suggested to him the
" answer that he made †."

* Ου γαρ ευθεως ημιν εαυΐκ την θεοτητα εξεκαλυπτεν, αλλα πρωτον μεν ενομιζετο ειναι προφητης, κ χριςΘ, απλως ανθρωπΘ, υςερον δε εφανη, δια των εργων κ των ρηματων, τϗτο οπερ ην. In Johan. Hom. 2. Opera, vol. 8. p. 20.

† Τω γαρ φαινομενω προσπλαιοντες, την κεκρυμμενην ηγνοϗν θεοτητα. ϗ γαρ αν εξεπλαγησαν, κελευοντα τη κτισει θεωρϗντες οι δημιϗργον
ειναι της κτισεως επιςαμενοι.—Τοσαυτης ϗν αγνοιας τας των ανθρωπων,
ψυχας περι αυΐϗ βοσκομενης, ϗδε των αποςολων ο χορος αγνοιας ελευ-
θερος εμενεν.—Ειδως δε την αγνοιαν, υποβαλλει τω Πετρω θεικως την
αποκρισιν. Or. 25. p. 138, 139. 141.

Job

Job the monk obferves, that "Chrift faid, *thy fins are forgiven thee*, without intimating that be himfelf forgave them, by his own authority *."

Photius fays, "when our Lord faid, *My Father is greater than I*, the difciples were ftill imperfect, and thought the Father much greater. This they had learned from the Mofaic law, which taught the Father rather than the Son. This alfo our Saviour himfelf had perpetually inculcated. This, therefore, being their fixed opinion, they faid, Shew us the Father, and it fufficeth us †." Afterwards, he fays, "they knew him to be God, after his fufferings and refurrection ‡."

* Οτι το μεν αφεωνται εκ εχει των ρηματων προφοραν, ως εξ ιδιας εξυσιας προφερομενην κ προσαγμα⊙. Photii. Bib. fect. 222. p. 622.

† Επει γαρ ετι ατελως ετοι διεκειντο περι τον θεον κ διδασκαλον, μειζονα τε πολλω τον πατερα ενομιζον. τετο μεν των μωσαικων νομων εμφανετερον, αυτοις τον πατερα η τον υιον καταγγελλοντων· τετο δε τε σωτηρος ανω κ κατω περιστρεφοντος αυτοις τον πατερα· επει αν τοιαυτη τις αυτοις ενεστηρικτο η δοξα, δια γαρ τετο κ ελεγον, δειξον ημιν τον πατερα, κ αρκει ημιν. Epift. 176. p. 263.

‡ Ibid. p. 270.

Theodoret

Theodoret says, that "before his suffer-
"ings all persons held such an opinion
"concerning him," viz. that he was a mere
man, " but after his resurrection and ascen-
"sion, the descent of the Spirit, and the
"various miracles which they performed
"by invoking his name, all the believers
"knew that he was God, and the only be-
"gotten Son of God*." This is expressed
in general terms, but it will appear hereafter, that it is to be understood with great
limitations; the knowledge of the divinity
of Christ being, according to Theodoret
himself, far from universal among the christians, long after the death of Christ.

Sometimes the Fathers speak of Peter as
knowing that Christ was God before his
death, by immediate revelation from the
Father. Chrysostom also says, that before
our Lord's resurrection, the apostles had
learned that God had a Son equal to the

---

* Προ μεν εν τε παθες τοιαυτας ειχον δοξας περι αυτε. μετα δε την αναςασιν, κ̀ την εις ερανες αναβασιν, κ̀ την τε παναγιε πνευματος επι φοιτησιν, κ̀ τας παντοδαπας θαυματεργιας ας επετελεν, καλεντες αυτε το σεβασμιον ονομα, εγνωσαν απαντες οι πιςευοντες, οτι κ̀ θεος εςι, κ̀ τε θευ μονογενης υιος. Ad Rom. i. 4. Opera, vol. 3. p. 11.

Father.

Father*. But, in general, it was their opinion, that even Peter, as well as the other apoſtles, was ignorant of this great truth, till the deſcent of the Spirit at Pentecoſt; and they thought that this was one of the great truths alluded to, when our Lord ſaid, that he had many things to teach his diſciples, of which he could not inform them before his death.

Cyril of Alexandria, deſcanting on this " text, ſays, they who were not renewed by " the new rule of living, and the new doc- " trine of the Spirit, to them the recent " preaching of the goſpel, and the ſublime " myſtery of the trinity, was not to be deli- " vered. Juſtly, therefore, was the interpre- " tation of higher things reſerved to the fu- " ture renovation of the Spirit. That before " the reſurrection of the Saviour, and the " coming of the Spirit, the diſciples were as " Jews, is eaſy to prove†." Auſtin, however,

---

* Εμαθου οτι υιος τυ θευ εϛι, κ) υιον εχει ο Θεὸς ομοτιμον. In Acta, vol. 8. p. 459.

† Qui enim nondum nova vivendi norma, novaque doctrina per ſpiritum reformati ſunt, iis prædicatio evangelii recens, et myſterium trinitatis ſublime tradendum non eſt. Jure igitur renovationi per ſpiritum futuræ, altiorum rerum

says, that "the doctrine of the divinity of
"Christ could not be one of the things
"that Christ would not reveal, because
"they were not able to bear it, though
"some had said so*." And yet this writer himself, as we shall see, acknowledges
that the divinity of Christ was not taught
with clearness, till it was done by the
apostle John. Origen supposed that the
things which our Saviour referred to were
what related to the abolishing of the Jewish
law †. But he thought that John was the
person who first taught the doctrine of
Christ's pre-existence and divinity.

rerum interpretatio reservatur. Quod autem ante resurrectionem salvatoris, et ante spiritus adventum, Judaice discipuli vivebant, facillimum est probare. In John, lib. 11. cap. 41. Opera, vol. 1. p. 963.

* In principio erat verbum, et verbum erat apud deum, et deus erat verbum, hoc erat in principio apud deum, et alia quæ sequuntur, quoniam postea scripta sunt, nec ea dominum Jesu dixisse narratum est cum hic esset in carne, sed hæc unus ex apostolis ejus ipso ac spiritu ejus sibi revelante conscripsit: ex his esse quæ noluit tunc dominus dicere, quia ea discipuli portare non poterant, quis me audiat tam temere ista dicentem. In John, Tr. 96. cap. 16. Opera, vol. 9. p. 478.

† Ad Celsum, lib. 2. p. 57.

Before I proceed to confider what the Fathers thought of the apoftles' fentiments and conduct on the day of Pentecoft, I fhall take notice of another reafon which they give for the care that was taken to conceal the knowledge of our Lord's divinity, which was *to deceive the devil*, left he, knowing him to be the Meffiah, fhould not have ventured to encounter him, and fo, not being conquered by him, and efpecially by means of his death, the great object of his miffion would not have been gained.

This thought firft occurs in epiftles afcribed to Ignatius, who fays, " the vir- " ginity of Mary, her delivery, and his " death, were concealed from the prince of " this world*." Jerom fays, that both the demons and the devil, rather fufpected, than knew the Son of God †. Chryfoftom, fpeaking of the myftery of the incarnation being

---

* Και ελαθε τον αρχοντα τȣ αιωνος τȣτȣ η παρθενια Μαριας, κỳ ο τοκετος αυτης, ομοιως κỳ ο θανατος τȣ κυριȣ, τρια μυϛηρια κραυγης, ατινα εν ησυχια θεȣ επραχθη. Ad. Eph. S. 19. p. 16.

† Jam dæmones quam diaboli fufpicari magis filium dei, quam noffe intelligendi funt. In Matt. cap. 8. Opera, vol. 6. p. 12.

concealed

concealed from many, says, "Why do I say
"many? Mary herself, when she carried him
"in her womb, did not know the secret. And
"why do I say men? The devil himself did
"not know it, for if he had known it, he
"would not afterwards have asked him upon
"the mount, saying, *If thou art the Son of
"God*; and he did this once, twice, and three
"times. On this account he said to John,
"who was beginning to reveal him, *hold now*;
"that is, be silent now. It is not yet time
"to reveal the secret of the incarnation; I
"must yet deceive the devil; keep silence
"now, for thus it becomes us *." Again,
he says, "the devil was at a loss to know
"whether Christ was God or not. †."

* Και τι λεγω τας πολλας, οπα γε αδε αυτη η κυοφορασα παρθενος ηδει το απορρητον. Και τι λεγω ανθρωπας, κὶ αυτον τον διαβολον ελανθανεν. αδε γαρ αν, ειπερ ηδει, ηρωτα αυτον μετα τοσατον χρονον επι τα ορας, ει υιος ει τα θεα, κὶ απαξ, κὶ δις κὶ τριτον τατο εποιει. διο κὶ τω Ιωαννη ελεγεν αρξαμενω αυτον εκκαλυπτειν: αφες αρτι· τατεςι, σιγα νυν, αδεπω καιρος τα γαρ εκαλυφθεναι το απορρητον της οικονομιας. ετι λανθανειν τον διαβολον βαλομαι. σιγα τοινυν φησι. ατω γαρ πρεπον εςιν ημιν. In Ps. 49. Opera, vol. 3. p. 289.

† Εν αμηχανια λοιπον ην, κὶ ετε οτι ανθρωπος ην ψιλος πιςευσαι ηδυνατο, δια τα περι αυτα λεχθεντα· αδε αυ παλιν παραδεξασθαι, οτι υιος ην τα θεου, δια το βλεπειν αυτον πεινωντα. In Matt. Opera, vol. 7. p. 119.

There is something pleasant in the manner in which the Fathers sometimes speak of the devil being deceived by the humanity of Christ. Cyril of Jerusalem says, "it was necessary that Christ should suffer for us, but the devil would not have come near him, if he had known this; for if *they had known, they would not have crucified the Lord of glory.* 1 Cor. ii. 8. The body, therefore, was the bait of death, that the dragon, thinking to swallow it down, might vomit up all that he had swallowed *."

Ruffinus also represents the divinity of Christ as concealed within his humanity, to catch the devil as with a bait; and to prove this, he adduces many passages of the Old Testament, especially that of Ezek. *I will draw thee out with my hook*, &c†.

---

* Εδει παθειν υπερ ημων τον κυριον, αλλ' ουκ αν ετολμησε προσελθειν ο διαβολος, ει ηδει τουτον. ει γαρ εγνωσαν, ουκ αν τον κυριον της δοξης εσαυρωσαν. δελεαρ τοινυν τω θανατω γεγονε το σωμα, ινα ελπισας καταπιειν ο δρακων, εξεμεση κ̣ τους ηδη καταποθεντας. Is. 25. 8. Cat. 12. Opera, p. 155.

† Ita et is qui habet mortis imperium rapuit quidem in morte corpus Jesu, non sentiens in eo hamum divinitatis inclusum; sed ubi devoravit, hæsit ipse continuo, et diruptis

CHAP. III. *his own Divinity.* 83

Theodoret says, that Christ concealed his divinity in his temptation by the devil; and says, that when the devil heard him speak as a man, he was encouraged to proceed with the temptation. He represents him as saying, "I heard the voice that came down "from heaven, calling you the Son of God, "but I shall not believe it till it appear by "facts*."

Job the monk also says, "it was neces- "sary that the mystery of the incarnation of "the logos should be concealed, both to "make it more acceptable to the hearers, "and also to deceive the devil †."

Basil of Seleucia says, that, "though the "demons called Christ the Son of God, "they did not know that he was God, be-

---

tis inferni claustris, velut de profundo extractus, trahitur ut esca cæteris fiat. In Symb. Opera, p. 179.

* Κρυπ]ει μεν την θεοτητα — ꭒκ απηγορευσε την νικην ακꭒσας ως ανθρωπ☉ ειη. Της μεν γαρ ανωθεν ελθꭒσης φωνης ηκꭒσα, φησι, τꭒ]ο σε καλεσꭒσης, απιϛω δε, εως αν λαβω την πειραν διδασκαλον. Opera, vol. 5. p. 46.

† Αναγκαιον δε ην το επισκιαζεσθαι το μυϛηριον της τꭒ λογꭒ σαρ- κωσεως δια δε το γενεσθαι τοις ακροωμενοις ευπαραδεκτον, κ̀ ινα τꭒ σκοτꭒς τον αρχοντα λαθη. Photii. Bib. S. 222. p. 622.

G 2   "cause

" cause all very good men are called *sons of*
" *God*, and Israel is called his first born *."

It was objected, that it was wrong in God to conquer the devil by deceiving him, the divinity of Christ being concealed under his human nature; but Gregory Nyssen replies, that " it was fair enough to deceive the de-
" ceiver †."

If it was imagined to be necessary that the devil, whose cunning and penetration was never thought very lightly of, should remain ignorant of our Lord's divinity, he must, no doubt, have concealed it with the greatest care, and have conducted himself in the most cautious manner. If the devil was not able to discover any thing of the matter, how could *men* find it out, and especially Jews, whose most sanguine expectations from the Messiah went no farther than to a man, born like other men? Certainly they

---

* Υιον μεν θευ καλυσι, θεον δε τεως τον υιον υκ επισανται. υιοι γαρ θευ κευλυνται, κ̓ οι διαρετης ακροτητα την προς θεον εχοντες οικειοτητα. ετω το πρωτοτοκος υιος μυ Ισραηλ. Or. 23. p. 128.

† Η μεν γαρ κἀ αξιαν αντιδοσις, δι ης ο απατεων ανταπαλαται το δικαιον δεικνυσιν. Or. 2. Opera, vol. 2. p. 515.

who

who thought that the devil continued ignorant of the pre-exiſtence and divinity of Chriſt till after his death, muſt have thought that all the Jews, and our Lord's diſciples, were ignorant of thoſe doctrines. If, as Chryſoſtom ſays, it was particularly neceſſary to conceal this great ſecret from our Lord's diſciples, leſt they ſhould have publiſhed it through joy, and alſo from his enemies, and the devil, leſt they ſhould have counteracted the deſign of his coming, we may take it for granted, that, in the opinion of the writers who have given us theſe repreſentations, it was no more ſuſpected at the time of Chriſt's death, that he had even pre-exiſted, or that he had had any thing to do in the making or governing the world, than that he was to be ſo great a perſonage before he was born.

Let us now ſee in what manner the apoſtles were ſuppoſed to have conducted themſelves in this reſpect after our Lord's aſcenſion, and after the deſcent of the Spirit on the day of Pentecoſt.

CHAPTER IV.

Of the Testimony of Athanasius to the Caution with which the Apostles divulged the Doctrines of the Pre-existence and Divinity of Christ.

AS the Testimony of Athanasius, on account of his known orthodoxy, and of course his unwillingness to make any needless concessions to his adversaries, may be thought to have more weight than any other, I shall, in the first place, produce *it*; and as exceptions have been made to it, I shall shew that, independent of any concurrent testimony of others of the Fathers, who have mentioned the subject, and which I shall produce hereafter, it clearly proves that, in his idea, the apostles thought it necessary to use great caution in divulging to the Jews so offensive a doctrine as that of the divinity of Christ; though, in consequence of their caution on this head, the Jewish christians did in their age continue unitarians,

unitarians, believing Chrift to be nothing more than a mere man, and alfo propagated the fame doctrine among the Gentile converts. The paffage itfelf is as follows:

"Will they affirm," fays he, "that the
"apoftles held the doctrine of Arius, becaufe
"they fay that Chrift was a man of Nazareth,
"and fuffered on the crofs? or becaufe they
"ufed thefe words, were the apoftles of
"opinion that Chrift was only a man, and
"nothing elfe? By no means: this is
"not to be imagined. But this they did
"as wife mafter-builders, and ftewards of
"the myfteries of God; and they had this
"good reafon for it. For the Jews of that
"age, being deceived themfelves, and hav-
"ing deceived the Gentiles, thought that
"Chrift was a mere man, only that he came
"of the feed of David, refembling other
"defcendants of David, and did not be-
"lieve either that he was God, or that the
"word was made flefh. On this account
"the bleffed apoftles, with great prudence,
"in the firft place, taught what related to
"the humanity of our Saviour to the Jews,
"that having fully perfuaded them, from his
"miraculous

" miraculous works, that Christ was come,
" they might afterwards bring them to the
" belief of his divinity, shewing that his
" works were not those of a man, but of
" God. For example, Peter having said
" that Christ was a man who had suffered,
" immediately added, he is the prince of
" life. In the gospel he confesses, thou
" art the Christ, the Son of the living God;
" and in his epistle, he calls him the bishop
" of souls *."

* Ουδεν γαρ αυτοις ατολμητον, ότι και αυτοι αποστολοι τα Αρειε εφρονεν. ανθρωπον γαρ αυτον απο Ναζαρετ, και παθητον του χριστον απαγγελλσιν, εκεινο τοινυν τοιαυτα φανταζομενα, ως επειδη τοις ρημασι τετοις εχρησαντο, μονον ανθρωπον ηδεισαν τον χριστον οι αποστολοι, η πλεον εδεν; μη γενοιτο· εκ εστιν εδε εις νεν ποτε τετο λαβειν· αλλα η τετο ως αρχιτεκτονες σοφοι, η οικονομοι μυστηριων θεε πεποιηκασι. η την αιτιαν εχεσιν ευλογον· επειδη γαρ οι τοτε Ιεδαιοι πλανηθεντες, η πλανησαντες Ελληνας, ενομιζον τον χριστον ψιλον ανθρωπον, μονον εκ σπερματος Δαβιδ αρχεσθαι, καθ ομοιοτητα των εκ του Δαβιδ αλλων γενομενων τεκνων· ετε δε θεον αυτον, εδε οτι λογος σαρξ εγενετο επιστευον. Τετε ενεκα, μετα πολλης της συνεσεως οι μακαριοι αποστολοι τα ανθρωπινα τε σωτηρος εξηγευντο πρωτον τοις Ιεδαιοις, ινα ολως πεισαντες αυτες, εκ των φαινομενων η γενομενων σημειων, εληλυθεναι τον χριστον, λοιπον η εις τα περι της θεοτητος αυτε πιστιν αυτες αναγαγωσιν, δεικνυντες οτι τα γενομενα εργα εκ εστιν ανθρωπε, αλλα θεε. αμελει Πετρος ο λεγων ανδρα παθητον τον χριστον, ευθυς συνηπτεν ετος αρχηγος της ζωης εστιν, &c. &c. De Sententia Dionysii, Opera, vol. 1. p. 553, 554.

There

There is a passage in the *Sermo Major de fide* of this writer, published in *Montfaucon's Collectio Patrum*, which bears some resemblance to this. Speaking of Peter preaching Christ as Jesus of Nazareth, a man approved of God, he says, "He calls "him a man, and not God, with respect "to the Jews, and others, who, like them, "considered things according to the flesh, "from that time to the present. And the "apostles of our Lord, and our Lord himself, answered concerning himself as a "man. Ye seek to kill me, a man who "has told you the truth*.

It has been said, that Athanasius is here speaking of the unbelieving Jews. The expression is, οι τοτε Ιεδαιοι *the Jews of that age*; which includes both the believing and unbelieving Jews. Had he been speaking of the Jews of his own time, it would, I own, have been probable that he meant the unbelieving Jews; but speaking as he

---

* Ανδρα τε αυτον φησι, και ε θεον, προς τες Ιεδαιες και τες ομοιως αυτοις κατα σαρκα φρονεντας εκ τοτε και νυν. και οι αποσολοι και αυτος ο κυριος περι εαυτε ανθρωπινως απεκρινατο λεγων. τι με ζητειτε αποκτειναι, ανθρωπον ος την αληθειαν υμιν λελαληκα. Vol. 2. p. 16.

does

does of the Jews at the very firſt promulgation of chriſtianity among them, it is moſt natural to ſuppoſe that he meant all the Jews. Paul, long after his converſion to chriſtianity, called himſelf a Jew. However, it will be ſufficiently evident from the whole tenor of the paſſage, that he muſt have meant the believing Jews principally, and in ſome reſpects, the believing Jews only, excluſive of the unbelieving ones. And in this conſtruction of the paſſage, I am by no means ſingular, but have the ſanction of trinitarians themſelves, as that of the Latin tranſlator and Beauſobre.

The Latin tranſlator of Athanaſius, a catholic, and certainly no unitarian, had ſo little ſuſpicion of any other meaning, that he renders χριτου in this place by *Jeſum*. The learned Beauſobre, a trinitarian, and therefore, an unexceptionable judge in this caſe, quoting this very paſſage, does not heſitate to pronounce that they were believing Jews who were intended by the writer, "Ces Juifs," he ſays, "ne ſont pas "les Juifs incredules, mais cieux qui fa- "ſoient profeſſion du chriſtianiſme. But
admitting

admitting that the Jews here meant were unbelieving Jews, they were such as the apostles wished to convert to christianity, and many of them soon became christians.

But the circumstance which decisively proves that the Jews Athanasius is speaking of were *christian Jews*, is their drawing the Gentiles into the belief of the simple humanity of Christ. For certainly the gospel was preached to the Gentiles by the believing, and not by the unbelieving Jews. If it be supposed that the doctrine Athanasius speaks of was not concerning *Jesus*, but the *Messiah in general*, how could it interest the Gentiles? The doctrine, therefore, must have been that concerning *Jesus*, and consequently, the preachers must have been christian Jews, and their proselytes christian Gentiles. It is ridiculous to suppose that the question could be interesting to any others.

Supposing, however, the whole body of the Gentiles (little as they were concerned in the question) to have been previously taught by the Jews, that their Messiah, whenever he should come, would be nothing

thing more than a man; if this was an opinion that they were as fully perſuaded of as Athanaſius repreſents the Jews, their teachers, to have been, the ſame caution muſt have been as neceſſary with reſpect to them, as with reſpect to the Jews themſelves, and for the ſame reaſon.

It has been ſaid, that Athanaſius ſays nothing about the *caution* of the apoſtles, but only ſpeaks of their *prudence*, in teaching what was more eaſy and neceſſary, before that which was more difficult and leſs neceſſary. But the term συνεσις, in the connexion in which it ſtands, can bear no other ſenſe than *caution*, and great caution, μετα πολλης της συνεσεως, and it appears from the whole tenor of the diſcourſe, that Athanaſius could have intended nothing elſe than to deſcribe the prudence, or extreme caution of the apoſtles, and to account for it. He evidently does not repreſent them as deferring the communication of the doctrine of the divinity of Chriſt, on account of its being more conveniently taught afterwards, as part of a ſyſtem of faith; but only leſt it ſhould have given offence to the Jews.

CHAP. IV.   *of Athanasius.*   93

If skill, or prudence, in these circumstances, be not the same thing with *caution,* I do not know what is meant by caution.

It has been said that Athanasius speaks of the *rapidity* with which Peter proceeded to teach the doctrine of the divinity of Christ. On the other hand, I find no trace of rapidity in this account of the apostles conduct. All that approaches to it is that, immediately after any mention of the humanity of Christ (which he speaks of as necessary on account of the Jewish prejudices) he says the apostles subjoin some expressions which might have led their hearers to the knowledge of his divinity; but the instances he produces are such as plainly confute any pretensions to their being a distinct and full declaration of that doctrine.

The first instance he gives us is from the speech of Peter to the Jews on the day of Pentecost, in which he says (Acts ii. 22.) " Ye men of Israel, hear these words, Jesus " of Nazareth, a man approved of God " among you, by miracles and wonders, and " signs, which God did by him in the midst
" of

"of you, as ye yourselves also know." In this Athanasius acknowledges, that Peter preached the proper humanity of Christ, but says that, immediately afterwards (referring to his discourse on the cure of the lame man in the temple) he called him *the prince of life* (Acts iii. 10.) " and killed the " prince of life whom God hath raised from " the dead."

Had the apostle meant that his audience should have understood him as referring to the divinity of Christ by that expression, his prudence must have lasted but a very short time indeed; probably not many days. If, therefore, his intention was, as Athasius represents it, to preach the doctrine of the humanity of Christ in the first place, and not to divulge the doctrine of his divinity till they were firmly persuaded of his messiahship, he could not *mean* to allude to his divinity in this speech, which was addressed not to the believing, but to the unbelieving Jews. At least, he could only have thought of doing it in such a manner as that his hearers might afterwards infer the doctrine from it; and it must have required great ingenuity,

ingenuity, and even a ſtrong prepoſſeſſion in favour of the divinity of Chriſt (the reverſe of which this writer acknowledges) to imagine that this expreſſion of *prince of life*, which ſo eaſily admits of another interpretation, had any ſuch reference. Moreover, in all the inſtances which Athanaſius produces concerning the conduct of the apoſtles in this reſpect, from the book of Acts, he does not pretend to find one in which the divinity of Chriſt is diſtinctly preached, though he quotes four paſſages in which his humanity is plainly ſpoken of.

Beſides, had Athanaſius thought that the apoſtle had preached the doctrine of the divinity of Chriſt with much effect, it is probable that he would have added this circumſtance to his narrative; as, from the object of the work in which the paſſage is introduced, it may be inferred, that he could not but have thought that it would have been ſufficiently to his purpoſe. For, certainly, if he could have added that, notwithſtanding their caution in preaching this extraordinary doctrine (againſt which he acknowledges the Jews had the ſtrongeſt prejudices)

judices) the apoſtles neverthelefs did preach it with effect, and that it was the general belief of the Jewiſh chriſtians in their time, he would have done it. It would certainly have favoured his great object in writing the piece, viz. the vindication of Dionyſius, in uſing a like caution with reſpect to the Sabellians, to have added, that this prudence, or caution, was not, in either of the two caſes, finally detrimental to the cauſe of truth. I therefore conſider the ſilence of Athanaſius on this head as a negative argument of ſome weight; and, upon the whole, I think that Athanaſius muſt have ſuppoſed that both the Jewiſh and Gentile churches were unitarian in the time of the apoſtles. At leaſt, he enables us to infer that it muſt have been ſo, which is quite ſufficient for my argument.

Now if this caution was requiſite in the firſt inſtance, and with reſpect to the firſt converts that the apoſtles made, it was equally requiſite with reſpect to the reſt, at leaſt for the ſake of others who were not yet converted, unleſs the firſt ſhould have been enjoined ſecrecy on that head. For whenever

whenever it had been known that the apostles were preaching not such a messiah as they expected, viz. a man like themselves, but the eternal God, the difference was so great, that a general alarm would have been spread, and the conversion of the rest of the Jews (to a doctrine which must have appeared so highly improbable to them) would have been impeded. We may therefore presume that the apostles must have connived at this state of ignorance concerning the divinity of Christ, in the Jewish christians, till there was little hope of making any farther converts among the Jews, and till the gospel began to be preached to the Gentiles.

Indeed, this must have been the case according to Athanasius's own account; for he, says, that these Jews, being in an error themselves, led the Gentiles into the same error. He must, therefore, be understood to say, that the Jewish converts, while (through the caution of the apostles) they were ignorant of the divinity of Christ, preached the gospel in that state to the Gentiles. And as he speaks of *Gentiles in general*, and without any respect to *time*, and also of their being actually brought over to that belief, it is impossible not to understand him of this caution, being continued till the gospel had been fully preached to the Gentiles as well as to the Jews. Besides, one of the instances that Athanasius here gives of the preaching of the simple humanity of Christ is taken from the discourse of the apostle Paul at Athens, which was about the year 53 after Christ; and, indeed, at this time the gospel had not been preached to any great extent among the Gentiles. For it was on this very journey that this apostle first preached the gospel in Macedonia and Greece.

If, according to Athanasius, the apostolical reserve with respect to the doctrine of the divinity of Christ continued till this time (and he says nothing concerning the termination of it) we may presume that this great doctrine, supposing it to have been known to the apostles, had not been publicly taught by them, till very near the time of their dispersion and death; and then I think it must have come too late, even from them.

For

For it appears from the book of Acts, that their mere *authority* was not sufficient to overbear the prejudices of their countrymen. At least, the communication of a doctrine of so extraordinary a nature, of which they had no conception, must have occasioned such an alarm and consternation, as we must have found some traces of in the history of the Acts of the apostles. It could not have been received without hesitation and debate.

If we can suppose that the apostles, some time before their death, did communicate this great and unexpected doctrine, the effects of such communication must have been very transient. For presently after the death of the apostles, we find all the Jewish christians distinguished by the name of Nazarenes, or Ebionites, and no trace of the doctrine of the divinity of Christ among them.

When all these things are considered, viz. that Athanasius acknowledged that it required great caution in the apostles to divulge the doctrine of the divinity of Christ, and that the gospel was preached with success among the Gentiles, while the Jews were

were ignorant of it, it can hardly be doubted, but that he muſt himſelf have conſidered the chriſtian church in general as unitarian in the time of the apoſtles, at leaſt till near the time of their diſperſion and death.

According to Athanaſius, the Jews were to be well grounded in the belief of Jeſus being the Chriſt, before they could be taught the doctrine of his divinity. Now, if we look into the book of Acts, we ſhall clearly ſee, that they had not got beyond the firſt leſſon in the apoſtolic age, the great burden of the preaching of the apoſtles being to perſuade the Jews that Jeſus was the *Chriſt*. That he was likewiſe *God*, they evidently left to their ſucceſſors, who, indeed, did it moſt effectually, though it required a long courſe of time to ſucceed in it.

CHAPTER V.

Of the concurrent Testimony of other Fathers to the caution of the Apostles, in teaching the Doctrines of the Pre-existence and Divinity of Christ.

I Have no great occasion to lay much stress on the testimony of Athanasius, as there is that of others of the Fathers sufficiently full and clear to the same purpose.

Chrysostom having said, that Christ taught his divinity by his works only, says, that " Peter also, in the beginning,
" used the same method. For that, in his
" first discourse to the Jews, he taught no-
" thing clearly concerning his divinity ;
" and because they were then incapable of
" learning any thing clearly concerning it,
" he dwelt upon his humanity ; that, being
" accustomed to this, they might be pre-
" pared for what they were to be taught
" afterwards. And if any person," he says,
" will attend to the whole of their preach-
" ing,

"ing, he will see what I say very clearly.
"For he calls him *a man*, and dwells upon
"his suffering and resurrection, and things
"belonging to the flesh. And Paul, when
"he speaks of his being *the Son of David*
"*according to the flesh*, teaches us nothing
"farther, that what belonged to the huma-
"nity might be acknowledged. But the
"son of thunder discourses concerning his
"mysterious and eternal existence; so that,
"omitting what he *did*, he relates what he
"*was* *."

The same writer says, that the apostles
concealed the doctrine of the miraculous
conception on account of the incredulity of

---

* Δ.α τετο κ̓ ο Πετρ۞ εν αρχη ταιω κεχρηται τω τροπω . κ̓ γαρ
ταυτην [πραξιν] προς Ιαδαιας εδημηγορει δημηγοριαν . κ̓ επειδη εδεν
περι της θεοτητ۞ αυτε τεως σαφες μαθειν ισχυον, δια τετο τοις περι της
οικονομιας ενδιαιρριβει λογοις· ινα τετοις η ακοη γυμνασθεισα τη λοιπη
προσδοποιησηι διδασκαλια. κ̓ ει βελοιτο τις την δημηγοριαν πασαν ανωθεν διελθειν, ευρησει τατο ο λεγω σφοδρα διαλαμπον . κ̓ γαρ ανδρα αυτον
καλει κ̓ αυτος, κ̓ τοις τε παθες κ̓ της αναστασεως κ̓ της κατα σαρκα
γεννησεως ενδιαιρριβει λογοις. κ̓ Παυλος δε. οι αν λεγη, τε γενομενε εκ
σπερματος Δαβιδ κατα σαρκα, εδεν ετερον ημας παιδευει, αλλ' ὁτι το
επομισεν επι της οικονομιας παρειληπται· ο και ημεις ομολογεμεν. αλλ'
ο της βροντης υιος περι της αρρητε και προαιωνιε ημιν υπαρξεως διαλεγεται εν. δια τετο το εποιησει αφεις, το ην εθηκεν. In John, Hom.
2. Opera, vol. 8. p. 20.

the

CHAP. V.   *of other Fathers.*   103

the Jews with respect to it, and that when they began to preach the gospel, they insisted chiefly on the resurrection of Christ. With respect to the former (and the same may, no doubt, be applied to the latter) he says, " he did not give his own opinion
" only, but that which came by tradition
" from the Fathers and eminent men. He,
" therefore, would not have his hearers to
" be alarmed, or think his account of it
" extraordinary *."

Thus, he says, that " it was not to give
" offence to the Jews, that Peter, in his
" first speech to them, did not say that
" *Christ* did the wonderful works of which
" he spake, but that *God* did them by him;
" that by speaking more modestly he might
" conciliate them to himself†." The same caution he attributes to him in " not saying
" that Christ, but that God spake by the

* Αλλα μη θορυβεισθε προς το παραδοξον τε λεγομενε . ε δε γαρ εμος ο λογος αλλα πατερων ημετερων θαυματων κ] επισημων ανδρα: In cap. Matt. 1. Hom. 3. vol. 7. p. 20.

† Ουκετι λεγει οτι αυτ⊙, αλλ' οτι δι αυτε ο θεος, ινα μαλλον τω μετριαζειν εφελκυσηται. In Acta Apostolorum, cap. 2. Hom. 6. vol. 8. p. 491.

H 4   " mouth

" mouth of his holy prophets, that by these
" means he might bring them gradually to
" the faith *."

After treating pretty largely of the conduct of the apostles, with respect to their insisting on the doctrine of the resurrection of Christ, rather than that of his divinity, immediately after the descent of the Holy Spirit, he says, " As to the Jews who had
" daily heard and been taught out of the
" law, *Hear, O Israel, the Lord thy God is*
" *one Lord, and besides him there is no other,*
" having seen him (Jesus) nailed to a cross,
" yea, having killed and buried him them-
" selves, and not having seen him risen
" again ; if they had heard that this person
" was God equal to the Father, would not
" they have rejected and spurned at it." I want words in English to express the force of the Greek in this place. The latin translator renders it, *nonne maxime omnes ab his verbis abhoruissent, ac resilissent et oblatrassent.*
" On this account," he adds, " they (the

---

* Ου λεγει ων ειπεν ο χριστ⸗, αλλ᾽ ων ελαλησεν ο θε⸗, ἔτι τω ϝυσκιαζειν μαλλον αυτες επαγομεν⸗ εις πιςιν ηρεμα. In Acta Apostolorum, Hom. 9. vol. 8. p. 511.

" apostles)

"apostles) brought them forwards gently
"and by slow degrees, and used great art in
"condescending to their weakness *."

Chrysostom represents the apostle as beginning his epistle to the Hebrews with saying, that "it was God who spake
"by the prophets, and not that Christ
"himself had spoken by them, because
"their minds were weak, and they were
"not able to bear the doctrine concern-
"ing Christ †. He even says, that when

* Πως δε αν Ιεδαιοι οι καθ εκασην ημεραν, μανθανονίες υπο τε νομε, Ακεε Ισραηλ, κυριος ο θεος σε κυρι<i>Θ</i> εις εσιν, κ, πλην αυτε εκ εσιν αλλος, επι ξυλε σαυρε ιδονίες προσηλωμενεν αυτον, μαλλον δε κ ταυρωσαντες κ θαψαντες, κ εδε ανασαντα θεασαμενοι, ακεοντες οτι θε<i>Θ</i> εσιν αυτ<i>Θ</i> ε<i>Θ</i>, κ, τω πατρι ισ<i>Θ</i>, εκ αν μαλισα παντων απεπηδησαν κ απερραγησαν. Διαυτι τετο ηρεμα, κ, καλα μικρον. αυτες προσειβαζεσι, κ, πολλη μεν κεχρηνιαι τη της συγκαταβασεως οικονομια.
In Acta Hom. 1. Opera, vol. 8. p. 447.

† Και θεα τι συνετως αυτο ειρηκε . ε γαρ ειπεν ο θε<i>Θ</i> ελαλησεν καιτοιγε αυτ<i>Θ</i>·ην ο λαλησας . αλλ' επειδη ασθενεις αυτων ησαν αι ψυχαι, κ, εδεπω ακεειν ηδυναντο τα περι τε χρισε, φησιν ο θε<i>Θ</i> δι αυτε ελαλησεν. In Heb. cap. 1. Opera, vol. 10. p. 1756. i. e.
"See how prudently he spoke : for he said God spake
"though it was himself that spake ; but because their
"minds were weak and they were not able to bear the
"things concerning Christ, he says *God spake by him.*"
N. B. The (ε) in the second clause of this passage must
be

"he there speaks of Christ as above the "angels," he still spake of his humanity. "See," says he, "his great caution, ορα την συνεσιν την πολλην*, the very expression used by Athanasius on a similar occasion.

But we find no trace of either Jews or Gentiles having received these sublime doctrines that Chrysostom alludes to in the age of the apostles. Nay we see that he himself represents the apostle Paul as obliged to use the same caution with respect to the Jews, when he wrote the epistle to the Hebrews, which was so late as A. D. 62. about two years before his death.

Theodoret observes, that " in the genea-"logy of Christ given by Matthew, this "writer did not add *according to the flesh*, "because the men of that time would not "bear it;" evidently meaning, that they would thereby have been led into a suspi-

---

be inserted by mistake for (ε) or some other particle, as it contradicts what is said in the close of the sentence, and the obvious sense of the whole. Or perhaps, the first ϛε⊙ should have been χρι⊙.

* In Heb. cap. 1. Opera, vol. 10. p. 1755.

cious

cion that, in the idea of the writer, he had some higher origin, and that they would have been offended at it. "But the apos-"tle Paul," he says, "could not avoid that "expression in his epistle to the Romans." He adds that, "before his death, not only "to the other Jews, but to the apostles "themselves, he did not appear as a God, "nor did his miracles lead them to form "that opinion of him†." This writer also

† Η γαρ τε κατα σαρκα προσθηκη, αινιτιεται ως τε θεε κ παιρος υιος εςιν αληθως κατα την θεοτητα. εδε γαρ επι των τετο μονον ονων ρπερ ορωνται, εςιν ευρειν το κατα σαρκα προσκειμενον. κ μαρτυς ο μακαριος Ματθαιος ο ευαγγελιςης· ειρηκως γαρ Αβρααμ εγεννησε τον Ισαακ, Ισαακ δε εγεννησε τον Ιακωβ, Ιακωβ δε εγεννησε τον Ιεδαν, κ πασαν εφεξης την γενεαλογιαν διεξελθων, αδαμε το κατα σαρκα προ-τεθεικεν. εχ ηςμοτε γαρ αυτοις ανθρωποις εςιν η τοιαυτη προσθηκη. εςαυθα δε, επειδη εκ ανθρωπος μονον εςιν, αλλα κ θεος προαιωνιος ο ενανθρωπησας θεος λογος, τε σπερματος τε Δαβιδ μνημονευσας ο θειος αποςολος, αναγκαιως το κατα σαρκα προτεθεικε, σαφως ημας διδαξας, πως μεν υιος εςι τε θεε, πως δε τε Δαβιδ εχρηματισε.—Προ μεν τε ςαυρε κ τε παθες, ο δεσποτης χριςος ε μονον τοις αλλοις Ιεδαιοις, αλλα κ αυτοις τοις αποςολοις εκ εδκ ει ε.ναι θεος. προσεπ-ταιον γαρ τοις ανθρωπινοις, εςθιοντα τε κ πινοντα, κ καθευδοντα, κ κο-πιωντα θεωμενοι, κ εδε τα θευματα αυτες προς ταυτην εποδηγει την δοξαν. αυτικα τοινυν το κατα την θαλατταν θεασαμενοι θαυμα ελεγον ποταπος εςιν ετος ο ανθρωπος, οτι κ η θαλασσα κ οι ανεμοι υποκεεσιν αυτω ; δια τοι τετο κ ο κυριος ελεγε προς αυτες. πολλα εχω λεγειν υμιν, αλλ' ε δυνασθε βαςαζειν αρτι.—Προ μεν εν τε παθες τοιαυτας

3

ειχον

says, that the apostles in mentioning the subjection of Christ to the Father (1 Cor. xv.) spake of him more lowly than was necessary for their advantage *."

Œcumenius also says, that " Peter in his " first speech, though by saying that *Christ* " *rose according to the flesh*, he intimated that " he was God, yet refers all to the Father, " that they might receive his sayings †." He makes the same observation on Peter's saying, the promise of the Spirit was from the Father. " He refers things to the Father,

ειχον δοξας περι αυτȣ. μετα δε την αναστασιν κ͵ την εις ȣρανȣς αναβασιν, κ͵ τȣ παναγιȣ πνευματος επιφοιτησιν, κ͵ τας παντοδαπως θαυματȣργιας ας επετελεν, καλȣντες αυτȣ το σεβασμιον ονομα, εγνωσαν απαντες οι πιστευοντες, οτι κ͵ θεος εστι, κ͵ τȣ θεȣ μονογενης υιος. In Rom. cap. 1. Opera, vol. 3. p. 15. Ed. Halæ.

* Ο μεν ȣν θειος αποστολος την εκ της ελληνικης μυθολογιας φυομενην υφορωμενος βλαβην, ταυτα προςεδειξε, ταπεινοτεροις χρησαμενος λογοις δια την εκεινων ωφελειαν. In 1 Cor. xv. Opera, vol. 3. p. 273.

† Και ȣδε ϋτως ηλθεν εις τον χριστον, αλλα παλιν εγκωμιαζεται ο Δαυιδ, δια τȣ, προφητης ȣν υπαρχεν, ινα δια την προς τιμην κ͵ το γενος το απ εκεινȣ, τȣ χριστȣ δεξωνται τον περι της αναστασεως λογον. κ͵ ȣκ ειπεν, οτι επηγγειλατο αυτω ο θεος αλλ' ο μειζον κ͵ απαραβατον εν, το ωμοσε το δε κατα σαρκα κηρυττοντος εστιν, ως κ͵ θεος χριστος, κ͵ συνεσιν εν τω πατρι. παντα δε τω πατρι ανατιθησιν, ινα τεως παραδεξωνται τα λεγομενα. Opera, vol. 1. p. 21.

" that

"that he might draw his hearers *." Again, he obferves, that he faid " the Father, and not " Chrift, promifed that appearance by Joel †." On another part of his fpeech, in which mention is made of *God glorifying his Son Jefus*, he fays; " he fpake humbly concern-" ing him ‡."

Quoting Theodoret, he " calls low dif-
" courfes concerning Chrift the *firft ele-*
" *ments*. To thofe who were not capable
" of a perfect faith, the preachers of the
" gofpel offered what relates to the huma-
" nity of Chrift. Thus the bleffed Peter
" preaching to the Jews, meafures his doc-
" trine by the weaknefs of his hearers.
" For he fays, *Jefus of Nazareth, a man*
" *approved of God among you*. And ye
" have need, he fays, from negligence,
" not being fuch (i. e. perfect) of milk,
" not of ftrong meat. He calls low dif-

---

* Και παλιντω πατρι ανατιθησι το γεγονος. οιδε γαρ ετω τες ακροατας επισπωμενος. Oecumen. vol. 1. p. 21.

† Κατ αρχας μεν γαρ τον πρωτα [πατερα] ελεγεν ε τον χριςον απαγγειλαϲθαι τετο δια Ιωηλ τε προφητε. Vol. 1. p. 21.

‡ Ετι των ταπεινοτερων εχεται —— δια τε ειπειν εκ ιδια δυναμει θαυματεργησαι —— τω προσθειναι τον παιδα. ε γαρ το αυθοδεξαςον εν: προσθηκη δοξης λαβειν. Ibid. p. 28.

courfes

" courses concerning Christ, those that re-
" late to the flesh, *milk*, and *strong meat*
" for the perfect, discourses concerning the
" divinity of Christ. For those, there-
" fore, who were babes in faith, there was
" need of low discourses, as milk is fit
" for babes; but for the perfect in faith,
" there was need of strong meat, the sublime
" philosophy concerning Christ. Every
" one, he says, who partakes of milk, that
" is, every one, who wants these low
" discourses concerning the humanity of
" Christ (for they are milk) is unskilful,
" and not a partaker of the word of righte-
" ousness. By the word of righteousness,
" he means the doctrine of the divinity of
" Christ, &c.*"

* ΑΛΛΟ. ϛοιχεια της αρχης των λογιων τȣ θεȣ, τȣς ταπεινοτερȣς περι χριϛȣ λογȣς εκαλεσε. τοις γαρ μηδε πω την πιϛιν εϛχηκοσι τελειαν, τα περι της ανθρωποτητος προσεφερον μονα, της αληθειας οι κηρυκες. ιδιως ο μακαριος Πετρος Ιȣδαιοις δημηγορων εμετρησε την διδασκαλιαν τη ασθενεια των ακȣοντων. Ιησȣν γαρ, εφη, τον Ναζωραιον, ανδρα απο τȣ θεȣ αποδεδειγμενον εις υμας. Και γεγονατε χρειαν εχοντες. Αυτοι γεγονατε, φησιν, εκ ραθυμιας, ȣκ οντες τοιȣτοι, γαλακτος κȢ ȣ ϛερεας τροφης. γαλα λεγει τȣς ταπεινȣς περι χριϛȣ λογȣς, τȣς περι της σαρκος: ϛερεαν δε τροφην, της τελειȣς τȣς περι της θεοτητος αυτȣ · τοις ȣν ετι νηπιοις την πιϛιν, εδει λογων ταπεινων (καταλληλον γαρ τοις νηπιοις το γαλα) τοις δε τελειοις την πιϛιν, της ϛερεας τροφης κȢ της υψηλης,

CHAP. V.   *of other Fathers.*   111

"Having called discourses concerning
"the humanity of Christ, the *first principles,*
"and those concerning his divinity *perfec-*
"*tion,* lest they should despond, as not
"being worthy of the most perfect dis-
"courses, he endeavours to give them those
"that were perfect. And he says so, but
"not in the same sense in which he had
"used the word *perfect* before, for they
"were not able to bear it. But he disposes
"his discourse in another manner, calling
"first principles, baptism, the imposition of
"hands, and the sign;" perhaps that of the
cross, "and perfection, the philosophy of
"works *"

υψηλης περι χριςυ φιλοσοφιας. πας γαρ ο μετεχων γαλακτος, πας γαρ. φησιν. ο μετεχων λογων ταπεινων, των περι της ανθρωποτητος τυ κυριυ (ηοι γας το γαλα) απειρος εςι κỳ αμετοχος λογυ δικαιοσυνης. λογον δεδικαιοσυνης λεγει, τον περι της θεοτητος τυ κυριυ· η ςερεα τροφη. ο υψηλος λογος, κỳ τα υψηλα περι χριςυ δογματα. In Heb. Opera, vol. 2. p. 353.

* Ανω ειπων αρχην τους περι ανθρωποτητος τυ κυριυ λογους, τελειο-τητα δε τους περι θεοτητος. ινα μη αδημονωσιν ηοι, ως μη αξιευμενοι των τε-λειοτερων λογων λεγειν τας τελειας πειραται. λεγει δε. υχ ως ατω τελειας εκαλεσε, (υ γαρ ισχυον ακυσαι.) αλλ' ετερως μεθοδευει τον λογον. αρχην μεν το βαπτισμα καλων, κỳ την εν αυτω των χειρων επιθεσιν κỳ σφραγιδα, τελειοτητα δε, την δι εργων φιλοσοφιαν, Photius in Œcumen. in Heb. vol. 2. p. 354.

Commenting

Commenting on Heb. v. 7. *he was heard,* " *in that he feared,* Œcumenius says, " this " he said on account of the weakness of his " hearers *." And again, speaking of *God having raised up Christ,* he says, " the di- " vine Paul often speaks in a low style; say- " ing, That the Father raised up Christ †."

Theophylact, commenting on Heb. i. says, " Why did he not say that Christ spake " to us? It was both because they were " weak, and not yet able to hear concerning " Christ, and to shew, that the Old and the " New Testament have the same author ‡."

I shall now proceed to shew, that, in the opinion of the same Fathers, the apostles thought it necessary to observe the same caution in teaching the doctrine of the divinity of Christ to the Gentiles, that had been requisite with respect to the Jews.

---

* Και εισακυσθεις. Τοσυλον, φησιν, εσηκυσθη, οτι κỳ ανεση. τυλο δε ειπε δια την ασθενειαν των ακυονλων, υπω μεγαλας εχονλων περι χριςυ δοξας. Των δε ταπεινων τυτων ρημαλων δυο αιλια, ηλε Carξ, κỳ η ασθενια των ακυονλων. In Heb. vol. 2. p. 349.

† Πολλαχυ γαρ ταπεινολερα ο θειος Παυλος; φθεγγομενος, τον παλερα φησιν αναςησαι τον χριςον. Ibid. p. 310.

‡ Δια τι δε υκ ειπεν, ελαλησεν ημιν ο χριςος; Αμα μεν, δια το ασθενεις ειναι αυλυς. κỳ μηπω δυνασθαι ακυσαι περι τυ χριςυ. αμα δε κỳ δεικνυων, ύλι η παλαια κỳ η καινη, ενος ετι κỳ τυ αυλυ. Vol. 2. p. 876.

CHAPTER VI.

Of the Caution observed by the Apostles in teaching the Doctrines of the Pre-existence and Divinity of Christ to the Gentile Converts.

THE apostles found the Jews fully persuaded concerning the doctrine of the divine unity, and on that account they are represented by the Fathers as cautious how they taught the doctrine of the divinity of Christ, lest their hearers should have been staggered at it, as if they had preached two Gods. The Gentiles were in a quite different situation, believing in a multiplicity of Gods; on which account it might be thought to require less caution to teach this favourite doctrine to them. But then, for the same reason for which it was thought improper for Moses and the prophets to teach it to the Jews, in the former periods of their history, when they were in danger of falling into idolatry, it was equally improper to insist upon it with the Gentiles, lest they should have been encouraged to persevere in the same system. Also, after they were brought to the worship of one God, they would have been no less averse to such a doctrine as the trinity than the Jews. On this account it was not less hazardous, according to Chrysostom, to teach the doctrine of the divinity of Christ to the Gentiles than it had been to the Jews.

In the passage, part of which I have quoted above, after observing, that if the apostles had not conducted themselves in this cautious manner with respect to the Jews, their whole doctrine would have appeared incredible to them, he adds, " and at Athens Paul calls
" him" (Jesus) " simply a man, and nothing
" farther, and for a good reason. For if
" they often attempted to stone Christ him-
" self, when he spake of his equality with
" the Father, and called him on that account
" a blasphemer, they would hardly have re-
" ceived this doctrine from fishermen, espe-
" cially after speaking of him as crucified.
" And why do I speak of the Jews? when
" at that time even the disciples of Christ
" himself were often disturbed and scanda-
" lized at him, when they heard sublime
                                " doctrines

" doctrines; on which account he said, *I*
" *have many things to say to you, but ye are*
" *not yet able to bear them.* And if they
" could not bear these things, who had liv-
" ed so long with him, and had received so
" many mysteries, and seen so many mira-
" cles, how could men, who were then first
" taken from their altars, idols, and sacri-
" fices, and cats, and crocodiles (for such
" was the worship of the heathens) and
" being then first brought off from these
" abominations, readily receive sublime doc-
" trines * ?"

Theodoret, commenting on 1 Cor. viii.
6. *To us there is one God the Father, and one*

* Εν δε Αθηναις κ̣ ανθρωπον αυτον απλως καλει ο Παυλος, ουδε πλεον
ειπων. εικοτως, ει γαρ αυτον τον χριστον διαλεγομενον περι της εις τον
πατερα ισοτητ(Θ)⁻, λιθασαιπολλακις επιχειρησαν, κ̣ βλασφημον δια τουτο
εκαλουν, σχολη γαρ παρα των αλιεων τουτον τον λογον εδεξαντο, κ̣ τουτο του
σταυρον προχωρησαντος. Και τι δει λεγειν τους Ιουδαιους · οπου γε κ̣ αυτοι
τοτε πολλακις οι μαθηται των υψηλοτερων ακουοντες εθορυβουντο κ̣ εσκανδαλιζοντο. δια τουτο κ̣ ελεγε πολλα εχω λεγειν υμιν αλλ' ου δυνασθε βασταζειν
αρτι. ει δε εκεινοι ουκ εδυναντο οι συγγενομενοι χρονον τοσουτον, κ̣ τοσουτων
κοινωνησαντες απορρητων, κ̣ τοσαυτα θεασαμενοι θαυματα, πως ανθρωποι
απο βωμων, κ̣ ειδωλων, κ̣ θυσιων, κ̣ αιλουρων, κ̣ κροκοδειλων, τοιαυτα
γαρ ην των ελληνων σεβασματα; κ̣ των αλλων των κακων τοτε πρωτον
αποσπασθεντες, αθροον τους υψηλους των δογματων εδεξαντο λογους. In
Acta, Hom. 1. Opera, vol. 8. p. 447.

Lord Jesus Christ, says, "Here he calls the
"one God, and the other Lord, lest he
"should give those who were just freed
"from heathenism, and had learned the
"truth, a pretence for returning to their
"heathenism and idolatry *."

Œcumenius, on the same place, says,
"The apostle speaks cautiously concerning
"the Father and the Son, calling the Father
"the one God, lest they should think there
"were two Gods; and the Son the one
"Lord, lest they should think there were
"two Lords. For if he had said *God and*
"*God,* the Greeks, from their ignorance,
"would have thought it had been poly-
"theism; or if he had said *Lord and Lord,*
"they would have thought there were many
"Lords. This is the reason why he now
"says, that the Father was God, and the
"Son Lord. For he had premised that with
"us there was but one God. Had he called
"both the Father and the Son God, and

* Εντανθα μεντοι τον μεν θεον προσηγορευσε, τον δε κυριον· ινα μη τοις εναγχος της Ελληνικης πλανης απαλλαγεισι, ϗ την αληθειαν μεμαθησι, παρασχη προφασιν εις την πολυθεον εξαπατην παλινδρομησαι. In Loc. Opera, vol. 3. p. 158.

"Lord

" Lord, he would have been found acting
" contrary to his own affirmation to the
" Greeks, and would have appeared to have
" introduced many Gods, and many Lords.
" Therefore he calls the Father God, and
" the Son Lord; condescending to the state
" of novices in the Greeks*." Again,
speaking of God having raised Christ from
the dead, he says, " the apostle herein con-
" descends to them as children, not that
" Christ was not able to raise himself †;"
Theodoret also, in his exposition of 1 Cor.
15. in which the apostle says, that *the Son
" was subject to the Father*, says, " the divine
" apostle, fearing the evil that might arise

---

* Διο και ὑιως ασφαλως τȣ πατρος και τȣ ὑιȣ εμνησθη· τον μεν πατερα ειπων ενα θεον, ινα μη δυο θεȣς νομισωσι, τον και υιον ενα κυριον, ινα μη δυο κυριȣς νομισωσιν· ει γαρ ειπε θεον και θεον, πολυθειαν αν εξ απειριας ενομισαν Ελληνες, η κυριον και κυριον, πολυκυριοτητα αν ενομισαν. ωστε και τȣ νυν ειπειν θεον πατερα και κυριον τον υιον αὐτη η αιτια. ην γαρ ὑποσχομενος παρ' ημιν ενα θεον ειναι. ει ȣν ειπεν και τον πατερα και τον υιον, θεον η κυριον, παλιν ευρισκετο τη οικεια ὑποσχεσει οσον προς Ελληνας εναντιȣμενος, και πολυθειαν η πολυκυριοτητα κατα το φαινομενον εισαγων. διο θεον ειπων τον πατερα, κυριον ειπε τον υιον, τη νηπιοτητι συγκαταβαινων των Ελληνων. Opera, vol. 1. p. 492.

† Ο δε θεος κ̀ τον κυριον ηγειρεν. Ετι νηπιοις ȣσιν, εδει συγκαταβαινειν, και προς την νηπιοτητα αυτων λαλειν. μη θορυβηθης ακȣσας οτι ο θεος τον χριστον ηγειρεν. ȣ γαρ επει ȣκ ισχυσεν ἑαυτον εγειραι, τȣτο φησιν. Ibid. p. 469.

" from

" from the Grecian mythology, added thefe
" things, fpeaking in low terms for their
" advantage *."

According to Œcumenius, thofe whom John, in his firft epiftle, addreffes as *children*, were thofe who were acquainted with the humanity of Chrift only, as the grown men were thofe who knew his divinity. Of the latter he fays, that " they knew him " that was from the beginning. But who " is from the beginning, but God the logos, " who was in the beginning with God?" He reprefents him as explaining his own meaning in the following manner : " Since " I knew that you will receive my writings " according to the difference in your ages, I " muft meafure my doctrine according to your " ages, and difcourfe with fome as children " who know the Father," he means God the Father only ; " but to others as fathers, who " know more than the children, and not as " the father only, but as without origin and " unfearchable, for he was in the begin- " ning. To thefe I muft addrefs more per-

* Ο μεν ων θειος αποστολος την εκ της Ελληνικης μυθολογιας φυομενην υφορωμενος βλαβην, ταυτα προστεθεικε, ταπεινοτεροις χρησαμενος λογοις δια την εκεινων ωφελειαν. Opera, vol. 3. p. 201.

" fect

"fect difcourfes *." Inconfiftently, however, with this, he fays, that " by thofe who "*deny the Son*, in this epiftle, are meant " they who fay that Chrift was a mere " man;" and yet he fays, that " by thofe " who *denied that Jefus was the Chrift*, were " meant the Gnoftics."

Theophylact, commenting on 1 Cor. i. 8. fays, " Since Paul was writing to the " Greeks, who worfhipped many Gods, " and many Lords, on this account he " does not call the Son God, left they " fhould think there were two Gods, as " being accuftomed to polytheifm. Nor " did he call the Father Lord, left they " fhould think there were many Lords. " For the fame reafon he made no mention

---

* Οις και εχειν την γνωσιν τε απ αρχης μαρτυρει. τις δε ο απ αρχης ; ει μη ο θεος λογος, ος ην εν αρχη προς τον θεον. Επει εν φησιν ετως υμας οιδα κατα τας των ηλικιων διαφορας δεξομενες τα παρ' εμε γραφομενα, αναγκη καμε παραμετρησαι τη διαθεσει της ηλικιας υμων την διδασκαλιαν, και τοις μεν ως παιδιοις επεγνωκοσι τον πατερα (λεγει δε τον θεον) διαλεχθηναι. τοις δε ως πατρασιν, οι πλεον εχεσι των παιδιων κατα την γνωσιν, το μη ως πατερα μονον επεγνωκεναι, αλλα και ως αναρχος και αδιεξιτητος . ην γαρ εν αρχη. τελοις δε και τελεωτερων αξιον παραθεσιν ποιησασθαι λογω. In John, Opera, vol. 2. p. 570.

" of the Holy Spirit, sparing the weakness
" of his hearers; as the prophets do not
" mention the Son clearly, on account of
" the Jews, lest they should think of a
" generation with passion*." In his Commentary on 1 Col. i. 12. he observes, that
" Paul mentions giving thanks to the Father only. He does the same," he says,
" in the epistle to the Corinthians, bringing them gradually to the doctrine concerning the Son †."

The same writer, in his Commentary on 1 Tim. ii. 5. *There is one God, and one mediator between God and Man, the man Christ Jesus*, says, " he does not speak plainly
" concerning the deity of Christ, because
" polytheism then abounded, and lest he

---

* Αλλ' επειδη προς ελληνας ην ο λογος αυ]ω, πολυθειαν πρεσβευον]ας κ πολυκυριο]η]α· δια τυ]ο, υ]ε κ τον υιον θεον ειπεν, ινα μη δυο θευς νομισωσιν, α]ε πολυθεια ενειθισμενοι· υ]ε κ τον πα]ερα κυριον, ινα μη πολλυς κυριυς κ παρ ημιν ειναι δοξωσι. Δια ταυ]ην δε την αι]ιαν, υδε τυ πνευμα]ος εμνησθη εν]αυθα, φειδομενος της ασθενειας των ακρο]ων· ωσπερ κ οι προφη]αι τυ υιυ σαφως υ μεμνην]αι, δια τυς Ιυδαιυς, ινα μη εμπαθη νομισωσι την γεννησιν. Opera, vol. 2. p. 226.

† Ουτω κ εν τη προς Κοριντηυς ποιει. Ηρεμα δε εμβιβαζει αυτυς εις τον περι υιυ λογον, Vol. 2. p. 631.

" should

" should be thought to introduce many
" gods; where, though he says, *one and
" one*, he does not put them together, and
" say *two*, but only *one and one*. Such is
" the caution of the scriptures. On this
" account he makes no mention of the
" Spirit, lest he should seem to be a poly-
" theist *."

Such abundant evidence as this, when there is nothing to oppose to it (and many more passages to the same purpose might, I doubt not, be collected, if it could be thought that they were at all wanting) must surely satisfy all the impartial, that, in the opinion of the christian Fathers, the doctrines of the pre-existence and divinity of Christ were considered as being of such a nature, as that it would not have been prudent to risk the communication of them either with Jews or Gentiles, on their first

* Ουκ ειπε δε φανερως κ̀ περι της θεοτητος τȣ χριϛȣ, επειδη πολυθεια τοτε εκρατει, κ̀ ινα μη νομισθη κ̀ αυτος πολλȣς θεȣς παρεισαγειν. οπȣγε ȣδε το, εις κ̀ εις, οταν λεγηται, προσηκει συντιθεναι, κ̀ λεγειν δυο, αλλα εις κ̀ εις. τοσαυτη γαρ η ευλαβεια της γραφης. δια τȣτο ȣκ εμνησθη ȣδε τȣ πνευματος, ινα μη δοξη πολυθεος ειναι. Vol. 2. p. 757.

conversion to christianity. And the plain inference from this is, that the orthodox Fathers must necessarily have supposed, that the christian church, in general, was at first unitarian, and that it continued to be so a considerable time. For none of them say, or hint, when this caution on the part of the apostles ceased; and they represent them as using it in the very latest of their writings, as in those from Paul after his confinement at Rome, and therefore not long before the destruction of Jerusalem. At that time, therefore, they must have thought that the great body of christians were unitarians, and without being considered as heretics on that account.

But the most decisive proof of this is their universally concluding, that the doctrines of the pre-existence and divinity of Christ were never taught clearly and explicitly till it was done by John, in the introduction to his gospel, which they supposed to have been published among the last of the books of the New Testament, and after the death of the other apostles.

CHAP-

CHAPTER VII.

Of John being thought to have been the first who clearly and boldly taught the doctrines of the Pre-existence and Divinity of Christ.

AS this is an article of considerable consequence, I shall produce a redundance of evidence in support of it; nothing being better calculated to satisfy us, that, in the opinion of the christian Fathers, the doctrines of the pre-existence and divinity of Christ were not generally received in the life-time of the other apostles; and, therefore, that simple unitarianism could not have been considered as any heresy in the early ages. These authorities I shall produce, as I have generally done others, nearly in the order of time in which the writers flourished. I shall only first observe, that John seems to have got the title of θεολογος, *divine*, from this circumstance, of his teaching the doctrine of the divine logos, which was supposed to be peculiar to him. This appellation

appellation is given to him in the title to the book of Revelation. It is mentioned by Athanasius in his Sermo Major de Fide*, and also by Cyril of Alexandria†. For a similar reason Isaiah is stiled Theologus by Eusebius, in Is. xxiv. 10.‡

I shall also remind my reader in this place, that this hypothesis of John having taught the doctrine of the divinity of Christ in the introduction of his gospel, does not occur in the earliest writers. These being nearer to the source of information, say that John had a view to the Gnostics only, both in his epistles, and the introduction to his gospel. This was the opinion of Irenæus, who wrote about the year 170; for which see this work, vol. I. p. 253. The first writer who says that John meant the unitarians, I believe, was Origen.

* Montfaucon's Collectio, vol. 2. p. 13.
† Hom. Opera, vol. 2. p. 75.
‡ Montfaucon's Collectio, vol. 2. p. 450.

SECTION I.

The Acknowledgments of the Christian Fathers that John was the first who taught the doctrines above-mentioned.

ORIGEN, though a zealous defender of the doctrines of the pre-existence and divinity of Christ, yet, as will appear in its proper place, only considered them as more sublime doctrines, fit for the more perfect christians. He says, that " John " alone introduced the knowledge of the " eternity of Christ to the minds of the " Fathers*." " John himself was trans- " formed into God, and so became partaker " of the truth, and then pronounced that " the *word* of God was in God from the " beginning †."

* Joannes sola ejus æterna in notitiam fidelium animarum introducit. Opera, vol. 2. p. 428.

† Sanctus itaque theologus in deum transmutatus, veritatis particeps, domini verbum subsistere in deo principio, hoc est deum filium in deo patre, pronunciat. . Ibid.

" No

"No one," says this writer, "taught the divinity of Christ so clearly as John, who presents him to us, saying, *I am the light of the world, I am the way, the truth, and the life, I am the resurrection, I am the gate, I am the good shepherd*, and in the Revelation, *I am the alpha and the omega, the beginning and the end, the first and the last*. We may therefore boldly say, that, as the gospels are the first fruits" (or the most excellent part) "of the scriptures, so the gospel of John is the first fruits of the gospels; the sense of which no person can conceive, except he who reclines on the breast of Jesus, and who receives from Jesus his mother Mary, and makes her his own. He must be another John, who was shewn by Jesus as another Jesus. For he who is perfect does not himself live, but Christ lives in him. And since Christ lives in him, he says to Mary concerning him, Behold thy Son, Christ himself*."

---

* Ουδεις γαρ εκεινων ακριβως εφανερωσεν αυτε την θεοτητα ως Ιωαννης, παραστησας αυτον λεγοντα, εγω ειμι το φως τε κοσμε, εγω ειμι η οδος, κỳ η αληθεια, κỳ η ζωη. εγω ειμι η αναςασις.

The meaning of this is, that, to have the knowledge of the sublime doctrines of the pre-exiſtence and divinity of Chriſt, as taught by John, a man muſt be a chriſtian *of the firſt claſs and rank*, far above the ordinary ſort. He muſt be a ſecond John, and a ſecond Jeſus, imbibing their ſpirit, and entering into their moſt profound meaning.

Euſebius, ſays, that " John began the " doctrine of the divinity of Chriſt, that " being reſerved for him, as the moſt " worthy *."

But he who wrote the moſt largely, and the moſt eloquently on this ſubject is Chry-

αναςασις. εγω ειμι η θυρα, εγω ειμι ο ποιμην ο καλος. και εν τη αποκαλυψει, εγω ειμι το α και το ω, η αρχη και το τελος, ο πρωτ@ και ο εσχατ@. τολμητεον τοινυν ειπειν απαρχην μεν πασων γραφων ειναι τα ευαγγελια, των δε ευαγγελιων απαρχην το κατα Ιωαννην, ε τον νεν εδεις δυναται λαβειν μη αναπεσων επι το ςηθ@ Ιησε, μηδε λαβων απο Ιησε την Μαριαν γενομενην και αυτε μητερα; και τηλικετον δε γενεσθαι δει τον εσομενον αλλον Ιωαννην, ως τε οιονει τον Ιωαννην δει-χθηναι οντα Ιησεν απο Ιησε—και γαρ πας ο τετελειωμεν@. ζη εκετι, αλλ' εν αυτω ζη χριςος, και επει ζη εν αυτω χριςο@, λεγεται περι αυτε τη Μαρια, ιδε ο υι@ σε ο χριςο@. Comment. in Johan. vol. 2. p. 5.

* Της δε θεολογιας απαρξασθαι, ως αν αυτω προς τε θειε πνευματος οια κρειττονι παραπεφυλαγμενης. ταυτα μεν εν ημιν περι της τε κατα Ιωαννην ευαγγελιε γραφης ειρησθω. Hiſt. lib. 3. cap. 24. p. 117.

foſtom. And it will be ſeen that the greatneſs of the myſtery, its alarming appearance to the Jews, and the extreme caution of the evangeliſts and apoſtles in divulging it, gave him great ſcope for magnifying the courage of John, in teaching what the other apoſtles had only ventured to hint at, and which was reſerved for him, as the *ſon of thunder*, and whoſe emblem was *the eagle*, to expreſs his ſoaring higher than any other that had gone before him.

"John," he ſays, "alone taught the eter-
" nal and ſuper-celeſtial wiſdom*." "John
" firſt lighted up the lamp of theology; and
" all the moſt diſtant churches running to
" it, lighted up their lamps of theology, and
" returned rejoicing, ſaying, *In the begin-
" ing was the logos*†."

Chryſoſtom repreſents all the preceding writers of the New Teſtament as children, who heard, but did not underſtand things, " and who were buſy about cheeſe-cakes

---

* Μονος την αιωνιον κȝ υπερκοσμιον φιλοσοφιαν κηρυξας. In John i, Opera, vol. 6. p. 235.

† Πρῳτη αναψασα τον της θεολογιας λυχνον, πασαι των περᾳων αι εκκλησιαι προς σε δραμυσαι, εκαςη την εαυτης λαμπαδα την θεολογιαν ανηψε, κȝ υπεςρεψε χαιρυσα, εν αρχη ην ο λογος. Ibid. p. 604.

" and

"and childish sports*, but John," he says, "taught what the angels themselves did not know before he declared it †;" and he represents them as his most attentive auditors. "Leaving the Father," he says, "he (John) discoursed concerning the Son, "because the Father, was known to all, if "not as a Father, yet as God, but the "unbegotten was unknown ‡."

Of the three first evangelists, he says, "they all treated of the fleshly dispensation, "and silently by his miracles, indicated his "dignity. The dignity of the logos of "God was hid, the arrows against the he- "retics were concealed, and the fortifica- "tion to defend the right faith was not "raised by the pious preaching. John, "therefore, the son of thunder, being the

---

* Οι γε αλλοι απαντες, καθαπερ τα παιδια τα μικρα, ακκυσι μεν, εκ ισασι δε απερ ακκυσιν, αλλα περι πλακευντίας επιοντίαι, κỳ αθυρμαία παιδικα. In Johan. 1. Opera, vol. 8. p. 2.

† Α μηδε αγγελοι πριν η τετον γενεσθαι ηδεισαν. μεθ' ημων γαρ δη και ετοι δια της Ιωαννε φωνης και δι ημων εμαθον απερ εγνωμεν. Ibid.

‡ Τι δηποτ' ευ τον πατερα αφεις, περι τε υιε διαλεγεται: ότι εκεινος μεν δηλος απασιν ην, ει κỳ μη ως πατηρ, αλλ' ως θεος, ο δε μονογενης ηγνοειτο. Ibid. p. 11.

"last

"last, advanced to the doctrine of the lo-
"gos," or the divinity of Christ*.

"*In the beginning was the word.* This
"doctrine was not published at first, for
"the world would not receive it. Where-
"fore Matthew, Mark, and Luke" (John
is here added, but it must be an interpola-
tion) "began at a distance. When they
"began the preaching, they did not imme-
"diately say what was becoming his dig-
"nity, but what would suit the hearers.
"Matthew, beginning his gospel, says,
"*The book of the generation of Jesus Christ,*
"*the son of David, the son of Abraham.*
"Why does he not say the *son of God?*

* Παντες εν εχωρησαν εις την της σαρκ⊙ οικονομιαν, κ̔ ηρεμα πως, δια των θαυμαιων, εγνωριζον την αξιαν. Εκρυπ]ε]ο δε ε]ι τε θεε λογε αξιωμα, Εκρυπ]ε]ο δε τα καια των αιρε]ικων ϐελη, κ̔ το της ορθης δοξης επι]ειχισμα εδεπο]ε τω κηρυγμα]ι της ευσεϐειας εγηγερ]ο. Ιωαννης τοινυν. ο υι⊙ της βρον]ης, τελευ]αιος, παρηλθεν επι την θεολογιαν. De Sigillis, Op. vol. 6. p 173. N. B. The sense of the passage absolutely requires εκρυπ]ε]ο and not εκηρυτ]ε]ο in both the clauses, and in the latter it is so rendered by the Latin translator, though not in the former. The observation, that the first verses in the gospel of John are a refutation of all heresies is common with the Fathers. No person, except one who is pretty well conversant with them, can imagine how often those verses occur in their writings.

"Why

" Why does he conceal his dignity by poor
" language? Why does he conceal from
" men the things relating to his deity?
" He answers, I am preaching to the Jews,
" who do not even believe him to be
" a good man. They would not believe
" Christ to be the son of Abraham, and
" will they believe his being called the son
" of God?—The blessed Mark, also, when
" he applied himself to writing a gospel,
" taking courage from what had been done
" before" (meaning perhaps, by Matthew)
" calls him *the Son of God*; but he imme-
" diately contracts his discourse, and cuts
" short what he had intended to say, that
" he might sooth his hearers. He there-
" fore, introduces what he had to say, con-
" cerning the Baptist, saying, *The begin-*
" *ning of the gospel of Jesus Christ, as it is*
" *written in Isaiah the prophet, &c.*"

" Luke follows in the third place, and
" goes a middle way. He touches upon
" the doctrine of the logos, but does not ex-
" plain, or unfold his dignity; but says,
" *Since many have undertaken to give an ac-*
" *count of what has come to pass among us, it*
" *seemed*

"seemed good to me also, who have attended
"to every thing from the beginning, to write
"in order as has been delivered to us, by those
"who were eye-witnesses and ministers of the
"*logos*. But though he mentions the lo-
"gos, he did not say that the logos was
"God. What then does he do? Touch-
"ing upon the subject, and considering that
"he was speaking in the ears of the dead,
"he conceals his dignity, and brings on
"the œconomy," i. e. the doctrine of the
incarnation or humanity of Christ. "There
"was a priest Zacharias, &c."

"John, therefore, the son of thunder,
"last of all advanced to the doctrine of his
"divinity, after those three heralds; and
"with great propriety he followed them,
"and they went before, lightening a little,
"as the lightning precedes the thunder, lest
"bursting from the clouds at once it should
"stun the hearer.—They therefore lighten-
"ed the *œconomy*, or the humanity of Christ,
"but he thundered out the *theology*," that
is, the doctrine of Christ's divinity *.

* Εν αρχη ην ο λογος . εκ ευθυς τουτο εκηρυχθη . Ου γαρ εχωρει ο
κοσμος . μακραν ημιν οι ευαγγελισται Ματθαιος, Μαρκος, Λουκας, κ̄ϳ
Ιωαννης.

Again, he introduces John as holding a soliloquy with himself, and saying, after

Ιωαννης. Οτε ηρξαντο τε κηρυγματος, εκ ευθυς ελαλησαν τα πρεποντα τη αξια, αλλα τα αρμοζοντα τοις ακροωμενοις. ο Ματθαιος, αρχην ποιησαμενος των ευαγγελιων, λεγει. βιβλος γενεσεως Ιησυ χριστου υιε Δαβιδ, υιε Αβρααμ. διατι, μη υιε θεε; διατι πτωχη λεξει κρυπτεις την αξιαν; διατι τοις ανθρωποις τα θεια καλυπτεις; παρα Ιεδαιοις φησι· κηρυτ7ω, τοις μη ανθρωπον δικαιον ειναι πιστευσι. Τον χριστον υιον Αβρααμ επω εδεξατο, κ̀ υιον θεε καταγγελλομενον ανεξοντα.—Παλιν ο μακαριος Μαρκος καθεις εαυτον εις το ευαγγελιον, κ̀ θαρσησας τοις προγεγυμνασμενοις, λεγει μεν υιον θεε, αλλ' ευθεως συνεστειλε τον λογον, κ̀ εκολοβωσε την εννοιαν, ινα μαλαξη τον ακροατην. Επαγει εν ευθεως τα καλα τον βαπτιστην λεγων, αρχη τε ευαγγελιε Ιησυ χριτε, καθως γεγραπται εν Ησαια τω προφητη.—Ο Λεκας ακολεθει τριτος, κ̀ μεσος χωρει μετα τετων, κ̀ απτεται μεν τε θεε λογε, ε μην ερμηνευει κ̀ αναπτυσσει την αξιαν. αλλα φησιν, επειδηπερ πολλοι επεχειρησαν ανατάξασθαι διηγησιν περι των πεπληροφορημενων εν ημιν πραγματων, εδοξε καμοι παρακολεθησαι τοις πασιν απαρχης γραψαι, καθως παρεδωκαν ημιν οι απ αρχης αυτοπται, κ̀ υπηρεται γενομενοι τε λογε. αλλα λογον μεν ειπεν, εκ ειπε δε οτι κ̀ θεος ην ο λογος. τι εν κ̀ αυτος ποιει· αψαμενος το ειναι, κ̀ εννοησας· οτι νεκραις ακοαις ενηχει, κρυπτει την αξιαν, κ̀ προφερει την οικονομιαν. εγενετο ιερευς· Ζαχαριας. κ̀ τα εξης τε ευαγγελιε. Ιωαννης τοινυν ο υιος της βροντης τελευταιος παρηλθεν επι την θεολογιαν. μετα τες τρεις εκεινες κηρυκας, κ̀ εικοτως ο μεν ηκολεθησεν, οι δε προελαβον, τα μικρα τεως αστραπτοντες, ωσπερ γαρ της βροντης προηγειται αστραπη, ινα μη αθροον εκεινη εκ των νεφων ραγεισα πληξη τον ακροντα. Ουτως επειδη εμελλε βροντιαν ο Ιωαννης, προελαβον οι τρεις ευαγγελισται δικην αστραπων, κ̀ οι μεν εγραψαν την οικονομιαν, ο δε βροντα την θεολογιαν. De Sigillis, Opera, vol. 6. p. 171, &c.

" considering

considering the progress of heresy, "Why
"do I delay? Why have I any longer pa-
"tience? Why do I not bring forth the
"mystery hid from ages? Why do I hide
"in myself, the wisdom which was before
"the ages, which I derive from the im-
"mortal fountain on which I lean? Why
"do I not publish what angels are ignorant
"of? Why do I hide from the ends of
"the earth what no one knows, except the
"Father? Why do I not write what Mat-
"thew, and Mark, and Luke, through a
"wise and praise-worthy fear, passed in
"silence, according to the orders that were
"given them. How shall I speak what
"was given me freely from above? Mat-
"thew, according to what was granted to
"him, wrote according to his ability.
"Mark, and Luke, in like manner, accord-
"ing to the supply of the Spirit, have writ-
"ten their books in a becoming manner.
"I also will write, and add to those before,
"the fourth fountain of life. For there
"remains to the divine voice the discourses
"of *the divinity*, and the world is in dan-
"ger

" ger on this quarter. I will write a book
" which will ſtop the mouths of all, who
" ſpeak unjuſtly of God. I will write a
" book which will hide all the wiſdom of
" the world. I will write a book which
" ſhall not be confined to what concerns
" man. For the church is provided with
" what Moſes wrote concerning theſe
" things, about the heavens and the earth,
" &c.

" But I, leaving all things which have
" come to paſs from time, and in time,
" will ſpeak of that which was without
" time, and is uncreated, about the logos
" of God, which was generated from the
" Father in an ineffable manner, about
" which Moſes dared not to ſpeak. But
" I am able to do all things, through Chriſt
" who ſtrengthens me."

" The apoſtle John having reaſoned thus
" within himſelf, and having the pen of a
" writer in his hand, and confidering how
" to begin the theology, rejoicing in ſpirit,
" but with a trembling hand, is carried up-
" wards, being in the body at Epheſus, but
" with a pure heart and holy ſpirit leaves
" the

" the earth," &c. Then representing himself as carried up into heaven, he says, that " fishing out of the Father's bosom the " doctrine of the divinity, he wrote in his " body on earth, *In the beginning was the* " *logos,* &c*."

* Ελογιζετο εν εαυτω λεγων, τι αναβαλλομαι; τι φησι μακροθυμω ετι; τι 8 προσφερω εις μεσον το απο των αιωνων κεκρυμμενον μυτηριον; τι αποκρυβω εαυτω την απο των αιωνων σοφιαν, ην εκ της αθανατε πηγης επιπεσων ειλκυσα; τι 8 δημοσιευω, ον αγγελοι αγνοουσι; τι 8κ αποκαλυπτω τοις περασι, ον 8δεις επιγινοσκει, ει μη ο πατηρ; τι 8 γραφω, οπερ Ματθαιος κỳ Μαρκος κỳ Λυκας δι επαινυμενην δειλιαν παρασιωπησαντες παρεδραμον, τελεσαντες τα προςεταγμενα αυτοις; οθεν λαλησω καγω κατα την δοθεισαν μοι δωρεαν ανωθεν. Ματθαιος μεν οσον εχωρει, εγραψε κατα την ιδιαν δυναμιν, Μαρκος δε κỳ Λυκας ομοιως κατα την τυ αγιυ πνευματος χορηγιαν τας εαυτων βιβλους θεοπρεπως εδογματισαν. γραψω καγω κỳ προσθεσω τοις εμπροσθεν την τεταρτην πηγην την ζωης. λειπει γαρ εις θεουσταν φωνην ο περι θεολογιας λογος, κỳ κινδυνευει ο κοσμος εν τω μερει τυτω. γραψω βιβλον, δι ης εμφραγη πασαν τομα λαλυν κατα θεον αδικιαν· γραψω βιβλον την καλυψασαν πασαν εν κοσμω σοφιαν. γραψω βιβλον 8 περι ανθρωπυ διηγυμενην. 8 γαρ λειπει τη εκκλησια, α περι τυτων εγραψε Μωσης· περι υρανυ τε κỳ γης κỳ θαλασσων κỳ ιχθυων κỳ πετεινων κỳ τετραποδων, κỳ ερπετων κỳ φυτων κỳ σπερματων κỳ φωτηρων κỳ βρωματων κỳ λοιπης κτισεως; εγω δε παντα τα απο χρονυ κỳ εν χρονω γινομενα καταλειψας λαλησω περι τυ αχρονυ κỳ ακτιςυ, τυ προ παντων των αιωνων εκ τυ πατρος αρρητως γεννηθεντος θευ λογυ, περι 8 Μωσης ετος ειπειν 8κ ισχυσεν. εγω δε παντα ισχυω εν τω ενδυναμυντι με χριςω. ταυτα εν εαυτω σκεπτομενος ο αποςολος Ιωαννης κỳ τον γραφικον καλαμον εν τη χειρι κατεχων, κỳ εννοων πως της θεολογιας αρξηται. χαιρων μεν τη ψυχη. τρεμων δε τη χειρι

Chrysostom introduces Matthew also reasoning on the subject of his saying so little, or rather nothing, of the divinity of Christ; and indeed, according to his account, it was a very dangerous and hazardous topic.—
" Now," says he, " let us awake, and arise,
" Behold the gates are open to us, but let us
" enter with great regularity, and with
" trembling; first passing the outer court.
" What is the outer court? The book of
" the generation of Jesus Christ, the son of
" David, the son of Abraham. What is
" that you say?" (says the hearer) " You
" promised to discourse concerning the
" only begotten Son of God, and now you
" talk of David, a man who lived a thou-
" sand generations ago, and say, that he was
" his father and ancestor? Hold" (says the evangelist) " and do not expect to learn
" every thing immediately; but slowly, and
" by degrees: For you are yet in the outer
" court, and only near the gate; and why
" are you in haste to get into the innermost

χειρι, μεταρσιος γινεται, κ̣ τω σωματι εν Εφεσω ων, τη καθαρα καρδια τω πνευματι μετεωρος υπηρχε, κ̣ εκ τ8 πατρικ8 κολπ8 την θεολογιαν αλιευσας, τω σωματι κατω εγραφεν, εναρχη ην ο λογ☉. De Johanne, Opera, vol. 6. p. 606, &c.

" recess?

"recess? You have not yet well examined all that is without: For I do not as yet relate to you the generation itself; nor indeed shall I do it after this; for it is inexplicable and ineffable." Then reciting the dread that the prophet Isaiah had of the subject, which led him to exclaim, *Who shall declare his generation*, he says, " it is not my business to treat of this generation, but of the earthly one, of which there were ten thousand witnesses; and concerning this I shall so discourse as the gifts of the spirit shall enable me: for I cannot even declare this with perfect clearness: for even this is very fearful. Do not, therefore, think that you hear a small thing, when you hear even this generation; but raise your whole soul, and be full of horror when you hear that God is come upon earth;" and then he proceeds to describe at large all the awfulness of the incarnation, and the miraculous conception *.

* Διαναςωμεν τοινυν κὴ μη καθευδωμεν, ιδȣ γαρ ορω τας πυλας ημιν ανοιγομενας· αλλ' εισιωμεν μεία ευλαξιας απασης κὴ τρομȣ, των προθυρων αυίων ευθεως επιβαινονίες. τινα δε ετι ταυία τα προθυρα; βιβλ۞ γενεσεως Ιησȣ χριςȣ υιȣ Δαβιδ υιȣ Αβρααμ. τι λεγεις; περι τȣ

CHAP. VII. *Divinity of Christ.* 139

But this was far short of the eternal generation from the Father.

"Do not think," says this writer, "that you understand every thing, when you are informed that he was conceived by the Spirit; for there are many things of which we are yet ignorant, and which we have to learn; as how he who is infinite can be comprehended in a woman; how he who sustains all things can be carried

τȣ μονογενȣς υιȣ τȣ θεȣ διαλεξασθαι επηγΓειλω, κͺ τȣ Δαϐιδ μνημονευεις, ανθρωπȣ μετα μυριας γενεας γενομενȣ : κͺ αυτον ειναι φης, και πατερα και προγονον : επισχες, και μη παντα αθροως ζητει μαθειν, αλλ' ηρεμα κͺ κατα μικρον. εν γαρ τοις προθυροις ετηκας ετι παρ αυτα τα προπυλαια. τι τοινυν σπευδεις προς τα αδυτα. ȣπω τα εξω καλως κατωπτευσας απαντα. ȣδε γαρ εκεινην σοι τεως διηγȣμαι την γεννησιν· μαλλον δε ȣδε την μετα ταυτα. ανεκφρατος γαρ κͺ απορρητος. Την γενεαν αυτȣ τις διηγησεται · ȣ τοινυν περι εκεινης ημιν ο λογος νυν, αλλα περι ταυτης της κατω, της εν τη γη γενομενης, της μετα μυριων μαρτυρων, κͺ περι ταυτης δε, ως ημιν δυνατον ειπειν δεξαμενοις την τȣ πνευματος χαριν, ȣτω διηγησομεθα. ȣδε γαρ ταυτην μετα σαφηνιας πασης παρατητται ενι · επει κͺ αυτη φρικωδεταιͺη. μη τοινυν μικρα νομισης ακȣειν, ταυτην ακȣων την γεννησιν · αλλ' ανατησον σȣ την διανοιαν κͺ ευθεως φριξον, ακȣσας οτι θεος επι γης ηλθεν, ȣτω γαρ τȣτο θαυματον κͺ παραδοξον ην, ως κͺ τȣς αγγελȣς χορεν υπερ τȣτων τησαντας την υπερ της οικȣμενης επι τȣτοις αναφερειν ευφημιαν. In Matt. 1. Opera, vol. 7, p. 12.

" about

"about by her; how a virgin can bring
"forth, and remain a virgin *."

On this subject, which affords so much scope for eloquence, Epiphanius writes as follows: " Wherefore the blessed John
" coming, and finding men employed about
" the humanity of Christ, and the Ebio-
" nites being in an error about the earthly
" genealogy of Christ, deduced from Abra-
" ham, carried by Luke as high as Adam,
" and finding the Cerinthians and Merin-
" thians maintaining that he was a mere
" man, born by natural generation of both
" the sexes, and also the Nazarenes, and
" many other heresies; as coming last (for
" he was the fourth to write a gospel) be-
" gan as it were to call back the wanderers,
" and those who were employed about the
" the humanity of Christ; and seeing some
" of them going into rough paths, leaving
" the strait and true path, cries, Whither
" are you going, whither are you walking,

---

* Μη δε νομισης το παν μεμαθηκεναι, εκ πνευματ@ ακχων η γαρ πολλα αγνοϋμεν ετι. Και τϋτο μανθανοντες, οιεν πως ο απειρ@ εν μητρα εστιν; πως ο παντα συνεχων κυοφορειται υπο γυναικος; πως τικτει η παρθεν@ και μενει παρθεν@. In Matt. i. Opera, vol. 7. p. 31.

" who

"who tread a rough and dangerous path,
"leading to a precipice? It is not so. The
"God, the logos, which was begotten by
"the Father from all eternity, is not from
"Mary only. He is not from the time of
"Joseph, he is not from the time of Sala-
"thiel, and Zorobabel, and David, and Abra-
"ham, and Jacob, and Noah, and Adam;
"but *in the beginning was the logos, and the
"logos was with God, and the logos was God.*
"The *was*, and the *was*, and the *was*, do
"not admit of his having ever not been *."

* Διο κ̀ Ιωάννης ελθων ο μακαρι۞, κ̀ ευρων τ૪ς ανθρωπ૪ς ησχολημενες περι την κα]ω χριςυ παρυσιαν, κ̀ την ι૬ιωναιαν πλανηθενlων δια την ενσαρκον χριςυ γενεαλο]ιαν, απο Αβρααμ κα]αγομενην, κ̀ λυκα αναγομενην αχρι τυ Αδαμ, ευρον δε Κηρινθιανυς, και Μερινθιανυς, εκ παρα]ριζης αυ]ον λεγον]ας ειναι ψιλον ανθρωπον, και τυς Ναζωραιυς, και αλλας πολ.ας αιρεςεις, ως κα]οπιν ελθων, τε]αρ]۞ γαρ ε]ος ευαγγελι[ε]αι, αρχε]αι ανακαλειδαι, ας ειπειν, τυς πλανηθεν]ας, και ησχολη-μενυς περι την κα]ω χριςυ παρυσιαν, και λεγειν αυ]οις (ας κα]οπιν βαινων, και οραν τινας εις τραχειας οδυς κεκλικο]ας και αθεν]ας την ευθειαν και αληθινην, ας ειπεν) ποι φερεδε, ποι βαδιζετε, οι την τραχειαν οδον και σκανδαλωδη και εις χασμα φερυσαν βαδιζοντες; ανακαμψατε. Ουκ ες ν υτως, υκ ες ιν απο Μαριας μονον ο θεος λογ۞, ο εκ πατρ۞ ανωθεν γε-γεννημεν۞, υκ ες ιν απο των χρονων Ιωσηφ τυ ταυτης ορμαςυ, υκ ες ιν απο των χρονων Σαλαθιηλ, και Ζοροβαβηλ, και Δαβιδ, και Αβραμ, και Ιακωβ, και Νωε, και Αδαμ, αλλ' εν αρχη ην ο λογος

Another passage in this writer, in nearly the same words, may be seen, p. 433, 434.

Jerom says, "John the apostle, whom Je-
"sus loved, the son of Zebedee, and brother
"of James, who was beheaded by Herod af-
"ter the death of Christ, wrote his gospel
"the last of all, at the intreaty of the bishops
"of Asia, again Cerinthus, and other here-
"tics, and especially the doctrine of the
"Ebionites, then gaining ground, who said
"that Christ had no being before he was
"born of Mary, whence he was compelled
"to declare his divine origin *."

Ambrose says, "If you enquire concern-
"ing his celestial generation, read the gos-

ο λογος, και ο λογῷ ην προς τον θεον, και θεος ην ο λογος. Το δε ην, και ην, και ην ουχ υποδεχεται τω μη ειναι ποτε. Hær. 69. sect. 23. Opera, vol. 1. p. 747.

* Joannes Apostolus quem Jesus amavit plurimum, filius Zebedæi, frater Jacobi Apostoli, quem Herodes post passionem domini decollavit, novissimus omnium, scripsit evangelium, rogatus ab Asiæ episcopis, adversus Cerinthum, aliosque hæreticos et maxime tunc Ebionitarum dogma consurgens, qui asserunt Christum ante Mariam non fuisse, unde et compulsus est divinam ejus naturam edicere. Opera, vol. 1. p. 273.

"pel

"pel of John *." "If there be any other things," says Austin, "which intimate to the intelligent the divinity of Christ, in which he is equal to the Father, John almost alone has introduced them into his gospel; as having drank more familiarly, and more copiously, the secret of his divinity, from the breast of our Lord, on which he was used to lean at meat †." On this account he compares John to an eagle ‡. "The other evangelists," he says, "who treat of the humanity of Christ, were like animals that walk on the earth; but John, contemplating the power of his divinity more sublimely, flies to heaven

---

* At vero de cælesta generatione si quæris lege evangelium sancti Joannis. In Luc. cap. 2. Opera, vol. 2. p. 26.

† Et si qua alia sunt quæ Christi divinitatem in qua æqualis est patri, recte intelligentibus intiment, pene solus Johannes in evangelio suo posuit: tanquam de pectore ipsius domini, super quod discumbere in ejus convivio solitus erat, secretum divinitatis ejus uberius et quodammodo familiarius biberit. De Consensu Evangelistarum, lib. 1. cap. 5. Opera, vol. 4. p. 374.

‡ Ibid. p. 528, 529.

"with the Lord*." "But now, with an
"open voice, he says, that he is God, and
"was always with God, laying open the
"myſtery of God †."

A very particular and copious account of the pre-eminence of John, in conſequence of his teaching the doctrines of the pre-exiſtence and divinity of Chriſt, which had been omitted by the other evangeliſts, may likewiſe be ſeen in the epiſtle of Paulinus, which I put in the notes ‡.

* Cæteri quippe evangeliſtæ, qui temporalem Chriſti nativitatem et temporalia ejus facta, quæ geſſit in homine, ſufficienter exponunt, et de divinitate pauca dixerunt, quaſi animalia greſſibilia cum domino ambulant in terra: hic autem pauca de temporalibus ejus geſtis ediſſerens, ſed divinitalis potentiam ſublimius contemplans, cum domino ad cœlum volat. In John Pref. Opera, vol. 9. p. 5. 275.

† Nunc autem aperta voce dicit eum eſſe deum et ſemper fuiſſe apud deum, ſacramentum patefaciens dei. Queſtiones Mixtæ, vol. 4. p. 858.

‡ Idem ultra omnium tempora apoſtolorum ætate producta poſtremus evangelii ſcriptor fuiſſe memoratur, ut ſicut de ipſo vas electionis ait, quaſi columna firmamentum adjiceret fundamentis eccleſiæ, prioris evangelii ſcriptores conſona auctoritate confirmans, ultimus auctor, in libri tempore,

Cyril of Alexandria says, that " John was the first who taught more sublime things*." Marius Mercator says, that the three former evangelists, having spoken of Christ as a man, John shewed him to be God †."

tempore, sed primus in capite sacramenti, quippe qui solus e quatuor fluminibus ex ipso summo divini capitis fonte decurrens, de nube sublimi tonat: in principio erat verbum, et verbum erat apud deum, et deus erat verbum: transcendit Moysen, qui usque ad caput mundi et visibilium creaturarum exordia scientiæ terminos, et faciem mentis extendit. Iste et evangelistis cæteris, vel ab humano salvatoris ortu, vel a typico legis sacrificio, vel a prophetico præcursoris baptistæ præconio, resurrectionis evangelium exorsis, altius volans penetravit et coelos. Neque in angelis stetit, sed archangelos quoque et omnes desuper creaturas, virtutes, principatus, dominationes, thronos, supergressus, in ipsum se creatorem ardua mente direxit, et ab illa ineffabili generatione ordiens, et coeternum et consubstantialem, et co-omnipotentem, et co-opificem patri filium nunciavit. Ad Amandum. p. 213.

* Joannes theologus, tonitrui filius, cui divina dignatione concessum, ut supra dominicum pectus recubuerit, indeque nobis sublimiora ac divina hauserit dogmata: cum excelientem erga nos dei benignitatem commendare vellet, primumque quæ diviniora sunt dixisset, utpote ista, in principio erat verbum. Hom. Opera, vol. 2. p. 75.

† Post quam præfationem subdescendens, ut ostenderet quem illi tres evangelistæ hominem scripserant, esse etiam deum. Opera, p. 165.

Cosmas Indicopleustes, describing John as *theologus,* and the chief of the evangelists, says, that " he wrote to supply the " defects of the former evangelists, and " especially in preaching clearly the divi- " nity of Christ, making that the founda- " tion of his work, all which had been " omitted by the others. Wherefore, be- " ginning at his divinity, he immediately " passed to his humanity *."

" John," says Nicephorus, " did not give " an account of the carnal generation of " Jesus, but he first taught his divinity; " this being reserved for him, as the most " worthy, by the Holy Spirit †."

" Wherefore, John," says Theophylact, " began with the divinity of Christ. For " whereas others had made no mention of " his existence before the ages, he taught

---

* Εξαιρετως δε κ̄ περι της θεοτητος τȣ χριςȣ φανερως κηρυξας, θεμελιον της αυτȣ συγγραφης αυτω προταξας· απερ απαντα παραλελειμμενα τοις αλλοις ην. αρξαμενος τοινυν απο της θεοτητος, μετελελυθεν ευθεως κ̄ επι την ανθρωποτητα αυτȣ. De Mundo, lib. 5. Montfaucon's Collectio, vol. 2. p. 248.

† Της δε θεολογιας καταρχεται, οια τινος κρειτ]ονος προς τȣ θειȣ πνευματος ταμιευθεισης αυτω. Hist. lib. 2. cap. 45. vol. 1. p. 214.

" that

"that doctrine, left the logos of God
"should have been thought to be a mere
"man, without any divinity*." "Again,"
he says, "John wrote left men should never
"think highly concerning Christ, and ima-
"gine that he had no being before he was
"born of Mary, and that he was not gene-
"rated from God the Father, which was the
"case with Paulus Samosatensis †." " As
"John," he says, "has more lofty things
"of Christ than any other of the evange-
"lists, so he has recorded some of a lower
"nature; to shew that, as he was God, so
"he was truly man ‡."

Lastly, an account of John's teaching the pre-existence and divinity of Christ, may

---

* Επει γαρ οι αλλοι εκ εμνησθησαν περι της προ αιωνων υπαρξεως τε θεε λογε, αυτ⊙ εθεολογησε περι ταυτης, ινα μη νομισθειη ο τε θεε λογ⊙ ψιλος ανθρωπος ειναι. In Matt. Pref. vol. 1. p. 1, 2.

† Δεος μεν ην μη ποτε τινες χαμαιπετεις κ̀ μηδεν υψηλον νοησαι δυναμενοι, νομισωσι τον χριτον τοτε πρωτον εις υπαρξιν ελθειν οτι απο Μαριας εγεννηθη, κ̀ ουχι προ αιωνων εκ τε πατρος γεννηθηναι, ο παντων πεπονθε Παυλ⊙ ο Σαμοσαλευς. In John, cap. 1. vol. 1. p. 553.

‡ Επει γαρ παρα παντας τες ευαγγελιστας υψηλοτερα περι τε κυριε φθεγγεται, κ̀ θεολογει μεγαλα τινα, δια τετο κ̀ εν τοις σωματικοις πολυ ταπεινοτερα φθεγγεται. οθεν κ̀ εν τω πωθει πολυ το ανθρωπινον εχειν φησιν, απο τετε δεικνυων

be seen in the orations of Nicetas the Paphlagonian*."

The late introduction of the doctrine of the divinity of Christ is observed by the emperor Julian. He says, that " none of " Christ's disciples, except John, said that " he made the heavens and the earth, and " that not clearly and plainly †."

SECTION II.

Reflections on the subject.

AFTER reading these testimonies, so copious, and so full to my purpose, and uncontradicted by any thing in antiquity, it is not possible to entertain a doubt with respect to the opinion of the christian Fathers on this subject. They must have

δεικνυων της σαρκος την αληθειαν ινα συ μαθης οτι ει δε θεος ην, αλλα κ͗ ανθρωπος ην. In John ii. vol. 1, p. 726.

* Combefis Auctuarium, vol. 1. p. 362.

† Ὡς δε υμεις θελετε, τον ουρανον κ͗ την γην απεργασαμενο. ου γαρ δη ταυτα τετολμηκε τις ειπειν περι αυτυ των μαθητων, ει μη μονο Ιωαννης, ουδε αυτος σαφως, ουδε τρανως. Cyr. Con. Jul. lib. 6. Juliani, Opera, vol. 2. p. 213.

thought

thought that the doctrines of the pre-existence and divinity of Christ had not been preached with any effect before the writing of John's gospel; and, consequently, that before that time the great body of christians must have been unitarians; and they are far from giving the least hint of any of them having been excommunicated on that account. On the other hand, the apprehension was, lest those who preached doctrines so new and offensive, as those of the pre-existence and divinity of Christ, should have been rejected with abhorrence.

When we consider how late the three first gospels were written, the last of them not long before that of John, which was near, if not after, the destruction of Jerusalem, and that, in the opinion of the writers above-mentioned, all this caution and reserve had been necessary, till that late period, on the part of the christian teachers; how is it possible that, in their idea, the christian church in general should have been well established in the belief of our Lord's divinity? It could only have been great and open zeal on the part of the apostles, and not the timid caution and management which these writers ascribe to them, that could have effectually taught a doctrine which, according to them, the people were ill prepared to receive. And the history of both Peter and Paul sufficiently prove that the influence of mere apostolical authority was not so great at that time as many persons now take it to have been. Whatever power they had, they were not considered as lords over the faith of christians.

The christians of that age required something more than the private opinion of an apostle. They required some super-natural evidence that his doctrine was from God; and we have no account of the apostles proposing to them this additional article of faith, and alledging any such evidence for it. Chrysostom says, " if the Jews were " so much offended at having a new law " superadded to their former, how much " more would they have been offended, if " Christ had taught his own divinity." May it not be supposed, therefore, that they would have required as particular evidence

of

of a divine revelation in the one cafe as in the other? And what remarkably ftrong evidence was neceffary to convince them that the obligation of their law did not extend to the Gentiles? Would they, then, have received what Chryfoftom confidered as the more offenfive doctrine of the two, without any pretence to a particular revelation on the fubject?

It may be faid, that all the caution of which we have been fpeaking was neceffary with refpect to the *unbelieving Jews* only, into whofe hands thefe gofpels, and the other writings of the New Teftament, might fall. But how impoffible muft it have been to conceal from the unbelieving Jews the doctrine of the divinity of Chrift, if it had been a favourite article with the believing Jews. If this had been the cafe, it could not but have been known to all the world; and, therefore, all the offence that it could have given would have been unavoidable. So that this fuppofed caution of the evangelifts, &c. would have come too late, and would have anfwered no purpofe whatever.

This caution, therefore, muſt neceſſarily have reſpected thoſe perſons into whoſe hands the goſpels, &c. were moſt likely to come, and who would give the moſt attention to them; and theſe were certainly the believing Jews, and the chriſtian world at large, and not unbelievers of any nation. We are authoriſed to conclude, that in the opinion of the writers who have ſpoke of it, of whatever weight that opinion may be, this caution in divulging the doctrine of the divinity of Chriſt was neceſſary with reſpect to the great body of chriſtians themſelves, and eſpecially the Jewiſh chriſtians. Conſequently, they muſt have ſuppoſed, that at the time of theſe publications, which was about A. D. 64, the doctrine of the divinity of Chriſt was not generally held by chriſtians, and that there would have been danger of giving them great offence if at that time it had been plainly propoſed to them by the apoſtles themſelves. At this period, therefore, it may be inferred, that, in the opinion of theſe writers, the chriſtian church was principally unitarian, believing only the ſimple

simple humanity of Chriſt, and knowing nothing of his divinity or pre-exiſtence.

From the acknowledgment which theſe orthodox Fathers could not help making (for certainly they would not do it unneceſſarily) that there were great numbers of proper unitarians in the age of the apoſtles, it ſeems not unreaſonable to conclude, that there were great numbers of them in the age immediately following, and in their own. And their knowledge of this might be an additional reaſon for the opinion that they appear to have formed of that prevalence in the apoſtolic age. Would theſe Fathers have granted to their enemies ſpontaneouſly, and contrary to truth, that the Jews were ſtrongly prepoſſeſſed againſt the doctrine of the divinity of Chriſt, and that the unitarians were a formidable body of chriſtians while the apoſtles were living, if it had been in their power to have denied the facts? The conſequence of making theſe acknowledgments is but too obvious, and muſt have appeared ſo to them, as well as it now does to others, which makes them ſo unwilling to make it after them.

I cannot

I cannot conclude this chapter without obferving, in how unworthy a manner, and how unfuitably to their real character and conduct, thefe Fathers reprefent the apoftles as acting. They were all *plain men*, far from being qualified, or difpofed, to act fo cunning a part, as is here afcribed to them. There is nothing like art or addrefs in the conduct of any of them, as related in the fcriptures, except that of Paul; and this was only with refpect to his preaching the gofpel to the uncircumcifed Gentiles, before it was generally approved of at Jerufalem; on which account, he informed the chief of the apoftles only with what he had done. But this was no fecret long, and indeed a thing of that kind could not, in its own nature, have been much of a fecret at any time. On all other occafions he failed not to inform thofe to whom he preached *of the whole counfel of God*; as he fays that he had done with refpect to the church of Ephefus, Acts xx. 27. Much lefs can it be fuppofed that he would have concealed a doctrine of fo great magnitude and importance as that of the pre-exiftent dignity

of

of his master; and, communicating it only to a few, have left it to be taught after his death. For it is not to be supposed that the other apostles were in the secret of John's intending to do it after their deaths.

Besides, the instructions of the apostles enjoined them to teach all that they knew, even what their master had communicated to them in the greatest privacy. Whereas upon this scheme, they must have suffered great numbers to die in the utter ignorance of the most important truths of the gospel, lest, by divulging it too soon, the conversion of others should have been prevented.

To these observations I would add, that as among the twelve apostles, there must have been men of different tempers and abilities, it is not probable that they should *all* have agreed in conducting themselves upon this plan, viz. of not divulging the doctrine of the divinity of their master till their hearers should be sufficiently persuaded of his messiahship. Some of them would hardly have been capable of so much refinement, and would certainly have differed about the *time* when it was proper to divulge

divulge fo great a fecret. Befides, the mother of Jefus, and many other perfons of both fexes, muft have been acquainted with it. For that this fecret was ftrictly confined to the twelve apoftles, will hardly be maintained. And yet we have no account either of their inftructions to act in this manner, or of any difference of opinion, or of conduct, with refpect to it.

Never, fure, was a more improbable hypothefis ever formed to account for any thing, than this of the chriftian Fathers to account for the late teaching of the doctrines of the pre-exiftence and divinity of Chrift. But their circumftances left them no alternative. They muft have had fome very cogent reafon for admitting that the teaching of thefe doctrines was fo late; and this could not have been any thing but the want of that *general prevalence,* which they would have had, if they had been taught with effect in the life-time of the apoftles, and which would have continued to their own times. They muft, therefore, have known that there were more unitarians in the church in the early ages than they could account

account for on any other hypothesis than that of the doctrines of the pre-existence and divinity of Christ, not having been taught till very late. At present, the facts which forced the Fathers upon this hypothesis are forgotten, and the orthodox themselves wonder that they should have adopted a scheme so absurd and improbable. But the different manner in which such an hypothesis is received, is a proof of a great difference in the circumstances and views of things in the different periods. We see nothing to make so strange an hypothesis necessary. They would not have had recourse to it, if it had not been necessary.

CHAPTER VIII.

Of the Nazarenes and the Ebionites, shewing that they were the same People, and that none of them believed the Divinity or Pre-existence of Christ.

WE have seen that, according to the unanimous and very express testimony of the christian Fathers (a testimony which is greatly against their own cause, and therefore, the more to be depended upon) there could not have been many persons who believed the doctrines of the pre-existence and divinity of Christ in the age of the apostles; one of the last books of the canon, viz. the gospel of John, being the first in which those doctrines were clearly published.

If we look into the gospels, and the book of Acts, we shall find that one part of their testimony is true, viz. that those *sublime doctrines*, as they call them, were not taught in an early period. For none of the three first gospels make the least mention of any thing

thing in the perfon or nature of Chrift fuperior to thofe of other men. In like manner, all the *preaching of Chrift*, of which we have an account in the book of Acts, is that Jefus was the Meffiah, whofe divine miffion was confirmed by miracles, efpecially that of his own refurrection, and by the gifts of the Spirit. And all the *controverfies* of which we find any account, either in that book, or in the epiftles, refpected either the *Jewifh teachers*, who would have impofed the obfervance of the law of Mofes upon all the Gentile converts, or elfe thofe who held the principles of the *Gnoftics*.

The erroneous doctrines of thefe perfons are diftinctly marked, fo that no perfon can read the New Teftament without perceiving that there were perfons who held thefe doctrines, and that they were the caufe of great uneafinefs to the apoftles. But there is no trace of any other opinions at which they took the leaft umbrage.

As to the effect of the publication of John's gofpel, from which fo much feems to have been expected by the chriftian Fathers, it is impoffible that we fhould learn

any

any thing concerning it in the New Testament, because that was one of the last of the books that was published. However, we have no account in ecclesiastical history that it produced any change at all in the sentiments of christians. Though it is said to have taught a new and a sublime doctrine, it does not appear to have been received with any degree of surprize. There are no marks of the publication having given any peculiar pleasure to some, or alarm to others; or that it occasioned the least division among christians on the subject.

We may, therefore, very safely conclude, that those christians for whose use this gospel was written, saw it in a very different light from those Fathers who gave the preceding account of it. We know, indeed, that to them it did not appear to teach any other doctrine than what was contained in the three former gospels. For by the *logos* of which John treats in this famous introduction, they never imagined to be meant *Christ*, and therefore they could see nothing of his personal pre-existence or divinity in it. In their opinion, the logos was that

wisdom

CHAP. VIII.   *the same People.*   161

wisdom and power of God, by which all things were made.

Though this gospel was written in Greek, there were not wanting among the Jewish christians men of learning who would not have failed to give an account of it to their more ignorant countrymen, or to translate it for their use, if it had been thought necessary. Yet, notwithstanding this, all the Jewish christians continued in the very same state in which the christian Fathers represent them to have been before the publication of this gospel, viz. believers in the *simple humanity* of Christ only, and acknowledging nothing of his pre-existence or divinity. The same was also the state of the Gentile christians in general, long after the publication of this gospel.

As no entire writings of any Jewish christians are come down to us, all that we know concerning them must be derived from the writings of the Gentile christians; and as these christians were trinitarians, and had very little communication with the Jewish christians, we cannot

not expect any favourable, or indeed any impartial accounts concerning them. If, however, we may depend upon the earliest accounts that we have of them, and those given by persons who were the best qualified to give us good information, they were all unitarians, and were distinguished from the Gentile christians by the name of *Ebionites*, or *Nazarenes*. But as it has been pretended by those who, being trinitarians themselves, were willing to believe that there *must* have been a body of ancient Jewish christians who thought as they do, and that the Ebionites or Nazarenes must have been sects who broke off from their communion; and as some of these persons have even said that these Ebionites, or Nazarenes, were subsequent to the destruction of Jerusalem by Titus; and others have fixed their origin so late as the desolation of Judea by Adrian, it may not be improper to shew that persons distinguished by the name of Ebionites and Nazarenes were supposed to have existed in the time of the apostles.

Irenæus,

Irenæus, who gives no other name to any Jewish christians besides that of Ebionites, whom he always speaks of as both denying the pre-existence and divinity of Christ, and likewise the miraculous conception, objects to the Gnostics, that they were of late date, but he says nothing of the Ebionites in that respect *. Eusebius says, that "the first heralds of our Saviour" (by whom he must have meant the apostles) "called those Ebionites, which in the He-"brew language signifies poor; who, not "denying the body of Christ, shewed their "folly in denying his divinity†."

---

* Reliqui vero qui vocantur Gnostici, a Menandro Simonis discipulo, quemadmodum ostendimus, accipientes initia, unusquisque eorum, cujus participatus est sententiæ, ejus et pater, et antistes apparuit. Omnes autem hi multo posterius, mediantibus jam ecclesiæ temporibus, insurrexerunt in suam apostasiam. Lib. 3. cap. 4. p. 206.

† Και αυτε δε τε σωτηρος ημων, οι πρωτοκηρυκες Εβιωναιες ωνομαζον Εβραικη φωνη, πτωχες. την δε διοιαν αποκαλυντες, τες ενα μεν θεον λεγοντας ειδεναι, χ) τε σωτηρος τω σωμα μη αρνεμενες, την δε τε υιε θεοτητα μη ειδοντας. Ec. Theol. lib. 1. cap. 14. p. 75.

Epiphanius makes both Ebion (for in his time it was imagined, that the Ebionites were so called from some particular person of that name) and Cerinthus, cotemporary with the apostle John; and he could not tell which of them was the older*. He likewise makes the Ebionites cotemporary with the Nazarenes, at the same time that he says they held that Christ was the son of Joseph †. Also, in the passage before quoted from him, as well as in that from Jerom, we find the names of both the Ebionites and the Nazarenes among those who gave so much alarm to the apostle John. It must

* Ναζωραιοι καθεξης τυτοις εποιται, αμα τε αυτοις οντες, η και προ αυτων, η συν αυτοις, η μετ αυτες ομως συγχρονοι. ε γαρ ακριβεστερον δυναμαι εξειπειν τινες τινας διεδεξαντο. Hær. 30. Opera, vol. 1. p. 149. H. 29. p. 116.

† Ουτος γαρ ο Εβιων συγχρονος μεν τυτων υπηρχεν, απ αυτων δε συν αυτοις ορμαται. Τα πρωτα δε εκ παρατριβης και σπερματθ ανδρος, τυτεστιν τε Ιωσηφ, τον χριστον γεγενησθαι, ελεγεν, ως και ηδε ημιν προειρηται, οτι τα ισα τοις αλλοις εν απασι φρονων, εν τυτω μονω διαφερετο, εν τω τω νομω τε Ιουδαισμυ προσανεχειν, κατα σαβατισμον, και κατα την περιτομην, και κατα τα αλλα παντα οσαπερ παρα τες Ιουδαιες ομοιως τοις Σαμαρειταις διαπρατ]εται. Hær. 30. p. 125, 126.

be

be owned, however, that, in no perfect
consistence with this account, Epiphanius
places the origin of the Nazarenes after the
destruction of Jerusalem. After mentioning the places where they resided, viz. Peræa, Cœle-Syria, Pella, and Cocabe, he says,
" there was their origin, after the destruc-
" tion of Jerusalem, when all the disciples
" lived at Pella; Christ having warned
" them to leave Jerusalem, and retire at the
" approach of the siege; and on this account
" they lived, as I said, in Peræa. Thence
" the sect of the Nazarenes had its origin*."

Sophronius, quoted by Theophylact, says,
that " John, besides having a view to Ce-
" renthus, and other heretics, wrote more
" especially against the heresy of the Ebio-
" nites, which was then very prevalent,
" who said that Christ had no being before

---

* Εκειθεν μεν η αρχη γεγονε μετα την απο των Ιεροσο-
λυμων μεταςασιν, παντων των μαθητων των εν Πελλη ωκη-
κοτων, χριςε φησαντος καταλειψαι τα Ιεροσυλυμα, κ̓ ανα-
χωρησαι επειδη ημελλε πασχειν πολιορκιαν. κ̓ εκ της τοιαυ-
της υποθεσεως την Περαιαν ωκησαντες; εκεισε ως εφην δια-
τριβον. εντευθεν η κατα τες Ναζωραιες αιρεσις ειχε την
αρχην. Hær. 29. Opera, vol. 1. p. 123.

" he

"he was born of Mary; so that he was
"under a necessity of declaring his divine
"origin *."

Cassian calls Hebion "the first heretic,
"laying too much stress on the humanity
"of Christ, and stripping him of his di-
"vinity†."

There can be no doubt, therefore, but that both Ebionites and Nazarenes were existing in the time of the apostles; and that there was no real difference between these two sects. And that both of them were equally believers in the simple humanity of Christ, is no less evident.

The testimony of Origen is clear and decisive to this purpose. He says, that "the word *Ebion*, in the Jewish language, "signifies *poor*, and those of the Jews who "believe Jesus to be the Christ are called

---

* Και μαλιςα τηνικαυλα τε των Εϐιωνιτων δογμαΐος ανακυψαντος, των φασκεν]ων τον χριςον προ Μαριας μη γεγενησθαι. οθε ηναγκα- σθη την θειαν γεννσιν αυία ειπειν. In John, vol. 1. p. 548.

† Quorum primus Hebion, dum incarnationem dominicam nimis asserit, divinitatis eam conjunctione nudavit. De Incarnatione, lib. 1. cap. 2. p. 962.

"*Ebionites*."

"*Ebionites* *." Here is no room left for any difference between the Ebionites and the Nazarenes; for the Ebionites comprehended all the Jewish christians; and, according to Origen, none of them were believers in the pre-existence or divinity of Christ. He says, there were two sorts of Ebionites, of whom one believed the miraculous conception, and the other disbelieved it, while both of them rejected the doctrine of his divinity. "And when you
" consider," says he, " the faith concern-
" ing our Saviour of those of the Jews who
" believe in Christ, some thinking him to
" be the son of Joseph and Mary, and
" others of Mary only, and the divine Spi-
" rit, but not believing his divinity †."

He mentions the two sects of Ebionites in the following passage. " There are some

---

* Εβιων τε γαρ ο πίωχος παρα Ιεδαιοις καλειται. Και Εβιωνα‑ οι χρηματιζεσιν οι απο Ιεδαιων τον Ιησεν, ως χριτον, παραδεξαμενοι. In Celsum, lib. 2. p. 56.

† Και επαν ιδης των απο Ιεδαιων πιτευοντων εις τον Ιησεν την περι τε σωτηρος πιτιν, ότε μεν εκ μαριας κ̣ τε Ιωσηφ οιομενων αυτον ειναι, ότε μεν εκ μαριας μεν μονης, κ̣ τε θεια πνευματο̄, ε μην κ̣ μετα της περι αυτε θεολογια, ᴄ ψει, &c. Comment. in Matt. Ed. Huetii, vol. 1. p. 427.

" heretics

"heretics who do not receive the epistles
"of Paul, as those who are called Ebionites,
"of both sorts *."

Eusebius gives the very same account of the two sorts of Ebionites, and makes no mention of any Nazarenes, as differing from them. "Others," he says, "whom a ma-
"lignant demon was not able to turn aside
"entirely from the love of Christ, finding
"them weak in some respects, reduced into
"his power. These by the ancients were
"called Ebionites, as those who think
"meanly concerning Christ — For they
"think him to be merely a man, like
"other men, but approved on account of
"his virtue, being the son of Mary's huf-
"band. Others called by the same name,
"leaving the absurd opinion of the former,
"do not deny that Christ was born of a vir-
"gin, but say, that he was of the Holy Spirit.
"However at the same time, they by no
"means allowing that Christ was God, the
"word, and wisdom, were drawn into the
"rest of their impiety." He then says,

† Εισι γαρ τινες αιρεσεις τας Παυλε επιστολας τε αποστολε μη προσιεμεναι, ωσπερ Εβιωναιοι αμφοτεροι. In Celsum, lib. 6. p. 274.

that

that "they maintained the observance of "the Jewish law, and that they used the "gospel according to the Hebrews." He says also, "that beggars are called Ebio- "nites*."

It may be clearly inferred, from a passage in a letter of Jerom to Austin, that though he was acquainted with the nominal distinc-

* Ἄλλως δὲ ὁ πονηρὸς δαίμων τῆς περὶ τὸν Χριστὸν τε Θεν διαθέσεως ἀδυνατῶν ἐκσεῖσαι, θατεραληπτες εὑρὼν εσφετεριζέτο. Ἐβιωναιες τελες οἰκείως επεφημιζον οἱ πρῶτοι, πτωχῶς καὶ ταπεινῶς τὰ περὶ τὰ χριςν δοξαζονίας. λιτον μὲν γὰρ αυτον κὴ κοινον ηγετο κατα προκοπην ηθες αυτον μονον ανθρωπον δεδικαιωμενον εξ ανδρος τε κοινωνιας κὴ τῆς Μαριας γεγενημενον · δειν δε παντως αυτοις της νομικης θρησκειας, ως μη αν δια μονης της εις τον χριστον πιστεως κὴ τα κατ' αυτην βιε σωθησομενοις. αλλοί δε παρα τετες της αυτης ονίες προσηγοριας, την μεν των ειρημενων εκτοπον διεδιδρασκον ατοπιαν, εκ παρθενε κὴ τε αγιε πνευματος μη αρνεμενοι γεγονεναι τον κυριον · ε μην εθ ομοιως κὴ ετοι προυπαρχειν αυτον, Θεον λογον ονία κὴ σοφιαν ομολογενίες, τη των προτερων περιείρεπουτο δυσσεβεια · μαλιστα δε κὴ την σωματικην περι τον νομον λατρειαν ομοιως εκεινοις περιεπειν εσπυδαζον. ετοι δε τε μεν αποστολε πασας τας επιστολας, αρνητεας ηγετο ειναι δειν, αποστατην αποκαλεντες αυτον τε νομε. ευαγτελιω δε μονω τω καθ Εβραιες λεγομενω χρωμενοι, των λοιπων σμικρον εποιετο λογον. κὴ το μεν Σαββατον κὴ τη Ιεδαικην αλλην αγωγην ομοιως εκεινοις παραφυλατίον. ταις δ' αυ κυριακαις ημεραις, ημιν τα παραπλησια εις μνημην της τε κυριε αναστασεως επε- τελεν. οθεν παρα την τοιαυτην εγχειρησιν της τοιασδε λελογχασι προ- σηγοριας, τε Εβιωναιων ονοματος, την της διανοιας πτωχειαν αυτων υπο- φαινοντος. ταυτην γαρ επικλην ὁ πτωχος παρ Εβραιοις ονομαζεται.
Hist. lib. 3. cap. 27. p. 121.

tion

tion between the Ebionites and Nazarenes, he did not confider them as really, or at leaft as materially, differing from each other. " If this be true," he fays, " we fall into " the herefy of Cherintus and Ebion, who, " believing in Chrift, were anathematized " by the Fathers on this account only, that " they mixed the ceremonies of the law " with the gofpel of Chrift, and held to the " new" (difpenfation) " in fuch a manner " as not to lofe the old. What fhall I fay " concerning the Ebionites, who pretend " that they are chriftians? It is to this very " day in all the fynagogues of the eaft, a " herefy among the Jews, called that of the " *Minci,* now condemned by the Pharifees, " and commonly called Nazarenes, who be- " lieve in Chrift the Son of God, born of " the virgin Mary, and fay, that it was he " who fuffered under Pontius Pilate, and " rofe again, in whom alfo we believe. But " while they wifh to be both Jews and " chriftians, they are neither Jews nor " chriftians *."

* Si hoc verum eft; in Cherinti et Hebionis hærefim dilabimur, qui credentes in Chrifto, propter hoc folum a patribus

That this account of the Nazarenes is only explanatory of the Ebionites, is evident from his saying, "What shall I say concerning the Ebionites!" After such an expression as this, we naturally expect that he should proceed to say something concerning them, which this author most evidently does; observing, that the same people who were called *Ebionites* (by the Gentiles) were called *Minei* and *Nazarenes* by the Jews. Had he meant to describe any other class of people, he would naturally have begun his next sentence with *Est et,* or *Est alia heresis,* and not simply *heresis est.* As to his speaking of *heresy* in the second sentence, and not *heretics,* as in

patribus anathematizati funt; quod legis cærimonias Christi evangelio miscuerunt, et sic nova confessi sunt, ut vetera non amitterent. Quid dicam de Hebionitis, qui christianos esse se simulant? Usque hodie per totas orientis synagogas inter Judæos hæresis est, quæ dicitur mineorum, et a Pharisæis nunc usque damnatur, quos vulgo Nazaræos nuncupant, qui credunt in Christum, filium dei, natum de virgine Maria, et eum dicunt esse, qui sub Pontio Pilato passus est, et resurrexit, in quem et nos credimus: sed dum volunt et Judæi esse, et christiani, nec Judæi sunt nec christiani. Opera, vol. 1. p. 634.

the

the first, it is a most trifling inaccuracy in language, the easiest of all others to fall into, and of no consequence to the meaning at all. Besides, Jerom's account of these two denominations of men is exactly the same; the Ebionites being *believers in Christ, but mixing the law and the gospel*; and the Nazarenes, *wishing to be both Jews and christians*, which certainly comes to the very same thing.

Stress has been laid on our author's saying, that the Ebionites *pretended* to be Christians; but Jerom calls them *credentes in Christo, believers in Christ*; and if they believed in Christ at all, they could not believe much less than he himself represents the Nazarenes to have done. It may be said, that they only pretended to be christians, but were not, because they had been excommunicated. But what had they been excommunicated for? Not for any proper imperfection of their faith in Christ, in which they were inferior to the Nazarenes, but *only (solum)* because they mixed the ceremonies of the law with the gospel of Christ; which, in other words, he asserts

of

of the Nazarenes alſo, when he ſays, they wiſhed to be both Jews and chriſtians. And though he does not ſay that the Nazarenes were *excommunicated*, he ſays they were *not chriſtians*, which is an expreſſion of the ſame import.

Had there been any foreign reaſon why we ſhould ſuppoſe that Jerom meant to diſtinguiſh between the Ebionites and the Nazarenes, we might have heſitated about the interpretation of his meaning, eaſy as it is. But certainly there can be no cauſe of heſitation, when it is conſidered that in this he agrees not with Epiphanius only, but with the whole ſtrain of antiquity, as is allowed by Le Clerc, and all the ableſt critics; and to interpret his meaning otherwiſe is to ſet him at variance with all other writers.

It is aſked, " Why were the Cerinthians " omitted? Jerom places them with the " Ebionites in the preceding ſentence: and if " the Nazarenes and the Ebionites were the " ſame people, it may, with equal clearneſs of " evidence, be inferred, that they were the " ſame people with the Cerinthians likewiſe."

I anſwer,

I anfwer, they were the fame people, as far as Jerom then confidered them, becaufe they were equally zealous for the law of Mofes.

It has been faid, that Auftin's anfwer to Jerom fhews, that he confidered them as different perfons. But Auftin only enumerates all the names that Jerom had mentioned, and whether the differences were real or nominal, great or little, it fignified nothing to him. He himfelf, in his *Catalogue of herefies*, makes a difference between the Ebionites and Nazarenes, but by no means that which makes the latter to have been believers in the divinity of Chrift, and the former not. And as it was a common opinion, efpecially in the Weft, that there was *fome* difference between them (though the writers who fpeak of it could never be certain in what it confifted) it was very natural in Auftin to mention them feparately, whether Jerom had made them the fame or not.

I find that Suicer, in his *Thefaurus*, under the article *Ebion*, makes the fame ufe of this paffage of Jerom that I have done, and confiders the Nazarenes as a branch of the Ebionites.

Ebionites. Sandius alfo draws the fame inference from this paffage. Hift. Ecclef. p. 4.

That the unbelieving Jews fhould call the chriftian Jews Nazarenes, is natural; becaufe that was the opprobrious appellation by which they had been diftinguifhed from the beginning. According to Tertullian, they called them fo in his time *. Agobard fays they did the fame when he wrote †. But it was not fo natural that this fhould be adopted by the Gentile chriftians, becaufe they had been ufed to regard that appellation with more refpect. When, therefore, they came to diftinguifh themfelves from the Jewifh chriftians, and to diflike their tenets, it was natural for them to adopt fome other appellation than that of *Nazarenes*; and the term *Ebionites*, given them likewife by their unbelieving brethren, equally anfwered their purpofe.

* Unde et ipfo nomine nos Judæi Nazarenos appellant per eum. Adv. Marcionem, lib. 4. fect. 8. p. 418.

† Quod autem dominum noftrum Jefum Chriftum et chriftianos in omnibus orationibus fuis fub Nazarenorum nomine cotidie maledicant. De Infolentia Judæorum, Opera, p. 63.

The term minei is from the Hebrew מנים *(minim)* which signifies *sectaries*, and is that by which the Jews, in all their writings, distinguish the christians.

It is something remarkable, that Justin Martyr does not use the term *Ebionite*, or any other expressive of dislike. Irenæus is the first who uses it, or who speaks of the Jewish unitarians with the least disrespect.

It is an argument in favour of the identity of the Nazarenes and Ebionites, that the former are not mentioned *by name* by any writer who likewise speaks of the Ebionites before Epiphanius, who was fond of multiplying heresies, though the people so called were certainly known before his time. The term Ebionites only occurs in Irenæus, Tertullian, Origen, and Eusebius. None of them make any mention of Nazarenes; and yet it cannot be denied, that they must have been even more considerable in the time of those writers, than they were afterwards.

The conduct of all these writers is easily accounted for on the suppositions, that, in the time of Justin Martyr, the Jewish christians,

tians, though all unitarians, and even difbelieving the miraculous conception, were not known by any opprobrious appellation at all; that afterwards they were firſt diſtinguiſhed by that of Ebionites; and that it was not till the time of Epiphanius (when ſuch writers as he, who wrote expreſsly on the ſubject of *hereſy*, made a parade of their learning, by recounting a multiplicity of hereſies) that the term Nazarenes, by which the unbelieving Jews ſtill continued to call the chriſtians among them, was laid hold of, as ſignifying a ſect different from that of the Ebionites.

Moſheim makes a doubt whether there was ſuch a perſon as *Ebion*, or not. I have ſeen no evidence at all that any perſon of that name ever exiſted. There is no founder of a ſect, of whoſe hiſtory *ſome* particulars have not been handed down to poſterity; but this is *vox et præterea nihil*. The term *Ebionite*, was alſo long prior to that of *Ebion*. They who firſt uſed this term, ſay nothing about the *man* from others, and they were too late to know any thing of him themſelves.

It must be more particularly difficult to account for the conduct of Eusebius, on the supposition either of there having been such a person as Ebion, or of there having been any distinction between the Ebionites and Nazarenes, since it was his business, as an historian, to have noticed both.

The opinion that the Ebionites and Nazarenes were the same people, is maintained by Le Clerc, and the most eminent critics of the last age. What Mr. Jones (who is remarkable for his caution in giving an opinion) says on this subject, is well worth quoting.

"It is plain, there was a very great "agreement between these two ancient "sects; and though they went under dif- "ferent names, yet they seem only to have "differed in this, that the Ebionites had "made some addition to the old Nazarene "system. For Origen expressly tell us, "Και Εξιωναιοι χρηματιζουσι οι απο Ιουδαιων τον Ιησουν ως χριστον παρα- "δεξαμενοι. *They are called Ebionites who "from among the Jews own Jesus to be the "Christ.* And though Epiphanius seems to "make their gospels different, calling one

πληρεςαλον,

" πληρεςατον, *more entire*, yet this need not
" move us. For if the learned Cafaubon's
" conjecture fhould not be right, that we
" fhould read the fame ε πληρεςατον, in both
" places (which yet is very probable for
" any thing that Father Simon has proved
" to the contrary) yet will the difficulty be
" all removed at once, by this fingle con-
" fideration; that Epiphanius never faw any
" gofpel of the Nazarenes. For though
" he calls it πληρεςατον, yet he himfelf fays,
" εκ οιδα δε ει τας γενεαλογιας περιειλον, *he did not know*
" *whether they had taken away the genealogy*,
" as the Ebionites had done; i. e. having
" never feen the Nazarene gofpel, for ought
" he knew, it might be the very fame with
" that of the Ebionites, as indeed it moft
" certainly was*."

In my opinion, Jerom has fufficiently decided this laft queftion. Could he have had
any other idea than that thefe two fects (if
they were two) ufed the fame gofpel, when
he faid, " In the gofpel ufed by the Na-
" zarenes and Ebionites, which is com-
" monly called the authentic gofpel of

* On the Canon, vol. 1. p. 386.

Matthew

"Matthew, which I lately tranflated from Hebrew into Greek, &c.*"

Farther, the peculiar opinions of the Ebionites and the Nazarenes are reprefented by the moft refpectable authorities as the very fame; only fome have thought that the Nazarenes believed the miraculous conception, and the Ebionites not. But this has no authority whatever among the ancients.

Epiphanius fays, in the middle of his firft fection relating to the *Ebionites*, that Ebion (whom in the twenty-fourth fection he makes to be cotemporary with the apoftle John) "borrowed his abominable rites from the Samaritans, his opinion (γνωμην) from the Nazarenes, his name from the Jews, &c.*" And he fays, in the beginning of the fecond fection, "he was cotemporary with the former, and

* In evangelio, quo utuntur Nazareni et Ebionitæ (quod nuper in Græcum de Hebræo fermone tranftulimus et quod vocatur a plerifque Matthæi authenticum). In Matt. 12, 13. Opera, vol. 6. p. 21.

† Σαμαρειῶν μεν γαρ κ̓ εχει το βδελυρον, Ιεδαιων τε το ονομα, Οσσαιων δε κ̓ Ναζωραιων κ̓, Νασαραιων την γνωμην—κ̓ χριτιανων βελεῖαι εχειν την προσηγοριαν. Hær. 30. fect. 1. p. 125.

"had

"had the same origin with them; and first he
"asserted that Christ was born of the com-
"merce and seed of man, namely, Joseph,
"as we signified above," referring to the
first words of his first section, "when we
"said that in other respects he agreed with
"them all, and differed from them only in
"this, viz. in his adherence to the laws of
"the Jews with respect to the sabbath,
"circumcision, and other things that were
"enjoined by the Jews and Samaritans.
"He moreover adopted many more things
"than the Jews, in imitation of the Sama-
"ritans *," the particulars of which he
then proceeds to mention.

In the same section he speaks of the Ebionites as inhabiting the same country with the Nazarenes, and adds that, "agree-
"ing together, they communicated of their
"perverseness to each other †." Then, in

* See note, page 164, in this volume.

† Ενθεν αρχεται της κακης αυτε διδασκαλιας, οθεν δηθεν κ̣ Ναζαρηνοι οι ανομοι προδεδηλωνται. Συναφθεις γαρ ετος εκεινοις, κ̣ εκεινοι τετω, εκατερος απο της εαυτε μοχθηριας τω ετερω μετεδωκε. Hær. 30. sect. 2. p. 125, 126.

the third section, he observes that, afterwards, some of the Ebionites entertained a different opinion concerning Christ, than that he was the son of Joseph; supposing that, after Elxæus joined them, they learned of him some fancy concerning Christ and the Holy Spirit*.

Concerning the Nazarenes, in the seventh section of his account of them, he says, that they were Jews in all respects, except that they "believed in Christ; but I do not "know whether they hold the miraculous "conception or not †." This amounts to no more than a doubt, which he afterwards abandoned, by asserting that the Ebionites held the same opinion concerning Christ with the Nazarenes, which opinion he expressly states to be their belief, that Jesus was a mere man, and the son of Joseph.

---

* Φαντασιαν τινα περι χριστ8 διηγειλαι, κỳ περι πνευματος αγιϛ. Hær. 30. sect. 3. p. 127.

† Περι χριστ8 δε 8κ οιδα ειπειν ει κỳ αυτοι τη των προσειρημενων περι Κηρινθον κỳ Μηρινθον μοχθηρια αχθεντες, ψιλον ανθρωπον νομιζ8σιν, η καθως η αληθεια εχει, δια πνευματ(Θ- αγι8 γεγενησθαι εκ Μαριας, διαβεβαιενται. Hær. 29. sect. 7. vol. I. p. 123.

As

As to any properly orthodox Nazarenes, i. e. believers in the pre-exiſtence or divinity of Chriſt, I find no traces of them any where. Auſtin ſays, that the Nazarenes were by ſome called Symmachians, from Symmachus, who is not only generally called an Ebionite, but who wrote expreſsly againſt the doctrine of the miraculous conception. How then could the Nazarenes be thought to be different from the Ebionites, or to believe any thing of the divinity of Chriſt, or even the miraculous conception, in the opinion of thoſe who called them Symmachians? Auſtin who mentions this, does not ſay that they were miſcalled.

Theodoret, who, living in Syria, had a good opportunity of being acquainted with the Nazarenes, deſcribes them as follows: " The Nazarenes are Jews who honour " Chriſt as a righteous man, and uſe the " goſpel according to Peter *." This account of the faith of the Nazarenes was

---

* Οι δε Ναζωραιοι Ιȣδαιοι εισι, τον χριϛον τιμωνϊες ως ανϑρωπον δικαιον, ᾗ τω καλȣμενω κατα Πεϊρον ευαγϊελιω κεχρημενοι. Hær. Fql. lib. 2. cap. 2. Opera, vol. 4. p. 219.

evidently

evidently meant to reprefent them as differing from the orthodox with refpect to the doctrine concerning Chrift; and is to be underftood as if he had faid, "they be-
"lieve him to have been nothing more
"than a righteous man, and a divine
"teacher" (for claiming to be fuch, he could not otherwife have been a righteous man) "but they do not believe in his
"pre-exiftence, or divinity." Orthodox perfons, who believe thefe doctrines, are never defcribed by any of the ancients as Theodoret has defcribed the Nazarenes.

In the paffage quoted from Epiphanius, in which he gives an account of the motives for John's writing his gofpel, it is evident, both that he confidered the Nazarenes as exifting at that time, and alfo that they ftood in as much need of being taught the preexiftence and divinity of Chrift as the Ebionites. In another place this writer compares the Nazarenes to perfons who, feeing a fire at a diftance, and not underftanding the caufe, or the ufe of it, run towards it, and burn themfelves; "So thefe Jews,"
he

he says, "on hearing the name of Jesus only,
"and the miracles performed by the apos-
"tles, believe on him; and knowing that his
"mother was with child of him at Nazareth,
"that he was brought up in the house of
"Joseph, and that, on that account, he was
"called a Nazarene (the apostles stiling him
"a man of Nazareth, approved by miracles,
"and mighty deeds) imposed that name
"upon themselves *." This can never agree
with this writer supposing that the Nazarenes believed in the divinity of Christ, or
indeed in the miraculous conception; much
less with their having an origin subsequent
to the times of the apostles. And he never
mentions, or hints at, any change of opinion in the Nazarenes.

That Austin did not consider the Nazarenes in any favourable light, is evident

* Ακusαντες γαρ μονον ονομα τe Ιησe, κ̣ θεασαμενοι τα θεοση-
μεια τα δια χειρων των αποσολων γνομενα, κ̣ αυτοι εις αυτον πιςευusι.
γνοντες δε αυτον εκ Ναζαρετ εν γαςρι εγκυμονηθεντα, κ̣ εν οικω Ιωσηφ
αναξραφεντα, κ̣ δια τeτο εν τω ευαγΓελιω Ιησeν Ναζωραιον καλεισθαι, ως κ̣ οι αποσολοι φασιν Ιησeν τον Ναζωραιον ανδρα, αποδεδειγμενον εν τε σημειοις κ̣ τερασι κ̣ τα εξης ; τeτo τo ονομα επιθεασιν
αυτοις, το καλεισθαι Ναζωραιeς. Hær. 29. sect. 5. Opera,
vol. I. p. 120.

from

from his calling them, in his anfwer to Jerom, *heretics*, " As to the opinion of thofe " heretics, who, while they would be both " Jews and chriftians, can neither be Jews " nor chriftians, &c.*" It is in thefe very words that Jerom had characterized thofe whom he had called Nazarenes. What more could Auftin have faid of the Ebionites? Can it be fuppofed that he would have fpoken of the Nazarenes in this manner, if he had thought them orthodox with refpect to the doctrine of the trinity; efpecially confidering that it was in an age in which the greateft account was made of that doctrine; fo that perfect foundnefs in that article might be fuppofed to have atoned for defects in other things. That Jerom did not confider the Nazarenes as orthodox, even if he did make them to be different from the Ebionites, is evident from his calling them *not chriftians*.

If we confider the general character of the Jewifh chriftians in the time of the

* Quid putaverint hæretici, qui qum volunt et Judæi effe et chriftiani, nec Judæi effe nec chriftiani effe potuerunt, &c. Opera, vol. 2. p. 75.

apoftles,

apostles, and particularly how apt they were to be alarmed at the introduction of any thing that was *new* to them, and had the least appearance of contrariety to the law of Moses, it will both supply a strong argument in favour of the truth of christianity, and against their receiving the doctrine of the divinity or pre-existence of Christ either then or afterwards. Their rooted prejudices against the apostle Paul (whose conversion to christianity must have given them great satisfaction) merely on account of his activity in preaching the gospel to the uncircumcised Gentiles (though with the approbation of the rest of the apostles) shows that they would not receive any *novelty* without the strongest evidence. Their dislike of the apostle Paul, we know from ecclesiastical history, continued to the latest period of their existence as a church, and they would never make use of his writings. But to the very last, their objections to him amounted to nothing more than his being no friend to the law of Moses.

The resemblance between the character of the Ebionites, as given by the early christian

tian Fathers, and that of the Jewish christians at the time of Paul's last journey to Jerusalem, is very striking. After he had given an account of his conduct to the more intelligent of them, they were satisfied with it; but they thought there would be great difficulty in satisfying others. "Thou "seest brother," say they to him, Acts xxi. 20. "how many thousands of Jews "there are who believe, and they are all "zealous of the law. And they are in- "formed of thee, that thou teachest all the "Jews who are among the Gentiles, to for- "sake Moses; saying that they ought not "to circumcise their children, neither to "walk after the customs. What is it "therefore? The multitudes must needs "come together, for they will hear that "thou art come. Do therefore this that "we say unto thee: We have four men who "have a vow on them; them take, and pu- "rify thyself with them, and be at charges "with them, that they may shave their "heads, and all may know that those things "whereof they were informed concerning "thee are nothing, but that thou thyself "also

" also walkest orderly and keepest the law."
So great a resemblance in some things, viz. their attachment to the law, and their prejudices against Paul, cannot but lead us to imagine, that they were the same in other respects also, both being equally zealous observers of the law, and equally strangers to the doctrine of the divinity of Christ. In that age all the Jews were equally zealous for the great doctrine of the *unity of God*, and their *peculiar customs*. Can it be supposed then that they would so obstinately retain the one, and so readily abandon the other?

I have not met with any mention of more than one orthodox Jewish christian in the course of my reading, and that is one whose name was Joseph, whom Epiphanius says he met with at Scythopolis, when all the other inhabitants of the place were Arians. Hær. 30. Opera, vol. 1. p. 129.

CHAPTER IX.

Of the supposed Church of Orthodox Jews at Jerusalem, subsequent to the Time of Adrian.

MOSHEIM speaks of a church of trinitarian Jews, who had abandoned the law of Moses, and resided at Jerusalem, subsequent to the time of Adrian. Origen, who asserts that all the Jewish christians of his time conformed to the law of Moses, he says, must have known of this church; and therefore he does not hesitate to tax him with asserting a wilful falsehood. Error was often ascribed to this great man by the later Fathers, but never before, I believe, was his veracity called in question. And least of all can it be supposed, that he would have dared to assert a notorious untruth in a public controversy. He must have been a fool, as well as a knave, to have ventured upon it.

Bodies

Bodies of men do not suddenly change their opinions, and much less their customs and habits; least of all would an act of violence produce that effect; and of all mankind the experiment was the least likely to answer with the Jews. If it had produced any effect for a time, their old customs and habits would certainly have returned when the danger was over. It might just as well be supposed that all the Jews in Jerusalem began at that time to speak Greek, as well as that they abandoned their ancient customs. And this might have been alledged in favour of it, that from that time the bishops of Jerusalem were all Greeks, the public offices were no doubt performed in the Greek language, and the church of Jerusalem was indeed, in all respects, as much a Greek church as that of Antioch.

Mosheim produces no authority in his Dissertations for his assertion. He only says, that he cannot reconcile the fact that Origen mentions, with his seeming unwillingness to allow the Ebionites to be christians. But this is easily accounted for from the attachment which he himself had to the doctrine

doctrine of the divinity of Christ, which they denied; and from their holding no communion with other christians.

All the appearance of authority that I can find in any ancient writer, of the Jewish christians deserting the law of their ancestors, is in Sulpicius Severus, to whom I am referred by Mosheim in his History. But what he says on the subject is only what follows: " At this time Adrian, thinking " that he should destroy christianity by " destroying the place, erected the images of " dæmons in the church, and in the place " of our Lord's sufferings; and because the " christians were thought to consist chiefly " of Jews (for then the church at Jerusalem " had all its clergy of the circumcision) " ordered a cohort of soldiers to keep con- " stant guard, and drive all Jews from any " access to Jerusalem; which was of service " to the christian faith. For at that time " they almost all believed Christ to be God, " but with the observance of the law; the " Lord so disposing it, that the servitude " of the law should be removed from the " liberty of the faith and of the church.
Then

"Then was Marc the first bishop of the Gentiles at Jerusalem*." Here the historian says, that the object of Adrian was to overturn christianity, and that the Jews were banished because the christians there were chiefly of that nation. According to this account, all the Jews, christians, as well as others, were driven out of Jerusalem, and nothing is said of any of them forsaking the law of Moses. Eusebius mentions the expulsion of the Jews from Jerusalem, but says not a word of any of the christians there abandoning circumcision, and their other ceremonies, on that occasion. Indeed, such a thing was in the highest de-

---

* Qua tempestate Adrianus, existimans se christianam fidem loci injuria perempturum, et in templo ac loco dominicæ passionis dæmonum simulachra constituit. Et quia christiani ex Judæis potissimum putabantur (namque tum Hierosolymæ non nisi ex circumcisione habebat ecclesia Sacerdotem) militum cohortem custodias in perpetuum agitare jussit, quæ Judæos omnes Hierosolymæ aditus arceret. Quod quidem christianæ fidei proficiebat; quia tum pene omnes Christum Deum sub legis observatione credebant, Nimirum id domino ordinante dispositum, ut legis servitus a libertate fidei atque ecclesiæ tolleretur. Ita tum primum Marcus ex Gentibus apud Hierosolymam episcopus fuit. Hist. lib. 2. cap. 31. p. 215.

gree improbable. Speaking of the desolation mentioned, Is. vi. he says, that " it was fulfilled in the time of Adrian, when the Jews, undergoing a second siege, were reduced to such misery, that, by the imperial orders, they were not suffered even to see the desolation of their metropolis at a distance*."

Independent of all natural probability, had Sulpitius Severus actually written all that Mosheim advances; whether is it from this writer, or from Origen, that we are more likely to gain true information on this subject. Origen, writing in controversy, and of course subject to correction, appeals to a fact as notorious in the country in which he himself resided, and in his own times, to which therefore he could not but have have given particular attention. Whereas Sulpitius Severus lived in the remotest part of Gaul, several thousand miles from Palestine, and

---

* Επληρωθο δε κ͵ αυΐη καΐα της Αδριανε χρονες, καθ ες δευΐεραν υπομεινανΐες Ιεδαιοι πολιορκιαν, εις τεΐο το κακον περιεστησαν, ως νομιζις κ͵ διαΐαγμασιν αυΐοκραΐοςικοις, μηδε εξ αποπΐε την ερημιαν της εαυΐων μηΐροπολεως θεωρειν επιΐρεπεσθαι. Montfaucon's Collectio, vol. 2. p. 379.

two

two hundred years after Origen, so that he could not have asserted the fact as from his own knowledge; and he quotes no other person for it. But, in reality, Sulpitius Severus is no more favourable to Mosheim's account of the matter than Origen himself; so that to the authority of both of them, of all ancient testimony, and natural probability, nothing can be opposed but a willingness to find orthodox Jewish christians somewhere.

The passage of Origen, which is a full contradiction to all that Mosheim has advanced concerning this orthodox Jewish church, consisting of persons who abandoned the law of Moses, at the surrender of Jerusalem to Adrian, is as follows: "He who "pretends to know every thing, does not "know what belongs to the *prosopopeia*. "For what does he say to the Jewish be- "lievers, that they have left the customs of "their ancestors, having been ridiculously "deceived by Jesus, and have gone over to "another name, and another mode of life; "not considering that those Jews who have "believed in Jesus have not deserted the "customs

" customs of their ancestors; for they live
" according to them, having a name agree-
" ing with the poverty of their legal obser-
" vances. For the word *Ebion*, in the
" Jewish language, signifies *poor*; and those
" of the Jews who believe Jesus to be the
" Christ, are called Ebionites *."

Can it be supposed that Origen would have ventured to write in this manner (even supposing that he had no principle of integrity to restrain him from telling a wilful lie) if he had known any such church of Jewish christians as Mosheim describes. Besides, Origen's account of things agrees with what all the ancients say on the subject. Eusebius says, that the bishops of Jerusalem were Jews till the time of Adrian †. The bishops

---

* Αλλα μη ποτε ο παντ' επαγγελλομεν⊕ ειδεναι, το ακολυθον υκ οιδε κατα τον τοπον της προσωποποιιας · τι αν ᴋ λεγει προς τας απο Ιυδαιων πιςευοντας, κατανοητεον. φησιν αυτας καταλιπονταϛ τον πατριον νομον, τω εψυχαγωγησθαι υπο τε Ιησυ, ηπατησθαι πανυ γελοιως · ᴋ απηυτομοληκεναι εις αλλο ονομα, ᴋ εις ολλον βιον. Μηδε τυτο κατανοησας, οτι δε απο Ιυδαιων εις τον Ιησυν πιςευοντες υ καταλελοιπασι τον πατριον νομον. Βιυσι γαρ κατ αυτον, επωνυμοι της κατα την εκδοχην πτωχειας τε νομυ γεγενημενοι. In Celsum, lib. 2. p. 56.

† Ως μεχρι της κατα Αδριανον Ιυδαιων πολιορκιας, πενteκαιδεκα τον αριθμον αυτοθι γεγονασιν επισκοπων διαδοχαι · υς παντας Εβραιυς φασιν οντας, ανεκαθεν την γνωσιν τε χριςυ γνησιως καταδεξασθαι. Hist. lib. 4. cap. 5. p. 143.

were

were Jews, because the people were so. It is natural, therefore, to suppose, that when the bishops were Greeks, the people were Greeks also. And this is what Nicephorus expressly asserts to have been the case. For he says, that " Adrian caused Jerusalem to " be inhabited by Greeks only, and per- " mitted no others to live in it*."

Origen is so far from saying, that any Jews abandoned circumcision, and the rites of their religion, that he says some of the Gentile christians conformed to them †.

Having consulted Eusebius, and other ancient writers to no purpose, for some account of these Jews who had deserted the religion of their ancestors, I looked into Tillemont, who is wonderfully careful and exact in bringing together every thing that relates to his subject; but his account

* Ελλησι δε μονοις την πολιν εδιδε, κ, κατοικειν επετρεπεν. Hist. lib. 3. cap. 24. vol. 1. p. 256.

† Quia non solum carnales Judæi de circumcisione carnis revincendi sunt nobis, sed nonnulli ex eis, qui Christi nomen videntur suscepisse, et tamen carnalem circumcisionem recipiendam putant: ut Ebionitæ, et si qui his simili paupertate sensus aberrant. In Gen. Hom. 3. Opera. vol. 1. p. 19.

of the matter differs widely indeed from that of Mosheim. He says (Hist. des Empereurs, tom. 2. part 2. p. 506) " The " Jews converted to the faith of Christ " were not excepted by Adrian from the " prohibition to continue at Jerusalem. " They were obliged to go out with the " rest. But the Jews being then obliged " to abandon Jerusalem, that church began " to be composed of Gentiles, and before " the death of Adrian, in the middle of the " year 138, Marc, who was of Gentile " race, was established their bishop." He does not say with Mosheim, that this Marc was chosen by the Jews who abandoned the Mosaic rites. Hist. vol. 1. p. 172.

Fleury, I find, had the same idea of that event. He says (Hist. vol. 1. p. 316.) " From this time the Jews were forbidden " to enter Jerusalem, or even to see it at " a distance. The city being afterwards " inhabited by Gentiles, had no other name " than Ælia. Hitherto the church of Je- " rusalem had only been composed of Jew- " ish converts, who observed the ritual of " the law under the liberty of the gospel ;
" but

"but then, as the Jews were forbidden to remain there, and guards were placed to defend the entrance of it, there were no other chriſtians there beſides thoſe who were of Gentile origin; and thus the remains of the ſervitude of the law were entirely aboliſhed."

I cannot help, in this place, taking ſome farther notice of what Moſheim ſays with reſpect to this charge of a wilful falſhood on Origen. Jerom, in his epiſtle to Pammachius (Opera, vol. 1. p. 496.) ſays, that Origen adopted the Platonic doctrine of the ſubſerviency of truth to utility, as with reſpect to deceiving enemies, &c. the ſame that Mr. Hume, and other ſpeculative moraliſts have done; conſidering the foundation of all ſocial virtue to be the public good. But it by no means follows from this, that ſuch perſons will ever indulge themſelves in any greater violations of truth, than thoſe who hold other ſpeculative opinions concerning the foundation of morals.

Jerom was far from ſaying, that "Origen reduced his theory to practice." He mentions no inſtance whatever of his having recourse to it, and is far, indeed, from vindicating any person in asserting, that to silence an adversary, he had recourse to the wilful and deliberate allegation of a notorious falshood.

Grotius also says, that it is well observed by Sulpitius Severus, that all the Jewish christians till the time of Adrian held that Christ was God, though they observed the law of Moses, in the passage which I have quoted from him. But the sense in which Grotius understood the term *God* in this place must be explained by his own sentiments concerning Christ. As to Sulpitius himself, he must be considered as having said nothing more than that, " almost all the Jews at Jerusalem were christians, though they observed the law of Moses." This writer's mere assertion, that the Jewish christians held Christ to be God, in the proper sense of the word, unsupported by any reasons for it, is not to be regarded.

CHAP.

CHAPTER X.

Of the supposed Heresy of the Ebionites and Nazarenes, and other particulars relating to them.

I Have observed that Tertullian is the first christian writer who expressly calls the Ebionites *heretics*. Irenæus, in his large treatise concerning *heresy*, expresses great dislike of their doctrine, always representing them as believing that Jesus was the son of Joseph; but he never confounds them with *the heretics*. Justin Martyr makes no mention of *Ebionites*, but he speaks of the *Jewish christians*, which has been proved to be a synonymous expression; and it is plain, that he did not consider all of them as heretics, but only those of them who refused to communicate with the Gentile christians. With respect to the rest, he says, that he should have

no

no objection to hold in communion with them*. He describes them as persons who observed the law of Moses, but did not impose it upon others. Who could these be but Jewish unitarians? For according to the evidence of all antiquity, and what is supposed by Justin himself, all the Jewish christians were such. It is probable, therefore, that the Nazarenes, or Ebionites, were considered as in a state of excommunication, merely because they would have imposed the law of Moses upon the Gentiles, and refused to hold communion with any, besides those who were circumcised; so that, in fact, they excommunicated themselves.

This circumstance may throw some light on the passage in Jerom, in which he speaks of the Ebionites as anathematized *solely* on account of their adherence to the Jewish law. The Ebionites, at least many of them, would have imposed the yoke of the Jewish law upon the Gentile christians. They

ial. p. 231.

would not communicate with those who were not circumcised, and of course these could not communicate with them; so that they were necessarily in a state of excommunication with respect to each other. This would also be the case with the Cerinthians, as well as the Ebionites; and therefore Jerom mentions them together; the separation of communion with respect to both arising, in a great measure, from the observance of the law of Moses; though Jerom might write unguardedly, as he often did, in confounding the case of the Cerinthians so much as he here does with that of the Ebionites.

Ruffinus makes the heresy of Ebion to consist in their enjoining the observance of the Jewish law*. The attachment of the Jews to their own law was certainly very great. Origen speaks of the Ebionites as

* Consilium vanitatis est quod Ebion docet, ita Christo credi debere, ut circumcisio carnis, et observatio sabbathi, et sacrificiorum solemnitas, cæteræque omnes observantiæ secundum legis literam teneantur. In Symbol. p. 189.

thinking

thinking that Chrift came chiefly for the fake of the Ifraelites*.

There is fomething very particular in the conduct of Tertullian with refpect to the Ebionites. He fpeaks of the herefy of Ebion (of which he makes but the flighteft mention in his Treatife againft herefy in general) as confifting in the obfervance of the Jewifh ceremonies †; and yet he fays, that " John in his epiftle calls thofe chiefly " antichrifts, who denied that Chrift came " in the flefh, and who did not think that " Jefus was the Son of God;" meaning, probably, a difbelief of the miraculous conception. " The former," he fays, " Marcion held, the latter Ebion ‡."

* Ουκ απεςαλην ει μη εις τα προβαία τα απολωλοία οικε Ισραηλ. εκ ελαμβανομεν ταυία ως οι πίωχοι τη διανοια Εβιωναιοι πίωχειας της διανοιας επωνυμοι (Εβιω γαρ ο πίωχος παρ Εβραιοις ονομαζεται) ωςε υπολαβειν επι της σαρκικης Ισραελιίας προηγεμενως τον χριςον εκδεδη- μηκεκαι. Philocalia, p. 16.

† Ad Galatas fcribens invehitur in obfervatores et de- fenfores circu:ncifionis et legis. Hebionis hærefis eft. De Præfcrip. fect. 33. Opera, p. 214.

‡ At in epiftola eos maxime antichriftos vocat, qui Chriftum negarent in carne veniffe, et qui non putarent Jefum

Upon the whole, the conduct of Tertullian very much resembles that of Irenæus, who, without classing the Ebionites with heretics, expresses great dislike of their doctrine.

It is certain, that the Ebionites were a very different set of persons from the Gnostics, and that they were utter strangers to the principles of that philosophy which were the cause of the prejudice that was entertained concerning *matter* and *the body*, and which led the Gnostics to recommend corporeal austerities, and abstinence from marriage. Epiphanius says, that " the Ebio-
" nites, and all such sects, were enemies to
" virginity and continence*."

This writer's hatred of the Ebionites, and of course his misrepresentation of them, are very conspicuous. But there is one thing which he lays to their charge, which, though absolutely incredible, it is not easy to ac-

---

Jesum esse filium dei. Illud Marcion, hoc Hebion vindicavit. De Præscrip. sect. 33. Opera, p. 214.

† Τα νυν δε απηγορευίαι παυlαπασι παρ αυlοις παρθενια τε κỳ εγκραlεια, ως κỳ παρα τοις αλλαις ομοιαις ταulη αιρεσεσι. Hær. 30. p. 526.

count for. For he says, that " the Ebio-
" nites revere water as a God*." Damascenus says the same after him. De Hæresibus, Opera, p. 690.

Another most extraordinary and highly improbable allegation of Epiphanius, with respect to the Ebionites, is his charging them with the peculiar doctrines of the Gnostics, which is contrary to the testimony, I may safely say, of all other ancient writers; it being commonly said by them, that the heresy of the Ebionites was the very reverse of that of the Gnostics. He says, however, that " some of
" the Ebionites held that Adam, who was
" first formed, and into whom God breathed
" the breath of life, was Christ. But others
" of them say that he was from above,
" that he was a spirit created before any
" others, before the angels, that he was
" lord of all, was called Christ, and made
" the sovereign of that age; that he came
" from thence whenever he pleased, as into
" Adam, and that he appeared in the form

---

* Το ὑδωρ αντι θεου εχουσι. Opera, vol. 1. p. 53.

CHAP. X. *Ebionites and Nazarenes.* 207

" of a man to the patriarchs, to Abraham,
" Isaac, and Jacob, and that it was the
" same who in the latter days, being clothed
" with the body of Adam, appeared as a
" man, was crucified, rose from the dead,
" and ascended into heaven*."

Again, speaking of the Ebionites in general, he says, " they assert that there were
" two beings created, viz. Christ and the
" devil; that Christ took the inheritance
" of the future age, and the devil of the
" present, and that the Supreme Being
" made this appointment at the request of
" them both. On this account, they say
" that Jesus was born of the seed of man,
" and became the son of God by adoption,
" by Christ coming into him from above,

---

* Τινες γαρ εξ αυτων κ̃ Αδαμ τον χριϛον ειναι λεγυσι, τον πρωτον πλασθεντα τε κ̃ εμφυσηθεντα απο της τυ θευ επιπνοιας. αλλοι δε εν αυτοις λεγυσιν ανωθεν μεν οντα, προ παντων δε κτισθεντα πνευματα οντα, κ̃ υπερ αγγελυς οντα, παντων τε κυριευοντα, κ̃ χριϛον λεγεσθαι, τον εκεισε δε αιωνα κεκληρωσθαι · ερχεσθαι δε ενταυθα οτε βυλειται, ως κ̃ εν τω Αδαμ ηλθε, κ̃ τοις πατριαρχαις εφαινετο ενδυομεν⸰ το σωμα. προς Αβρααμ ελθων κ̃ Ισαακ κ̃ Ιακωβ. ο αυτος επ' εσχατων ων ημερων ηλθε, κ̃ αυτο το σωμα τυ Αδαμ ενεδυσατο, κ̃ ωφθη ανθρωπος, κ̃ εϛαυρωθη, κ̃ ανεϛη, κ̃ ανηλθεν. Hær. 30. sect. 3. p. 127.

" in

"in the form of a dove. But they say that he was not generated from God the Father, but created by him, as one of the archangels, though greater than they; for that he is lord of the angels, and of all things that were made by the Almighty; that he came and taught what is contained in their gospel, saying, *I am come to destroy sacrifices, and if you will not cease to sacrifice, wrath shall not cease with respect to you.* These and such like things are taught by them *."

In another passage he ascribes these doctrines not to Ebion himself, but to his

---

* Δυο δε τινας, ως εφην, συνιςωσιν εκ θευ τεταγμενυς, ενα μεν τον χριςον, ενα δε τον διαβολον. κỳ τον μεν χριςον λεγυσι τυ μελλοντ۞- αιωνος ειληφεναι τον κληρον, τον δε διαβολον τυτον πεπιςευθαι τον αιωνα, εκ προςαγης δηθεν τυ παντοκρατορος κατα αιτησιν εκατερων αυτων· κỳ τυτυ ενεκα Ιησυν γεγενημενον εκ σπερματ۞- ανδρος λεγυσι, κỳ επιλεχθεντα, κỳ υτω κατα εκλογην υιον θευ κληθεντα, απο τυ ανωθεν εις αυτον ηκοντ۞ χριςυ εν ειδη περιςερας. υ φασκυσι δε εκ θευ πατρος αυτον γεγεννησθαι, αλλα εκτιςθαι, ως ενα των αρχαγγελων, μειζονα δε αυτων οντα, αυτον δε κυριευειν, κỳ αγγελων κỳ παντων απο τυ παντοκρατορ۞ πεποιημενων, κỳ ελθοντα κỳ υφηγησαμενον, ως το παρ αυτοις ευαγγελιον καλεμενον περιεχει, οτι ηλθον καταλευσαι τας θυσιας, κỳ εαν μη παυσησθε τε θυειν, υ παυσεται αφ' υμων η οργη. και ταυτα και τοιαυτα τινα εςιν τα παρ' αυτοις επιτηδευματα. Hær. 30. sect. 16. p. 140.

followers

followers. "Ebion himself," he says, "held that Christ was a mere man, born as other men are; but they who from him are called Ebionites, say that God had a superior power called his son, that he assumed the form of Adam, and put it off again*."

That this representation, which is wholly Epiphanius's own, is founded on some mistake, cannot be doubted; and I think it most probable, that he has confounded the doctrines of the Ebionites with those of the Cerinthians, who agreed with them in some things, especially in Jesus being a mere man, born as other men are. But he most grosly misrepresented both the Ebionites and the Cerinthians, in saying that they rejected sacrifices, and taught that Christ preached against them. For according to the testimony of all antiquity, both these sects insisted on the observance of the Jewish law.

* Ποτε μεν ο αυτος Εβιων λεγων εκ παρατριβης ψιλον ανθρωπον αυτον γεγεννησθαι. αλλοτε δε οι απ' αυτου Εβιωναιοι, ανω δυναμιν εκ θεου κεκτησθαι υιον, και τουτον κατα καιρον τον Αδαμ ενδυεσθαι τε και εκδυεσθαι. Hær. 30. sect. 34. p. 162.

This is all that I have been able to collect concerning the *heresy* of the Ebionites, excepting that Optatus charges them with maintaining that "the Father suffered, and not the Son*." But it was no uncommon thing to charge all unitarians with being patripassians. No early accounts of the Ebionites say any such thing of them. Their doctrine was simply, that Christ was a man, but *a man approved of God by signs and wonders, and mighty deeds, which God did by him.*

I must here remark, that no person, I should think, can reflect upon this subject with proper seriousness, without thinking it a little extraordinary that the Jewish christians, in so early an age as they are spoken of by the denomination of Ebionites, should be acknowledged to believe nothing either of the divinity, or even of the preexistence of Christ, if either of those doctrines had been taught them by the apostles. Could they so soon have deserted so important an article of their faith, and so

* Ut Hebion, qui argumentabatur patrem passum esse, non filium. Lib. 4. p. 91.

lately

lately *delivered to the saints*; and having once believed Chrift to be either the Supreme God, or a fuper-angelic fpirit, have contrary to the general propenfity of human nature (which has always been to aggrandize, rather than to degrade a lord and mafter, becaufe it is in fact to aggrandize themfelves) come univerfally to believe him to be nothing more than a mere man, and even the fon of Jofeph and Mary?

CHAPTER XI.

Of the sacred Books of the Ebionites.

THE Ebionites being Jews, and in general acquainted with their own language only, made use of no other than a Hebrew gospel, which is commonly said to have been that of Matthew, originally composed in their language, and for their use. This I think highly probable, from the almost unanimous testimony of antiquity. But this is a question which I shall not make it my business to discuss.

"The Ebionites," says Irenæus, "make use of the gospel of Matthew only*." Jerom had seen this gospel, and translated it from Hebrew into Greek, and without giving his own opinion, says, that "it was by most persons called the authentic gospel of "Matthew."

* Ebionitæ etenim eo evangelio quod est secundum Matthæum solo utentes. Lib. 3. cap. 11. p. 220.

CHAP. XI.   *of the Ebionites.*   213

" Matthew*." Theodoret says concerning both the kinds of Ebionites, that they received no other gospel than that of Matthew†.

But it is evident from Epiphanius, that the Ebionites did not consider the two first chapters of Matthew's gospel as belonging to it; for their copies were without them, beginning with the third chapter. " The " gospel of the Ebionites began thus, It " came to pass in the days of Herod king " of Judea, in the time of Caiaphas the " high-priest, a person whose name was " John came baptizing with the baptism " of repentence in the river Jordan ‡." Here, however, there must be some mistake, as it was not in the time of Herod

---

* In Matt. cap. 12. Opera, vol. 6. p. 21.

† Αλλη δε παρα ταυτην συμμορια, την αυτην επωνυμιαν εχυσα· Εβιωνεις γαρ κ̓ ἕτοι προσαγορευονται · τα αλλα μεν απαντα συνομολογει τοις προτεροις, τον δε σωτηρα κ̓ κυριον εκ παρθενυ γεγεννησθαι φησιν· ευαγγελιω δε τω κατα Ματθαιον κεχρηνται μονω. Hær. Fab. lib. 2. cap. 1. vol. 4. p. 328. Ed Halæ.

‡ Οτι εγενετο, φησιν, εν ταις ημεραις Ηρωδυ βασιλεως της Ιυδαιας επι Αρχιερεως Καιαφα ηλθε τις Ιωαννης ονοματι βαπτιζων βαπτισμα μετανοιας εν τω ποταμω Ιορδανη, κ̓ τα εξης. Hær. 30. Opera, vol. 1. p. 138.

king of Judea, but of Herod the Tetrarch, or king of Galilee; and the inaccuracy is probably to be afcribed to Epiphanius himfelf. That this writer quoted only from his memory, and inaccurately, is evident from his giving the beginning of this gofpel in another place fomewhat differently, as follows: " It came to pafs in the days " of Herod king of Judea, John came bap- " tizing with the baptifm of repentance, " in the river Jordan; who was faid to be " of the race of Aaron the prieft, the fon " of Zacharias and Elizabeth; and all men " went out to him *."

This writer, who was fond of multiplying fects, and who makes that of the Nazarenes to be different from that of the Ebionites, fays concerning the latter, that " he did " not know whether they had cut off the " genealogy from the gofpel of Matthew †."

---

* Οτι εγενετο εν ταις ημεραις Ηρωδε τε βασιλεως της Ιεδαιας, ηλθεν Ιωαννης βαπτιζων βαπτισμα μετανοιας εν τω Ιορδανη ποταμω, ος ελεγετο ειναι εκ γενες Ααρων τε ιερεως, παις Ζαχαριε και Ελισαβετ, και εξηρχοντο προς αυτον παντες. Hær. 30. fect. 13. p. 138.

† Εχεσι δε το κατα Ματθαιον ευαγγελιον πληρεςατον Εβραιςι. παρ' αυτοις γαρ σαφως τετο, καθως εξ αρχης εγραφη Εβραικοις
γραμμασιν

Meaning, perhaps, the whole of the introduction, as far as the third chapter.— It must be observed, however, that in the copy of this gospel which Jerom translated, there was the second chapter, if not the genealogy. For in this gospel there was, *out of Egypt I have called my son,* and *he shall be called a Nazarene*.*" This I am willing to explain in the following manner. Originally the Jewish christians did not believe the doctrine of the miraculous conception. Both Justin Martyr and Irenæus represent them as disbelieving it, without excepting any that did. Origen is the first who has noticed two kinds of Ebionites, one believing the miraculous

γραμμασιν ετι σωζεται. εκ οιδα δε ει και τας γενεαλογιας τας απο τε Αβρααμ περιειλον. Hær. 29. vol. 1. p. 124.

* Mihi quosque a Nazaræis, qui in Berœa, urbe Syriæ, hoc volumine utuntur, describendi facultas fuit; in quo animadvertendum quod ubicunque evangelista, sive ex persona sua, sive ex persona domini salvatoris, veteris scripturæ testimoniis utitur, non sequatur septuaginta translatorum auctoritatem, sed Hebraicam, e quibus illa duo sunt. Ex Ægypto vocavi filium meum, et quoniam Nazaræus vocabitur. Catalogus Scriptorum, Opera, vol. 1. p. 267.

conception, and the other denying it. Probably, therefore, their original copies of the gospel had not the two first chapters, which contained that history; but after some time, those of the Jewish christians who gave credit to the story, would naturally add these two chapters from the Greek copies; and it might be a copy of this kind that Jerom met with.

Epiphanius likewise says, that " the " Ebionites made use of the travels of " Clement*." This being an unitarian work, they might be pleased with it; but it is not probable that they would read it in the public offices of their churches, or consider it in the same light with one of the books of scripture.

It is agreed on all hands that the Ebionites made no use of the epistles of Paul, because they did not approve of the slight which he seemed to put upon the law of Moses, which they held in the greatest possible veneration.

* Χρωνται δε και αλλοις τισι βιβλιοις, δηθεν ταις περιοδοις καλεμενοις Πέτρε, ταις δια Κλημεντ@ γραφεισαις. Hær. 30. Opera, vol. 1. p. 139.

Epiphanius

Epiphanius says farther concerning the Ebionites, that "they detest the pro-"phets *." This, however, I think altogether as improbable, as what he says of their revering water as a god. He is the only writer who asserts any such thing, and as far as appears from all other accounts, the Ebionites acknowledged the authority of all that we call the canonical books of the Old Testament. Symmachus, whose translation of the scriptures into Greek is so often quoted, and with the greatest approbation, by the learned Fathers, was an Ebionite; and Jerom says the same of Theodotion. They both translated the other books of the Old Testament, as well as the Pentateuch, and, as far as appears, without making any distinction between that and the other books; and can this be thought probable, if they had not considered them as entitled to equal credit? Besides, our Saviour's acknowledgment of the authority of the whole of the Old Tes-

* Αυτος [Κλημης] γαρ εγκωμιαζει Ηλιαν, κỳ Δαβιδ, και Σαμψων, και παντας της προφητας, ὑς ὑτοι βδελυτίονται. Hær. 30. p. 139.

tament

tament is so express, that I cannot readily believe that any christians, Jews especially, acknowledging his authority, would reject what he admitted.

Lastly, the authority of Epiphanius is, in effect, contradicted by Irenæus, who says, that " the Ebionites expounded the " prophecies too curiously *." Grabe says, that Ebion (by which we must understand some Ebionite) wrote an exposition of the prophets, as he collected from some fragments of Irenæus's work, of which he gives some account in his note upon the place †.

* Quæ autem sunt prophetica curiosius exponere nituntur. Lib. 1. cap. 26. p. 102.

† Ipsum Ebionem εξηγησιν των προφητων scripsisse, colligo ex fragmentis hujus operis, quæ ante paucos dies Parisiis accepi, en MS. codice collegii Claromontani descripto, a viro humanissimo, R. P. Michaele Loquien, inter addenda ad specilegium hæreticorum sæculi 1. suo tempore, deo volente, publicanda. Ibid.

CHAP-

CHAPTER XII.

Of Men of Eminence among the Jewish Christians.

THOUGH it is probable, that the Jewish christians in general were poor, and therefore had no great advantage of liberal education, which might be one means of preserving their doctrine in such great simplicity and purity; yet it appears that there were some men of learning among them. Jerom mentions his being acquainted with such during his residence in Palestine; and there are three persons among them who distinguished themselves by translating the Old Testament from Hebrew into Greek, viz. Aquila, Theodotion, and Symmachus; though the last of them only was a native of Palestine, and born a Samaritan. Eusebius says, that " Theodotion and Aquila were both Jewish " proselytes, whom the Ebionites follow-
" ing,

"ing, believe Christ to be the son of
"Joseph*." According to Epiphanius,
Theodotion was first a Marcionite, and then
a Jewish convert †. Aquila is said to have
flourished about the year 130, Theodotion
about 180, and Symmachus about 200.
Whatever was thought of the religious
principles of these men, the greatest account was made of their versions of the
Hebrew scriptures by learned christians of
all parties, especially that of Symmachus,
which is perpetually quoted with the greatest respect by Origen, Eusebius, and others.
Jerom, speaking of Origen, says, that "be-
"sides comparing the version of the sep-
"tuagint, he likewise collated the versions
"of Aquila of Pontus, a proselyte, that
"of Theodotion an Ebionite, and that of
"Symmachus, who was of the same sect;
"who also wrote commentaries on the
"gospel of Matthew, from which he en-

---

* Ὡς Θεοδοτίων ἡρμήνευσεν ὁ Ἐφέσιος, καὶ Ἀκύλας ὁ Ποντικος, αμφοτεροι Ιουδαιοι προσηλυτοι· οις κατακολουθησαντες οι Εβιωναιοι, εξ Ιωσηφ αυτον γεγενησθαι φασκουσι. Hist. lib. 5. cap. 8. p. 221.

† Θεοδοτίων τις Ποντικ[Ο]- απο της διαδοχης Μαρκιωνος του αιρεσιαρχου του Σινωπιτου. De Mensuris, Opera, vol. 2. p. 172.

"deavoured

" deavoured to prove his opinion*." In so great eftimation was Symmachus held, that Auftin fays the Nazarenes were fometimes called Symmachians †.

I referve the account of Hegefippus to the laft, becaufe it has been afferted that, though he was a Jewifh chriftian, he was not properly an Ebionite, but orthodox with refpect to his belief of the trinity. But that he was not only a Jewifh chriftian, but likewife a proper Ebionite, or a believer in the fimple humanity of Chrift, may, I think, be inferred from feveral circumftances, befides his being a Jewifh chriftian; though, fince Origen fays that none of them believed the divinity of Chrift, we ought to have fome pofitive evidence before we admit that he was an exception.

* Aquilæ fcilicet Pontici profelyti, et Theodotionis Hebionei, et Symmachi ejufdem dogmatis, qui in evangelium quoque κατα Ματθαιον fcripfit commentarios, de quo et fuum dogma confirmare conatur. Catalogus Scriptorum, Opera, vol. 1. p. 294.

† Et tamen fi mihi Nazareorum objiceret quifquam quos alii Symmachianos appellant. Contra Fauftum Man. Opera, vol. 6. p. 342.

That

That Hegesippus was an Ebionite, may be inferred from his giving a list of all the heresies of his time, in which he enumerates a considerable number, and all of them Gnostics, without making any mention of the Ebionites.

He being a Jewish christian himself, could not but be well acquainted with the prevailing opinions of the Jewish christians, the most conspicuous of which, it cannot be denied, was the doctrine of Christ's being a mere man. Now can it be supposed, that if he himself had been what is now called an orthodox christian, that is, a trinitarian, or even an Arian, he would wholly have omitted the mention of the Ebionites in any list of heretics of his time, had it been ever so short a one; and this consists of no less than eleven articles? Also, can it be supposed that Eusebius, who speaks of the Ebionites with so much hatred and contempt, would have omitted to copy this article, if it had been in the list?

Their not being inserted in the list by such a person as Eusebius, must, I think,
satisfy

CHAP. XII. *among Jewish Christians.* 223

satisfy any person, who has no system to support, with respect to this article. A stronger negative argument can hardly be imagined. As to Hegesippus himself, we must judge of his feelings and conduct as we should of those of any person at this day in a situation similar to his. Now, did any subsequent ecclesiastical historian, or did any modern divine, of the orthodox faith, ever omit Arians, or Socinians, or names synonymous to them (who always were, and still are, in the highest degree obnoxious to them) in a list of heretics?

Had the faith of the early christians been either that Christ was true and very God, or a superior angelic spirit, the maker of the world, and of all things visible and invisible under God; and had Hegesippus himself retained that faith, while the generality, or only any considerable number of his countrymen, had departed from it, it could not but have have been upon his mind, and have excited the same indignation that the opinions of the Arians and Socinians excite in the minds of those who are called orthodox at this day. Nay, in his circumstances,

such

such a defection from that important article of faith in his own countrymen, after having been so recently taught the contrary by the apostles themselves, whose writings they still had with them, must have excited a much greater degree of surprize and indignation, than a similar defection would have occasioned in any other people, or in any later times.

It is said to be as remarkable that Hegesippus should have omitted the Cerinthians as the Ebionites. But I see nothing at all extraordinary in the omission of the Cerinthians in this list of heretics by Hegesippus, as they were only one branch of the Gnostics, several of whom are in his list; and it is not improbable that these Cerinthians, having been one of the earliest branches, might have been very inconsiderable, perhaps extinct in his time. I do not know that they are mentioned by any ancient writer as existing so late as the time of Hegesippus; and as they seem to have been pretty much confined to some part of Asia Minor, and especially Galatia, which was very remote from the seat of the Ebionites,

he

he might not have heard much about them. Whereas the Ebionites were at that very time in their full vigour, and though their opinions (being then almost universal in what was called the catholic church) had not begun to give offence, they were afterwards the object of the most violent hatred to the other christians, and continued to be so as long as they subsisted.

That Hegesippus, though an unitarian himself, should speak as he does of the state of opinions in the several churches which he visited, as then retaining *the true faith*, is, I think, very natural. The only heresy that disturbed the apostle John, and therefore other Jewish christians in general, was that of the Gnostics; and all the eleven different kinds of heresies, enumerated by this writer, are probably only different branches of that one great heresy. If, therefore, the churches which he visited were free from Gnosticism, he would naturally say that they retained the true faith. For as to the doctrine of the personification of the logos, held then by Justin Martyr, and perhaps a few others, it was not, in its origin, so very alarming a thing; and very probably this plain man had not at all confidered its nature and tendency, if he had heard of it. The author of the Clementine Homilies, though cotemporary with Hegefippus, and unqueftionably an unitarian, makes no mention of it.

Hegefippus, as an unitarian, believed that all the extraordinary power exerted by Chrift was that of the Father refiding in him, and fpeaking and acting by him; and he might imagine that thefe philofophizing chriftians, men of great name, and a credit to the caufe, held in fact the fame thing, when they faid that this *logos* of theirs was not the logos of the Gnoftics, but that of John the evangelift, or the wifdom and power of God himfelf. And though this might appear to him as a thing that he could not well underftand, he might not think that there was any herefy, or much harm in it. Had he been told (but this he could only have had from infpiration) that this fpecious perfonification of the divine logos would, about two centuries afterwards, end in the doctrine of the perfect equality of the Son with the Father,

this

this plain good man might have been a little startled.

That Eusebius, and others, should speak of Hegesippus with respect (from which it has been argued that he could not possibly have been an Ebionite) appears to me nothing extraordinary, though it should have been known to them that he was one, considering that they quote him only as an historian; and supposing, what is very probable, that he did not treat particularly of doctrinal matters, but confined himself to the acts of the apostles, and other historical circumstances attending the propagation of the gospel; especially as he was the only historian of that age, and had always been held in esteem. A man who is once in possession of the general good opinion, will not be censured lightly, especially by such men as Eusebius.

Can it be supposed also that Eusebius, in expressly quoting ancient authorities against those who held the opinion of the simple humanity of Christ, would not have cited Hegesippus, as well as Irenæus, Justin Martyr, and others, if he
could

could have found any thing in him for his purpose? This may be considered as a proof that there was nothing in his work unfavourable to the doctrine of the Ebionites. A negative argument can hardly be stronger than this.

Had there been any pretence for quoting Hegesippus as a maintainer of the divinity of Christ, he would certainly have been mentioned in preference to Justin Martyr, or any others in the list; not only because he was an earlier writer, but chiefly because he was one of the Jewish christians, who are well known not to have favoured that opinion.

The manner in which Eusebius speaks of Hegesippus's quoting the gospel of the Hebrews, is such as led him to think that he was a Hebrew christian. "He quotes some things "from the gospel according to the Hebrews "and the Syriac, and especially in the He- "brew tongue, shewing that he was one of "the Hebrew christians *." We may, therefore, conclude, that he quoted it with respect; and this was not done ex-

* Εκ τε τȣ καθ Εβραιȣς ευαγʆελιȣ κȷ τȣ Συριακȣ, κȷ ιδιως εκ της Εβραιδος διαλεκτȣ τινα τιθησιν, εμφαινων εξ Εβραιων εαυτον πεπιστευμεναι. Hist. lib. 4. cap. 24. p. 184.

cept by those who were Ebionites, or who favoured their opinions. As Hegesippus wrote in Greek, he must have been acquainted with the Greek gospels, and therefore must have quoted that of the Hebrews from choice, and not from necessity.

Lastly, the manner in which Hegesippus speaks of James the Just, is much more that of an unitarian, than of a trinitarian.— " James the Just," says Eusebius, " is re-" presented by Hegesippus as saying, Why " do you ask me concerning Jesus the son " of man * ?" This looks as if both James and the historian were unitarians; the phrase *son of man*, being probably synonymous to a *prophet*, or a person having a divine commission, and certainly not implying any nature properly divine.

Valesius, the learned commentator on Eusebius, has intimated a suspicion, that the works of Hegesippus, as well as those of Papias and the Hypotyposes of Clemens Alexandrinus, were neglected and lost, on

* Τι με επερωτατε περι Ιησȣ τȣ υιȣ τȣ ανθρωπȣ. Hist. lib. 2. cap. 23. p. 79.

account of the errors they were supposed to contain*. This I cannot help thinking highly probable, and those errors could hardly be any other than the unitarian doctrine, and the things connected with it. Indeed, there were no errors of any consequence ascribed to that early age besides those of the Gnostics, and of the unitarians. The former certainly were not those that Valesius could allude to with respect to Hegesippus, because this writer mentions the Gnostics very particularly as heretics. Though Clemens Alexandrinus was not an unitarian, yet he never calls unitarians *heretics*; and since, in his accounts of *heretics in general*, which are pretty frequent in his works, he evidently means the *Gnostics only*, and therefore virtually excludes unitarians from that description of men; it is by no means improbable but that, in those writ-

---

* Porro ii Clementis libri continebant brevem et compendiariam utriufque testamenti expositionem, ut testatur Photius in bibliotheca. Ob errores autem quibus scatebant, negligentius habiti, tandem perierunt. Nec alia, meo quidem judicio, causa est, cur Papiæ et Hegesippi, aliorumque veterum libri interciderint. In Euseb. Hist. lib. 5. cap. 11.

ings of his which are lost, he might have said things directly in favour of unitarians.

In this passage Valesius also mentions the writings of Papias, as having, in his opinion, been lost for the same reason. Now Papias has certainly been supposed to be an Ebionite. Mr. Whiston has made this very probable from a variety of circumstances. See his *Account of the ceasing of Miracles*, p. 18. In the same tract he gives his reasons for supposing Hegesippus to have been an Ebionite, and he expresses his wonder, " that he should have had the good fortune " to be so long esteemed by the learned for " a catholic," p. 21, &c. In this Mr. Whiston may be supposed to have been sufficiently impartial, as he was an Arian, and expresses great dislike of the Ebionites; as, indeed, Arians always have done.

It is to be lamented that we know so very little of the history of the Jewish christians. We are informed, that they retired to Pella, a country to the east of the sea of Galilee, on the approach of the Jewish war, that many of them returned to Jerusalem when that war was over, and that they continued there till the city was taken by Adrian. But what became of those who were driven out of the city by Adrian, does not appear. It is most probable that they joined their brethren at Pella, or Beræa in Syria, from whence they had come to reside at Jerusalem; and indeed what became of the whole body of the ancient christian Jews (none of whom can be proved to have been trinitarians) I cannot tell. Their numbers, we may suppose, were gradually reduced, till at length they became extinct. I hope, however, we shall hear no more of them as an evidence of the antiquity of the trinitarian doctrine.

A few of the Nazarenes remained, as Epiphanius says, in the Upper Thebais and Arabia. He also speaks of the Ebionites as existing in his own time, and joined by the Ossens*. Austin says that they were in small numbers even in his time †.

* Μονοι δε τινες εν σπανει ευρισκονται, η ωϛ εις, η δυο Ναταρηνοι υπερ την ανω Θηϐαιδα, κ̓ επεκεινα της Αραϐιας. Hær. 20. Opera, vol. 1. p. 46.

† Ji sunt quos Faustus Symmachianorum vel Nazarenorum, nomine commemoravit, qui usque ad nostra tempora jam quidem in exigua, sed adhuc tamen vel in ipsa, paucitate perdurant. Contra Faustum Man, Opera, vol. 6, p. 351.

CHAPTER XIII.

Unitarianism was the Doctrine of the primitive Gentile Churches.

HAVING proved, as I think I may presume that I have done, to the satisfaction of every impartial reader, that the great body of Jewish christians always were, and to the last continued to be, unitarians; believing nothing concerning the pre-existence or divinity of Christ, it may with certainty be concluded, that the Gentile converts were also universally unitarians in the age of the apostles, and that, of course, the great majority of the common people must have continued to be so for a very considerable time. There is no maxim, the truth of which is more fully verified by observation and experience, than that great bodies of men do not soon, or without great causes, change their opinions. And the common people among christians, having no recollection of the apostles having taught

taught the pre-exiſtence or divinity of Chriſt, would not ſoon receive ſuch ſtrange doctrines from any other quarter.

In what manner the ſpeculative and philoſophizing chriſtians came to receive theſe doctrines, and what plauſible arguments they uſed to recommend them, I have fully explained. But ſuch cauſes would affect the learned long before they reached the unlearned; though, in time, the opinions of thoſe who are reſpected for their knowledge, never fail to diffuſe themſelves among the common people, as we ſee to be the caſe in matters of philoſophy, and ſpeculation in general.

Actual phenomena, I ſhall undertake to ſhew, correſpond to this hypotheſis, viz. that the Gentile chriſtians were at firſt univerſally unitarians; that for a long time a majority of the common people continued to be ſo, being till after the council of Nice, pretty generally in communion with the trinitarians, without abandoning their own opinion. It will alſo appear, from the moſt indiſputable evidence, that the Arian hypotheſis, which makes Chriſt to have been

a great

a great pre-exiftent fpirit, the maker of the world, and the giver of the law of Mofes, was equally unknown to the learned and to the unlearned, till the age of Arius himfelf. As to the opinion of Chrift having been a pre-exiftent fpirit, but either not the maker of world, or not the giver of the law, it is quite modern, being entirely unknown to any thing that can be called antiquity.

SECTION I.

Prefumptive Evidence that the Majority of the Gentile Chriftians in the early Ages were Unitarians.

BOTH the ftrongeft *prefumptions*, and the moft direct pofitive *evidence*, fhow that the common people among the Gentile chriftians, were unitarians, at leaft between two and three hundred years after the promulgation of chriftianity.

1. That unitarians muft have been in communion with what was in early times called

called the *catholic church*, is evident from there being no *creed*, or formulary of faith, that could exclude them. And we have seen that a creed was formed for the express purpose of excluding the Gnostics, who, of course, could not, and we find did not, join the public assemblies of christians, but formed assemblies among themselves, entirely distinct from those of the catholics.

There was no creed used in the christian church, besides that which was commonly called *the apostles*, before the council of Nice, and even after that there was no other generally used at baptism. This creed, as has been seen, contains no article that could exclude unitarians; and there was nothing in the public services that was calculated to exclude them. The bishops and the principal clergy, zealous for the doctrine of the trinity, might, of their own accord harangue their audiences on the subject, or they might pray as trinitarians; but if the unitarians could bear with it, they might still continue in communion with them, there being no law, or rule, to exclude them.

Accord-

Accordingly, we find that all the unitarians continued in communion with the catholic church till the time of Theodotus, about the year 200, when it is poffible that, upon his excommunication, fome of his more zealous followers might form themfelves into feparate focieties. But we have no certain account of any feparate focieties of unitarians till the excommunication of Paulus Samofatenfis, about the year 250, when, after him, they were called *Paulians*, or *Paulianifts*. Others alfo, about the fame time, or rather after that time, formed feparate focieties in Africa, on the excommunication of Sabellius, being, after him, called Sabellians.

2. The very circumftance of the unitarian Gentiles having *no feparate name*, is, of itfelf, a proof that they had no feparate affemblies, and were not diftinguifhed from the common mafs of chriftians. Had the unitarians been confidered as heretics, and of courfe formed *feparate focieties*,' they would as certainly have been diftinguifhed by fome particular name, as the Gnoftics were, who were in that fituation. But the Gentile

Gentile unitarians had no name given them till the time of Epiphanius, who ineffectually endeavoured to impofe upon them that of *Alogi**.* As to the terms Paulians, Sabellians, Noetians, or Artemonites, they were only names given them in particular places from local circumftances.

When bodies of men are formed, diftinguifhed from others by their opinions, manners, or cuftoms, they neceffarily become the fubjects of converfation and writing; and it being extremely inconvenient to make frequent ufe of periphrafes, or defcriptions, particular names will be given to them. This is fo well known, that there can hardly be a more certain proof of men not having been formed into feparate bodies, whether they were confidered in a favourable, or an unfavourable light, than their never having had any feparate name given them; and this was indifputably the cafe with the Gentile unitarians for the fpace of more than two hundred years after

---

* Φασκεσι τοινυν οι Αλογοι· ταυτην γαρ αυτοις τιθημι την επωνυμιαν· απο γαρ της δευρο ὑτως κληθησονlαι. Hær. 51. Opera, vol. I. p. 423.

the

the promulgation of christianity. The Jewish unitarians using a different language, and living in a part of the world remote from other christians, had little communication with the Gentiles, and therefore, of course, had assemblies separate from theirs; but for that reason they had a particular name, being called *Ebionites*.

The name by which the Gentile unitarians were sometimes distinguished before the separation of any of them from the catholic church, was that of *Monarchists*, which was probably assumed by themselves, from their asserting the monarchy of the Father, in opposition to the novel doctrine of the divinity of the Son. Had it been a name given them by their enemies, it would probably have been of a different kind, and have implied some reproach.

As to the term *Alogi*, given to the unitarians by Epiphanius, it may be safely concluded, that it was imposed on a false pretence, viz. their denying the authenticity of the writings of the apostle John, and their ascribing them to Cerinthus, for which there is no evidence besides his own; and
he

he does not pretend to have had it from the unitarians themselves. It is sufficiently evident that there could not have been any christians who rejected all the writings of John before the time of Eusebius, who considers very particularly the objections that had been made to the genuineness of all the books of the New Testament. And that the same people should reject these books after the time of Eusebius, and not before, is highly improbable. Epiphanius himself ascribes this rejection to the Alogi in general, and not to those of his time only; and he supposes the heresy of Alogi to have been an old one, of which that of Theodotus was a branch*."

The proof that Origen, Chrysostom, and the Fathers in general, give of their not being heretics, is that they had no particular name, besides that of christians. All therefore, that Chrysostom and others could alledge, as a proof that themselves and their friends were of the orthodox faith, and no heretics, might have been alledged by the

* Ανεϛη παλιν Θεοδοῖ۞ τις αποσπασμα υπαρχων εκ της προειρημενης Αλογȣ αιρεσεως. Hær. 54. Opera, vol. 1, p. 462.

whole

CHAP. XIII.   *originally Unitarian.*   241

whole body of unitarians before the time of Theodotus.

3. This argument will have double force, if we consider how exceedingly obnoxious the sentiments of the unitarians must have appeared, if they had been different from those of the generality of christians at that time. In what light they would have been regarded then, may be easily judged of by the treatment which they receive at present, wherever the trinitarian doctrine is established, and that of the unitarians is professed by the smaller number. In these circumstances, it is a fact which no person can deny, that unitarians have, in all countries, been regarded with the greatest possible abhorrence, and treated as impious blasphemers. It is considered as a great stretch of moderation to tolerate them at all. There are many instances in which even Arians would not allow that the unitarians were christians. This now would certainly have been the case in the primitive times, if the unitarians had been in the same situation, that is, if they had been the *minority*, and trinitarians, or even Arians, the majo-

rity. For, human nature being the same, the influence of the same circumstances will likewise be the same, as universal experience shews. For no sooner were the trinitarians the majority, and had the favour of government, than they took the severest measures against those who openly avowed themselves to be unitarians. The same also was their treatment from the Arians, when they were in power, as the history of Photinus testifies.

It is well known with what severity Calvin proceeded against Servetus, when the doctrine which he defended was far from being novel, and Calvin himself was exposed to persecution. Even in these circumstances he thought that to write against the doctrine of the trinity was a crime for which *burning alive* was no more than an adequate punishment; and almost all the christian world, not excepting even the meek Melancton, justified his proceedings. Now, since the minds of men are in all ages similarly affected in similar circumstances, we may conclude, that the unitarian doctrine, which was treated with so much respect

respect when it was first mentioned, was in a very different predicament then, from what it was at the time of the reformation. The difference of *majority* and *minority*, and nothing else, can account for this difference of treatment.

4. Another, and no inconsiderable argument in favour of the antiquity of the proper unitarian doctrine among christians, may be drawn from the *rank* and *condition* of those who held it in the time of Tertullian. He calls them *simplices et idiotæ*, that is, *common* or *unlearned people*; and such persons are certainly most likely to retain *old* opinions, and are always far less apt to innovate than the learned, because they are far less apt to speculate. Whenever we endeavour to trace the oldest opinions in any country, we always enquire among the *idiotæ*, the common people; and if they believe one thing, and the learned another, we may conclude with certainty, that which ever of them be *true*, or the more probable, those of the common people were *the more ancient*, and those of the learned and speculative the more *novel* of the two.

In most cases the more novel opinions are most likely to be true, considering the gradual spread of knowledge, and the general prevalence of prejudice and error; but in some cases the probability is on the side of the more ancient opinions; and it is evidently so in this. The true doctrine concerning the person of Christ must be allowed to have been held by the apostles. They, no doubt, knew whether their master was only a man like themselves, or their maker. Their immediate disciples would receive and maintain the same doctrine that they held, and it must have been some time before any other could have been introduced, and have spread to any extent, and especially before it could have become the prevailing opinion. We naturally, therefore, look for the *genuine* doctrine of christianity, concerning the person of Christ, among those who, from their condition and circumstances, were most likely to maintain the old opinion, rather than among those who were most apt to receive a new one. Surely, then, we have a better chance of finding the truth on this subject among these

these *idiotæ*, the common and unlearned people, than with such men as Justin Martyr, who had been a heathen philosopher, Irenæus, or any other of the learned and speculative christians of the same age.

On the contrary, supposing the christian religion to have been gradually corrupted, and that, in a long course of time, the corrupt doctrine should become the most prevalent among the common people; the reformation of it, by the recovery of the genuine doctrine, is naturally to be looked for among the learned and the inquisitive, who, in all cases, will be the *innovators*. This is remarkably the case in the present state of things. The common people in the Roman catholic countries are bigots to the old established faith, while the learned are moderate, and almost protestants. In protestant countries the common people still adhere most strongly to the doctrine of their ancestors, or those which prevailed about the time of the reformation, while the learned are every where receding farther from them; they being more inquisitive, and more enlightened than the unenquiring vulgar

vulgar. But still, if any man should propose simply to enquire what were the opinions most generally received in this country a century ago (which was about the space that intervened between Victor and the time of the apostles) we should think him very absurd, if he should look for them among the learned, rather than among the common people. We have experience enough of the difficulty with which the bulk of the common people are brought to relinquish the faith of their ancestors.

Dissenters in England are well situated for judging of the truth of the general maxim, that large bodies of men do not soon change their opinions. Notwithstanding the dissenters have no legal bonds, but are perfectly free to adopt whatever opinions they please; yet, as they were universally Calvinists at the time of the reformation, they are very generally so still. The ministers, as might be expected, are the most enlightened, and have introduced some reformation among the common people; but a majority of the ministers are, I believe, still Calvinists.

No

No person at all acquainted with history can entertain a doubt with respect to the general maxim, that great bodies of men do not soon change their opinions. It appeared when our Saviour and the apostles preached the gospel with all the advantage of miracles; and it appeared in the christianizing of the Gentile world. How long did the ignorant country people, in particular, continue *pagans*, a word borrowed from their being chiefly the inhabitants of villages? Does not the history both of the corruption, and of the reformation of christianity prove the same thing? How many yet believe the doctrine of transubstantiation? and what I think as much a case in point, how many yet believe the doctrine of the trinity?

Is it then at all probable, that when the doctrine of the simple humanity of Christ is acknowledged to have been held by the *idiotæ*, or *common people*, and who are expressly said to have been the greater part of the believers *(major credentium pars)* this should not have been the general opinion a century before that time; but, on the contrary,

contrary, that of the deity of Chrift, which was held by Tertullian, and other learned chriftians, and who fpeak of the common people as being fhocked *(expavefcunt)* at their doctrine? Sufficient caufe may be affigned why the learned in that age fhould be inclined to adopt any opinion which would advance the perfonal dignity of their mafter; and the fame caufes would produce the fame effect among the common people, but it would be more flowly, and acquire more time, as appears to have been the fact.

It may be faid, that the teftimony of Tertullian is exprefsly contradicted by Juftin Martyr, who (in giving an account of the circumftances in which the Platonic philofophy agreed, as he thought, with the doctrine of Mofes, but with refpect to which he fuppofed that Plato had borrowed from Mofes) mentions the following particulars, viz. the power which was after the firft God, or the logos, " affuming the figure of " a crofs in the univerfe, borrowed from the " fixing up of a ferpent (which reprefented " Chrift) in the form of a crofs in the wil-
" dernefs;

CHAP. XIII. *originally Unitarian.* 249

" derness; and a third principle, borrowed
" from the spirit, which Moses said moved
" on the face of the water at the creation;
" and also the notion of some *fire*, or con-
" flagration, borrowed from some figurative
" expressions in Moses, relating to the anger
" of God waxing hot. These things, he
" says, we do not borrow from others, but
" all others from us. With us you may
" hear and learn these things from those
" who do not know the form of the letters,
" and who are rude and barbarous of speech,
" but wise and understanding in mind, and
" from some who are even lame and blind,
" so that you may be convinced that these
" things are not said by human wisdom,
" but by the power of God *."

But all that we can infer from this passage is, that these common people had learned from Moses that the world was made by

* Ου τα αυτα εν ημεις αλλοις δοξαζομεν, αλλ' ο παντες τα ημετερα μιμεμενοι λεγεσι. παρ ημιν εν εςι ταυτα ακεσαι και μαθειν παρα των εδε τες χαρακτηρας των ςοιχειων επιςαμενων, ιδιωτων μεν κ βαρβαρων το φθεγμα, σοφων δε κ πιςων τον νεν οντων, κ πηρων κ χηρων τινων τας οψεις· ως συνειναι, ε σοφια ανθρωπεια ταυτα γεγονεναι, αλλα δυναμει θεε λεγεςθαι. Apol. p. 88.

the

the power and wisdom (or the logos) of God; that the serpent in the wilderness represented Christ; and that there was a spirit of God that moved on the face of the waters: in short, that these plain people had been at the source from which Plato had borrowed his philosophy. It is by no means an explicit declaration that these common people thought that the logos and the spirit were persons distinct from God. Justin was not writing with a view to that question, as Tertullian was; but only meant to say how much more knowledge was to be found among the lowest of the christians, than among the wisest of the heathen philosophers.

Besides, Justin is here *boasting* of the knowledge of these lower people, and it favoured his purpose to make it as considerable as he could; whereas Tertullian is *complaining* of the circumstance which he mentions; so that nothing but the conviction of a disagreeable truth could have extorted it from him. The same was the case with respect to Athanasius.

That

That the common people in Justin's time should understand his doctrine concerning the personification of the logos, is in itself highly improbable. That this logos, which was originally in God the same thing that reason is in man, should, at the creation of the world, assume a proper personality, and afterwards animate the body of Jesus Christ, either in addition to a human soul, or instead of it, is not only very absurd, but also so very *abstruse*, that it is in the highest degree improbable, a *priori*, that the common people should have adopted it. The scriptures, in which they were chiefly conversant, could never teach them any such thing, and they could not have been capable of entering into the philosophical refinements of Justin on the subject. Whereas, that the common people should have believed as Tertullian and Athanasius represent them to have done, viz. that there is but one God, and that Christ was a man, the messenger or prophet of God, and no *second God* at all (the rival as it were of the first God) is a thing highly credible in itself, and therefore requires less external evidence.

5. Another

5. Another ground of prefumption, that the unitarians were not confidered as heretics, or indeed in any obnoxious light, and confequently of their being in very great numbers in early times, is, that no treatifes were written againft them. As foon as ever Gnoftics made their appearance, they were cenfured with the greateft feverity, and exprefs treatifes were written againft them. Whereas the unitarians were firft mentioned without any cenfure at all, afterwards with very little; and no treatife was written exprefsly againft them before Tertullian's againft Praxeas, with whom he was, on other accounts, much offended. About the fame time, it is fuppofed, that Caius wrote the treatife called *The Little Labyrinth*, quoted by Eufebius. Before this time there were fome voluminous writers among chriftians, and feveral treatifes were written exprefsly againft herefy, but all the herefies then noticed were thofe of the Gnoftics. Irenæus's treatife againft herefy fhews, that the Gnoftics only were confidered as coming under that defcription. The Ebionites indeed are cenfured in it, but no mention is

made of the Gentile unitarians, though they were the majority of the common people among christians a long time after this.

His censures of Gentile unitarians is, at least indirect, as they held the same doctrine concerning Christ that the Ebionites did; and it must always be considered, that Irenæus lived in Gaul, where there were no Ebionites, and perhaps not many unitarians, as they abounded most in those countries in which christianity was first planted.

Theophilus of Antioch, about the year 170, wrote against heresies, but only his book against Marcion is mentioned by Eusebius. Hist. lib. 4. cap. 24. p. 187. He also mentions many of the works of Melito, bishop of Sardis, but none of them were against the unitarians. Lib. 4. cap. 26. p. 188. Rhodon, he also says, wrote against the Marcionites. Lib. 5. cap. 13. p. 225. We have also the first book of a large work of Origen's against heresy; and it is very evident, as I have observed, from his introduction, that he had no view to any besides the Gnostics. Can it be doubted then, but that

that there would have been treatises written expressly against the unitarians long before the time of Tertullian, if they had been considered in any obnoxious light, or had not been a very great majority of the christian world.

6. That the unitarian doctrine was very prevalent, even among learned christians, in the age which followed that of the apostles, and was then supposed to be that which was taught by them, may, with considerable probability, be inferred from the *Clementine Homilies*, and *Recognitions*, of which some account was given, vol. 1. p. 113. What is particularly remarkable relating to this work (for the two were originally the same) is, that, though it was written by a philosopher, and upon subjects which related to the doctrine concerning the person of Christ, it contains no mention of that doctrine which made so great a figure afterwards, and which in time bore down all before it, viz. that of the personification of the logos. No person, I should think, could peruse that work with care, without concluding, that the orthodoxy of the subsequent period

riod had made but little progress then. The same questions are discussed, and the same objections are answered, but on quite different principles, and without taking the least notice of any different principles.

If we cannot infer from this circumstance, that such a system as that of Justin Martyr, or the orthodoxy of the third century, did not exist, or was not much prevalent, so as to have attracted much notice, in the second; it must at least be allowed, as I observed before, that the writer of this work, being indisputably a man of genius and learning, would ascribe to Peter and Clement such opinions, and such a mode of answering the Gnostics, as he thought would pass for theirs. And as the work was probably a very popular one, from the different editions and modifications of it (being published afterwards, with Arian, and again with trinitarian adulterations) and used, as Epiphanius says, by the Ebionites as a sacred book, we may likewise infer, that the theological doctrines of it were generally *thought* to be those of the apostolic age, though with such additions as the
philo-

philosophy of the times could supply. A man must have had less knowledge and less judgment than the writer of this work was evidently possessed of, to have put into the mouths of Peter and Clement unitarian doctrines, and unitarian modes of answering the Gnostics, if it had not been supposed that Peter and Clement, though no philosophers, were at least unitarians.

To the passages quoted from this work before, I shall here add another, in which, contrary to the orthodox doctrine of the world not having been made by God himself, but by the logos, and without noticing any such doctrine, he gives a fine enumeration of the attributes of the one true God, and represents him as the *demiurgus*, the immediate maker of the world, and all the several parts of it, the heavens and the heavenly bodies, the earth and water, mountains and seas, fountains and fruits, &c. &c.*

* Διο, ω τεκνον κλημης, επεχε, μη αλλο τι φρονησης περι τε θεε, η οτι αυτος μον۞ εςιν θεος, κ̄ κυρι۞, κ̄ πατηρ, αγαθος κ̄ δικαι۞, δημιεργος, μακροθυμος, ελεημων, τροφευς ευεργεΐης, φιλανθρωπιαν νομι-Ίευων, αγνειαν συμβελευων, αιωνι۞, αιωνιες ποιων, ασυγκρι]۞, ταις των αγαθων ψυχαις οικιζομεν۞, αχωρη]۞ κ̄ χωρεμεν۞, ο εν απειρω

Dr. Lardner obferves (Credibility, vol. 2. p. 819.) that the Clementine Homilies and Recognitions deferve a more particular examination than has yet been given to them. And indeed, in the view in which I have mentioned them, and alfo, in many others, they are juftly intitled to it; as they contain a particular account of the opinions of thofe times, efpecially of the manner in which chriftianity was treated and defended by philofophers. More may be learned concerning the theology and philofophy of thofe times, from this fingle work, than from many others. It is true that the philofophical doctrines in it are abfurd enough; but the age afforded no better, and they are exhibited in a very pleafing drefs.

ρω Τον μεγαν αιωνα ως κεντρον πηξας, ο ουρανον εφαπλωσας, κὴ γην πιλωσας, υδωρ ταμιευσας, αερα εν ουρανω διαθεις, πηγας γη βρυσας, καρπους εκφυσας, ορη υψωσας, θαλασσαν περιορισας, ανεμους τε κὴ πνευματα διαλαξας · ο το περιεχον σωμα εν απειρω πελαγει πνευματι βελης ασφαλης ασφαλισαμενος. Hom. 2, fect. 45. p. 632.

SECTION II.

Direct Evidence in Favour of the Gentile Christians having been generally Unitarians.

BUT there is no occasion to argue in this manner from circumstances, and the nature of the thing, since it appears from the evidence of all history, so as never to have been questioned by any writer of reputation, that the unitarians had not any places of worship separate from those of other christians in early times. It was allowed by Mosheim, a zealous trinitarian, who says, (Hist. vol. 1. p. 191) " However, ready many " have been to embrace this erroneous doc- " trine, it does not appear that this sect " formed to themselves a separate place of " worship, or removed themselves from " the ordinary assemblies of christians." But does it not also follow from the same fact, that these unitarians were not expelled from christian societies by others, as they certainly would have been, if they had been considered as heretics ?

" In

"In former times," says Nicephorus, "all who were called christians, though they held different opinions, being considered in the same light by the Gentiles, and suffering from them, made little account of their differences, while they were exposed to equal hardships, on which account they easily joined in the common assemblies; and having frequent intercourse, while they were few in number, did not divide into parties*." In these circumstances, however, the Gnostics held separate assemblies, and as the violence of persecution did not make the orthodox receive *them* into their assemblies, so neither would they have admitted the unitarians, if they had been at all obnoxious to them.

That unitarians were included among those who, holding different opinions, were

---

* Επι μεν γαρ των ανω χρονων οσοι κλησει χριϛε εσεμνυνονlο ει, κϳ διαφοροι ταις δοξαις ησαν, ϗοι ϖανlες ϖρος των τα Ελληνων θαυμαζονlων ενομιζονlο · κϳ κακως εξ εκεινων ϖασχονlες, απολυπραγμονηlον το διακρινεσθαι ειχον, κοινας υφιϛαμενοι συμφορας · δια τι κϳ ραϛα καϑ' εαυlας συνιονlες. εκκλησιαζον · ϖυκνην τε την ομιλαν εχονlες, ει δε ολιγοι ησαν, ομως εκ εις ϖολλα διελυθησαν. Hist. lib. 8. cap. 52. vol. 1. p. 661.

considered by the orthodox as *fellow christians*, is evident from the following passage of Origen; but it will be more evident from other passages which I shall have occasion to quote from him hereafter. It is only to be observed, that the unitarians are here described as being *patripassians*; but these were only the more philosophical of the unitarians, as I shall show in its proper place. "It is allowed," he says, "that as in the great multitude of believers, "who admit of difference of opinion, there "are some who say that the Saviour is God "over all; but we do not say so, who be-"lieve him when he said, *My Father is* "*greater than I?* *"

Eusebius, describing two sorts of heretics, one of whom denied the humanity of Christ, and the other his pre-existence and divinity, says, that the former were *out of the church*; but he is so far from saying the same of the latter, that he particularly com-

---

* Εϛω δε, τινας ως εν πληθει πιϛευονῖων, κ̓ δεχομενων διαφωνιαν, δια την προπέιειαν αποϊιθεσθαι τον σωηρα ειναι τον επι πασι θεον· αλλ' ετι γε ημεις τοιετον, οι πειθομενοι αυτω λεγονῖι, Ο πατηρ, ο πεμψας με, μειζων με εϛι. Ad Celsum, lib. 8. p. 387.

plains

plains that Marcellus, one of them, even presided in it, being then bishop of Ancyra*.

That Chrysostom considered almost all the christians as being unitarians in the age of the apostles has been shewn already; and yet he says, that in their time there was no heresy †." This, however, could not be strictly true, because there were Gnostics in the time of the apostles; but they were few compared with their numbers afterwards. On this account, it is said by several of the ancients, that heresy began in the time of Adrian, when the most distinguished of the Gnostics made their appearance. Cyprian says, that " the worst of the

---

* Των γαρ ἑτεροδοξων, οἱ μεν, μη προειναι μηδε προϋπαρχειν τον υιον τȣ θεȣ φανῖες, ανθρωπον ενα αυῖον τοις λοιποις ὁμοιον, ὑποθεμενοι εξ ανθρωπȣ, υιοθεσια τεῖιμησθαι αυῖον εφασαν, κ̓ τȣῖο δονῖες, αθανατον κ̓ αιελευῖη αυῖο τιμην κ̓ δοξαν κ̓ βασιλειον αιωνιον ὡμολογησαν. οἱ δε τον ανθρωπον αρνησαμενοι, υιον ειναι θεȣ. θεον προονῖα ὑφεϛησανῖο· αλλ' οἱ μεν της εκκλησιας αλλοῖριοι, μεχρι τοσȣῖε πλανης ελασαν· ὁ δε της εκκλησιας τȣ θεȣ τοσουῖοις καθηγησαμενος χρονοις, την ὑπαρξιν αναιρει τȣ υιȣ τȣ θεȣ, τω αυῖȣ λειῖȣργησας θυσιαϛηρια. Contra Marcellum, vol. I. p. 33.

† Τοῖε τοινον, ἡνικα εκηρυτῖον αυῖοι καῖα την οικȣμενην ἁπασαν, ἁιρεσις ȣδεμια ἠν. Ser. 61. Opera, vol. 5. p. 809.

" heresies

"heresies did not rise till after the time of
"the apostles *."

That the common people among christians were actually unitarians in the early ages, and believed nothing of the pre-existence or divinity of Christ before the council of Nice, we have as express a testimony as can be desired in the case. These sublime doctrines were thought to be above their comprehension, and to be capable of being understood and received by the learned only. This we see most clearly in the general strain of Origen's writings, who was himself a firm believer, and a zealous defender, of the pre-existence and divinity of Christ.

"This," says he, "we ought to under-
"stand, that, as the law was a shadow of
"good things to come, so is the gospel
"as it is understood by the generality.
"But that which John calls the everlast-
"ing gospel, and which may be more
"properly called the *spiritual*, instructs the

* Et hoc, cum nondum hæreticæ pestes acriores prorupissent. Epist. 1, Opera, p. 211. 219.

"intelligent

" intelligent very clearly concerning the
" Son of God. Wherefore the gospel must
" be taught both corporeally and spiritually,
" and when it is necessary we must preach
" the corporeal gospel, saying to the carnal,
" that we know nothing but Jesus Christ
" and him crucified. But when persons
" are found confirmed in the spirit, bring-
" ing forth fruit in it, and in love with
" heavenly wisdom, we must impart to
" them the logos returning from his bo-
" dily state, in that he was in the begin-
" ning with God *."

" Some are adorned with the logos itself,
" but others with a logos which is a-kin to
" it, and seeming to them to be the true

* Και τuτο δε ειδηναι εχρην, ὁτι ωσπερ εςι νομ☉ σκιαν παρεχων των μελλονlων αγαθων, υπο τu καθ' αληθειαν καταγγελλομενu νομu δηλuμενων; ειω κ) ευαγγελιον σκιαν μυςηριων χριςu διδασκει, το νομιζομενον υπο πανlων των ενlυγχανονlων νοεισθαι. Ὁδε φησιν Ιωαννης ευαγγελιον αιωνιον, οικειως αν λεχθησομενον πνευμαlικον, σαφως παριςησι τοις νοuσι τα πανlα ενωπιον περι υιu τu θεu.—Διοπερ αναγκαιον πνευμαlικως κ) σωμαlικως χριςιανιζειν· κ) οπu μεν χρη το σωμαlικον κηρυσσειν ευαγγελιον, φασκονlα μηδεν ειδεναι τοις σαρκικοις η Ιησuν χριςον κ) τuτον εςαυρωμενον, τuτον ποιηlεον. επαν δε ευρεθωσι καιπληρισμενοι τω πνευμαlι, κ) καρποφορuνlες εν αυlω, ερωνlες τu uρανιu σοφιας, μεlαδοlεον αulοις τu λογu, επανελθονl☉ απο τu σεσαρκωσθαι, εφ ο ην εν αρχη προς τον θεον. Comment. in Johan. vol. 2. p. 9.

" logos;

" logos; who know nothing but Jesus Christ
" and him crucified, who look at the word
" made flesh *."

" There are," says he, " who partake of
" logos which was from the beginning, the
" logos that was with God, and the logos
" that was God, as Hosea, Isaiah, and Jere-
" miah, and any others that speak of him
" as the logos of God, and the logos that
" was with him; but there are others who
" know nothing but Jesus Christ and him
" crucified, the logos that was made flesh,
" thinking they have every thing of the
" logos when they acknowledge Christ ac-
" cording to the flesh. Such is the multi-
" tude of those who are called christians †."

* Οι μεν γαρ αυτω τω λογω κεκοσμηνται. Οι δε παρακειμενω τιν αυτω, κỳ δοκεντι ειναι αυτω τω πρωτω λογω, οι μηδεν ειδοτες, ει μη Ιησεν χριστον, κỳ τετον εσαυρωμενον, οι τον λογο νσαρκα ορωντες. Comment. vol. 2. p. 49.

† Ουτω τοινυν οι μεν τινες μετεχεσιν αυτε τε εν αρχη λογε, κỳ προς τον Θεον λογε, κỳ Θεε λογε, ωσπερ ωσηε κỳ ησαιας κỳ ιερεμιας, κỳ ει τις ετερος τοιετον εαυτον παρεστησεν ως τον λογον κυριε, η τον λογον γενεσθαι προς αυτον. ετεροι δε οι μηδεν ειδοτες ειμη Ιησεν χριστον κỳ τετον εσαυρωμενον, τον γενομενον σαρκα λογον, το παν νομιζοντες ειναι τε λογε χριστον κατα σαρκα μονον γινωσκεσι. τετο δε εστι το πληθος των πεπιστευκεναι νομιζομενων. Comment. in Johan. vol. 2. p. 49.

Again, he says, "the multitudes" (i. e. the great mass or body) "of believers are instructed in the shadow of the logos, and not in the true logos of God, which is in the open heaven*."

But nothing can be more decisive than the evidence of Tertullian to this purpose, who, in the following passage, which is too plain and circumstantial to be misunderstood by any person, positively asserts, though with much peevishness, that the unitarians, who held the doctrine of the divinity of Christ in abhorrence, were the greater part of christians in his time.

"The simple, the ignorant, and unlearned, who are always the greater part of the body of christians, since the rule of faith," meaning, probably, the apostles creed, "transfers the worship of many gods to the one true God, not understanding that the unity of God is to be maintained but with the œconomy; dread this œconomy; imagining that

---

* Τα δε πληθη των πεπιστευκεναι νομιζομενων τη σκια τε λογε, κ̀ εχι τω αληθινω λογω θεε εν τω ανεωγοτι ερανω τυγχανοντι, μαθητευειν. Comment. in Johan. vol. 2. p. 52.

"this

" this number and difposition of a trinity is
" a divifion of the unity. They, there-
" fore, will have it that we are worfhippers
" of two, and even of three Gods, but that
" they are the worfhippers of one God
" only. We, they fay, hold the monarchy.
" Even the Latins have learned to bawl
" out for the monarchy, and the Greeks
" themfelves will not underftand the œco-
" nomy *."

It is hardly poffible in any words to defcribe the ftate of things more clearly than

---

* Simplices enim quippe, ne dixerim imprudentes et idiotæ, quæ major femper credentium pars eft, quoniam et ipfa regula fidei a pluribus diis feculi, ad unicum et deum verum transfert; non intelligentes unicum quidem, fed cum fua œconomia effe credendum expavefcunt ad œconomiam. Numerum et difpofitionem trinitatis, divifionem præfumunt unitatis; quando unitas ex femetipfa derivans trinitatem, non deftruatur ab illa, fed adminiftretur. Itaque duos et tres jam jactitant a nobis prædicari, fe vero unius dei cultores præfumunt.——Quafi non et unitas inrationaliter collecta, hærefim faciat, trinitas rationaliter expenfa, veritatem conftituat. Monarchiam, inquiunt, tenemus. Et ita fonum vocaliter exprimunt etiam Latini, etiam opici, ut putes illos tam bene intelligere monarchiam, quam enunciant. Sed monarchiam fonare ftudent Latini, œconomiam intelligere nolunt etiam Græci. Ad Praxeam, fect. 3. p. 502.

Tertullian

Tertullian here does. It is the language of strong feeling and complaint, the cleareſt of all proofs that he did not mif-ſtate things on that ſide, as it would have been for the purpoſe of his argument to have repreſented the unitarians as being inconſiderable on account of their numbers, as well as deſpicable on account of their want of learning.

Whoever Tertullian meant by the *ſimplices* and *idiotæ*, for any thing that appears, he meant the whole body of them. His language is general and unlimited. However, I am far from being willing to conſtrue him rigorouſly, and am ready to allow that ſome of the ſimple and unlearned perſons he deſcribes might profeſs to believe the doctrine of the trinity, though he ſays nothing of it. But, making all reaſonable deductions on this account, he aſſerts a palpable falſehood, and againſt himſelf, if a very great majority of them were not unitarians.

On the whole, it is impoſſible not to infer from this paſſage, that, in the time of Tertullian, the great body of unlearned chriſtians were unitarians. Common ſenſe
cannot

cannot put any other conſtruction on this paſſage, and Tertullian is far from being ſingular in this acknowledgment. It is made, in different modes, by ſeveral of the Fathers, even later than the age of Tertullian.

That Tertullian conſidered the more ſimple and unlearned people as thoſe among whom the unitarian doctrine was the moſt popular, is evident from his ſaying, that " the tares of Praxeas grew up, while many " ſlept in the ſimplicity of doctrine *."

That the word *idiota* in Latin, or ιδιωτης in Greek, ſignifies a man ſimply *unlearned*, and not *a fool*, would be an affront to the literature of my readers to attempt to prove.

Athanaſius alſo, like Tertullian, acknowledged that the unitarian doctrine was very prevalent among the lower claſs of people in his time. He calls them the οι πολλοι, *the many*, and deſcribes them as perſons of low underſtanding. " It grieves," he ſays, " thoſe who ſtand up for the holy faith,

* Fruticaverant avenæ Praxeanæ hic quoque ſuperſeminatæ, dormientibus multis in ſimplicitate doctrinæ. Ad Praxeam, lib. 1. p. 511.

"that *the multitude,* and especially persons of low understanding, should be infected with those blasphemies. Things that are sublime and difficult are not to be apprehended, except by faith; and ignorant people must fall, if they cannot be persuaded to rest in faith, and avoid curious questions *."

This being the language of *complaint,* as well as that of Tertullian, it may be the more depended on for exhibiting a state of things very unfavourable to what was called the orthodoxy of that age. And it was not the doctrine of Arius, but that of Paulus Samosatensis, that Athanasius is here complaining of.

These *humble christians* of Origen, who got no farther than *the shadow of the logos,* the *simplices,* and *idiotæ* of Tertullian, and the *persons of low understanding* of Athanasius, were

---

* Λυπει δε κ̀ νυν τες ανεχομενες της αγιας πιστεως, ηπερι των αυτων βλασφημιων βλαπτεσα τες πολλες· μαλιστα τες ηλατιωμενες περι την συνεσιν. Τα γαρ μεγαλα κ̀ δυσκαταληπτα των πραγματων πιστει τη προς τον Θεον λαμβανεται. Οθεν οι περι την γνωσιν αδυνατεντες αποπιπτεσιν, ει μη πεισθειεν εμμενειν τη πιστει, κ̀ τας περιεργες ζητησεις εκτρεπεσθαι. De Incarnatione verbi contra Paulum Samosatensem, Opera, vol. I. p. 591.

probably

probably the *simplices credentium* of Jerom, who, he says, " did not understand the scrip-
" tures as became their majesty." For had these simple christians (within the pale of the church) inferred from what John says of the logos, and from what Christ says of himself, that he was, personally considered, equal to the Father, Jerom would hardly have said, that " they did not understand
" the scriptures according to their ma-
" jesty," for he himself would not pretend to a perfect knowledge of the mystery of the
" trinity. " For these simple christians," he says, " the earth of the people of God
" brought forth hay, as for the heretics it
" brought forth thorns *." For the intelligent, no doubt, it yielded richer fruits.

From all these passages, and others quoted before, I cannot help inferring, that the doctrine of Christ being any thing more

---

* Quod dicitur super terram populi mei, spinæ et fœnum ascendent, referre potest et ad hæreticos, et ad simplices quosque credentium, qui non ita scripturam intelligunt ut illius convenit majestati. Unde singula singulis coaptavimus, ut terra populi dei hæreticis spinas, imperitis quibusque ecclesiæ fœnum afferat. Jerom in Isai. xxxii. 20. Opera, vol. 4. p. 118.

than

than a man, the whole doctrine of *the eternal logos*, who was *in God*, and who *was God*, was long considered as a more abstruse and refined principle, with which there was no occasion to trouble the common people; and that the doctrine of the simple humanity of Christ continued to be held by the common people till after the time of Athanasius, or after the council of Nice. And if this was the case then, we may safely conclude, that the unitarians were much more numerous in a more early period, as it is well known that they kept losing, and not gaining ground, for several centuries.

CHAPTER XIV.

An Argument for the Novelty of the Doctrine of the Trinity, from the Manner in which it was taught and received in early Times.

THE subject of this chapter properly belongs to the Twelfth, as it relates to a *circumstance* from which it may be *inferred*, that the unitarian doctrine was held by the the majority of christians in the early ages; but I reserve it for a distinct consideration in this place, because it requires a more particular discussion, and will receive much light from what was advanced both in the Twelfth and Thirteenth chapters.

One proof of the *antiquity* of a doctrine is its being found among the common people, in preference to the learned; the former being the least, and the latter the most apt to innovate; so that from the doctrine of the simple humanity of Christ being held by the common people in the time of Tertullian,

lian, Origen, and Athanasius, it may be concluded with certainty, that it was the doctrine which they had received from their ancestors, and that it originated with the apostles themselves.

There is also another mark by which we may distinguish what opinions are *new*, and what are *old*, whenever they are apprehended to be of much consequence; and that is by the manner in which they are advanced by the patrons of them, and that in which they are received by those who disapprove of them. The innovator will be timid and modest, and the asserter of an old opinion will be bold and confident. A new opinion will alarm and terrify; but an old one will be treated with respect. This maxim we see exemplified every day, and in no case more remarkably than with respect to these very doctrines of the pre-existence and divinity of Christ.

If we look back into the state of things in this country about a century, or half a century ago, we shall find the trinitarians shocked at the doctrine of the humanity of Christ, and endeavouring to bear it down with the greatest confidence and violence. On the other hand, all the defences of what is called the Socinian doctrine, were written with the greatest modesty, and with the air and manner of an apology. Let us now, by this maxim, judge how things stood with respect to this very doctrine in the time of Justin Martyr, Origen, and Tertullian.

As the doctrine of the humanity of Christ was then chiefly held by the common people, who were not writers, and as no work of any unitarian, written after the controversy was started, has been preserved to us, we labour under great disadvantages in this respect. But notwithstanding this, circumstances enow may be collected from the writings of the trinitarians, to enable us to judge how both themselves, and the unitarians, thought and felt with respect to it; and circumstances furnished in this indirect manner by adversaries, are often the least suspicious intimations of the real state of things.

On this principle, it will, I think, sufficiently appear, that it was with great difficulty that the generality of christians were

recon-

reconciled to the doctrine of the deity of Chrift, and that of the trinity in any form. It is evident, that the lower clafs of chriftians was much ftaggered by it, and exceedingly offended when they *did* hear of it; which could never have been the cafe if it had then been fuppofed to have been the doctrine of the apoftles, and to have been delivered by them as the moft effential article of chriftian faith, in which light it is now reprefented. Such terms as *fcandalizare, expavefcere*, &c. ufed by Tertullian, Novatian, &c. and ταρασσειν, &c. by Origen, can only apply to the cafe of fome *novel* and *alarming* doctrine, fomething that men had not been accuftomed to. We may, therefore, take it for granted, that it had not been much heard of among the common people at leaft; and if fo, that it had never been taught by the apoftles.

Admitting that the apoftles had taught any doctrines of a peculiarly fublime nature (which the Fathers pretend to have been the cafe with refpect to the pre-exiftence and divinity of Chrift) yet, as all their teaching was in public, and there were no fecrets among them (Paul, for instance, having solemnly assured the elders at Ephesus, that *he had not shunned to declare unto them the whole council of God*) the common people must at least have heard of these sublime doctrines, and have been accustomed to the sound of the language in which they were expressed. And had they known that those doctrines had been taught by the apostles to any of their body, though not to themselves, they would have learned to respect what they did not understand, and was not meant for their use. They could never have been *offended* and *staggered* at things which they and their fathers before them had always been in the hearing of.

I shall not recite in this place all the passages which show how much the common people were offended at the doctrines of the pre-existence and divinity of Christ. Many of them have already passed before the eye of the reader, and many others will be produced in different connexions. It will be found, that even at and after the council of Nice, the unitarians continued to speak their sentiments with the greatest freedom, and

and always exclaimed againſt the prevailing doctrines, as no leſs *new* than *abſurd*. Little were thoſe writers who have inadvertently recorded theſe circumſtances aware of the value of the information which they were hereby giving to poſterity. Had Tertullian, Origen, and others, thought more highly than they did of the common people, we ſhould probably never have known from them what their opinions and feelings were. But, happily for us, theſe writers thought meanly of the common people, and ſpeaking of them with contempt, or pity, have, without deſign, given us very uſeful and valuable lights into this very important circumſtance in the hiſtory of their times.

I ſhall now give an account of the manner which the doctrines of the pre-exiſtence and divinity of Chriſt were firſt propoſed by the moſt learned and diſtinguiſhed perſons of their age; and we ſhall find that it was with much diffidence, and the air of an *apology*, as if they were ſenſible that the doctrines were *new*, and might not eaſily recommend themſelves. For this purpoſe I ſhall, in the firſt place, produce an extract from

from the writings of Juftin Martyr, who was probably the firft who publicly maintained thefe doctrines.

He reprefents Trypho as faying, concerning the doctrine of the incarnation, " it is fo extraordinary, that it can never " be proved. That this Chrift was a God, " exifting before the ages, and then born " a man, is not only extraordinary, but ri-" diculous. To this I anfwered, I know " that this doctrine appears ftrange, and " efpecially to thofe of your race," that is, to the Jews*. It is evident from this paffage, that Juftin thought that this doctrine would appear ftrange to others, befides the Jews; and as he proceeds, it will appear that he took care not to lay too much ftrefs on this new doctrine, left he fhould not be able to prove it fatisfactorily.

" It will not follow that he is not the " Chrift, though I fhould not be able to prove

---

* Παραδοξες τις γαρ ωδε και μη δυναμενΘ- ολως αποδειχθηναι δοκει μοι ειναι. το γαρ λεγειν σε, προυπαρχειν θεον οντα προ αιωνων τετον τον χριστον, ειτα και γεννηθηναι ανθρωπον γενομενον υπομειναι, και οτι εκ ανθρωπος εξ ανθρωπε, ε μονον παραδοξον δοκει μοι ειναι, αλλα και μωρον. Καγω προς ταυτα εφην, οιδ' οτι παραδοξΘ- ο λογΘ- δοκει ειναι, και μαλιστα τοις απο τε γενες υμων. Dial. p. 232, 233.

" that

"that he pre-exifted, as God, the fon of him that made all things, and that he became a man by the virgin; it being proved that he is the Chrift, the Son of God, whoever he was; though I fhould not prove that he pre-exifted, but was a man of the fame paffions with ourfelves, having flefh, and being fubject to his Father's will. It will be right to fay, that in this only I have been miftaken, and not that he is not the Chrift, though he fhould appear to be a man born as other men are, and to be made Chrift by election. For there are fome of our race, who acknowledge him to be Chrift, but hold that he was a man born like other men. With them I do not agree, nor fhould I do fo, though ever fo many, being of the fame opinion, fhould urge it upon me; becaufe we are commanded by Chrift himfelf, not to obey the teachings of men, but what was taught by the holy prophets and himfelf." Trypho fays, " They who fay that he was a man, born like other men, and that he became Chrift by election," i. e. the appointment of God, "seem to hold a doctrine more "credible than yours. For all of us ex- "pect that Christ will be a man, born like "other men, and that Elias will come to "anoint him. If, therefore, this person "be the Christ, he must by all means be "a man born like other men*."

This diffidence of Justin agrees remarkably well with the supposition, that the

---

* Ουκ απολλυται το τοιχτον ειναι χριστον τε θετ εαν αποδειξαι μη δυναμαι ότι και προυπηρχεν, υιος τε ποιητα των ολων θεος ων, και γεγεννηται ανθρωπος δια της παρθενε. Αλλα εκ παντος αποδεικνυμενν ότι άτιος εστιν ο χριστος ο τε θετ, όστις έτιος εται, εαν δε μη αποδεικνυω ότι προυπηρχε και γεννηθηναι ανθρωπω ομοιοπαθης ημιν, σαρκα εχων, καθα την τε πατρος βαλην, υπεμεινεν, εν τετω πεπλανηθαι με μονον λεγειν δικαιον, αλλα μη αρνεισθαι ότι ὑιος ετιν ο χριστος, εαν φαινηται ως ανθρωπω εξ ανθρωπων γεννηθεις, και εκλογη γενομενω εις τον χριστον ειναι αποδεικνυνται. Και γαρ εισι τινες, ω φιλοι ελεγον, απο τε ημετερα γενας ομολογευντες αυτον χριστον ειναι, ανθρωπον δε εξ ανθρωπων γενομενον αποφαινομενοι. Οις, ε συντιθεμαι, εδ αν πλειτοι ταυτα μοι δοξασαντες ειποιεν, επειδη εκ ανθρωπειοις διδαγμασι κεκελευσμεθα υπ αυτε τε χριστα πειθεσθαι, αλλα τοις δια των μακαριων προφητων κηρυχθεισι και δι αυτε διδαχθεισι. Και ο Τρυφων, εμοι μεν δοκεσιν, ειπεν, οι λεγοντες ανθρωπον γεγονεναι αυτον και κατ εκλογην κεκρισθαι, και χριστον γεγονεναι, πιθανωτερον υμων λεγειν, των ταυτα απερ φης λεγοντων. και γαρ παντες ημεις τον χριστον ανθρωπον εξ ανθρωπων προσδοκωμεν γενησεσθαι. και τον Ηλιαν χρισαι αυτον ελθοντα. εαν δε ετιος φαινηται ων ο χριστος, ανθρωπον μεν εξ ανθρωπων γενομενον εκ παντος επιτασθαι δει. Dial. p. 233.

unitarians

unitarians were originally no less than the whole body of christians, and that the trinitarians were the innovators, appearing at first modest and candid, as was natural while they were a small minority, though they grew bold and imperious when they became the majority.

Independently of any nice construction of this passage, we may safely say, that if the doctrine of the simple humanity of Christ had not been at least a *very general* opinion in the time of Justin, he would never have spoken of it with so much tenderness and respect as he has done, considering how very different it was from his own opinion, his defence of which has sufficiently the appearance of an apology. He even intimates some degree of doubt with respect to his opinion, when he says that, if he should not be able to prove it, the fundamental doctrine of christianity, viz. that of the messiahship of Jesus, would not be affected by it. Why should he provide this retreat, if he had not had some secret suspicion of the ground on which he stood. He calls the unitarians *some*, as if they

they were the minority; but the term is indefinite, and may apply to the majority; and from the complexion of the whole paſſage, I have no doubt but that Juſtin was aware that it was ſo, and that, with a view to this, he added, that he ſhould not be influenced by that conſideration.

That Juſtin's language is that of a man who knew that he was advancing a *new* opinion, is evident, as I ſaid, from the general air and complexion of it; and the more we attend to it, the more ſenſible we ſhall be of the juſtneſs of this conſtruction.

1. Let it be conſidered, that in this place, as well as in his writings in general, he *labours* the proof of the pre-exiſtence of Chriſt, ſhewing that it is conſonant to the principles of Platoniſm, and alſo deducible from the writings of Moſes, and other parts of the Jewiſh ſcriptures, without referring to any other writer in ſupport of what he advances.

2. He does not uſe a ſingle acrimonious expreſſion againſt thoſe who differed from him with reſpect to it, which is juſt as any man would do who ſhould write in defence of

of a novel, or not very prevalent opinion, and one, of which himself was the principal abettor.

3. He talks of not being overborne by the authority of any number of men, even his fellow chriftians, but would adhere to the words of Chrift, and the fenfe of fcripture; which is a ftile almoft peculiar to thofe whofe opinions are either quite novel, or at leaft not very prevalent.

4. The phrafe, " neither do I agree with " the majority of chriftians, who may have " objected to my opinion," which is nearly the moft literal rendering of the paffage (though I would not be underftood to lay much ftrefs on that circumftance) will naturally be conftrued to mean that the majority actually did make the objection, or that Juftin fufpected they might make it.

When I confider thefe circumftances, and alfo how apt all perfons are to make their own party more numerous than it really is, I am inclined to think that even, if the paffage might bear fuch a conftruction as that Juftin meant to infinuate that the majority were with him, yet that it would not be be the moſt natural conſtruction, or a ſufficient authority to conclude that ſuch was the fact. I therefore think that, upon the whole, the paſſage has all the appearance of an apology for an opinion different from that which in his time was commonly received on the ſubject.

I am no doubt, influenced in my conſtruction of this particular paſſage by the perſuaſion that I have, from other independent evidence, that the unitarians were in fact, the majority of chriſtians in the time of Juſtin; that he therefore knew this to be the caſe, and could not mean to inſinuate the contrary. Another perſon having a different perſuaſion concerning the ſtate of opinions in that age, will naturally be inclined to put a different conſtruction upon this paſſage. In this caſe I only wiſh that he would ſuſpend his judgment till he has attended to my other arguments, and afterwards he may perhaps ſee this paſſage in the ſame light in which I do.

The word γένος I think, refers to natural deſcent; and I therefore conclude that Juſtin here meant not chriſtians in general, but

but Gentile christians in particular; because, as he is opposing the opinion concerning Christ, which made him to be a *man born of men*, not to the doctrine of the miraculous conception, but only to his pre-existence (though I think it probable, that most, if not all, who believed in the *simple humanity*, were also in that age believers in the *natural birth* of Christ) the only idea that he had in his mind, and to which he attended, was that of his *simple humanity*, and we have positive evidence that this was the doctrine of all the Jewish christians, so that he could not speak of some of them holding it and others not. Whereas the Gentile christians were divided on that subject; and some of them, even later than this, viz. in the time of Origen, held that in the strictest sense of the expression, Jesus was a man born of man, being the son of Joseph as well as of Mary. I therefore think that Justin meant the Gentile christians, omitting the Jewish christians, whose sentiments he might suppose to have been well known to the learned Jew, with whom he was
con-

conversing. It was as if he had said, Not only do those christians who are of *your race*, viz. Jews, believe Christ to be a mere man, born as other men are, but there are also some of *our race*, viz. Gentile christians, who hold the same opinion.

I shall conclude this article with observing, that, without attending to minute criticisms, it is quite sufficient for my purpose, that these ancient unitarian christians, whether they held the miraculous conception or not, whether they were Jews or Gentiles, or whether Justin meant to represent them as strictly speaking the majority of christians, or otherwise, were not treated by him as *heretics*. From this circumstance alone, it may be concluded, that they were very numerous, because, whenever unitarians have not been very numerous, and have not made a respectable figure among christians, they have always been considered with great abhorrence, and have been cut off from communion with those of the orthodox persuasion.

With

With what rancour does Eusebius treat this class of christians, both in his History, and in his Treatise against Marcellus of Ancyra, when we know from Athanasius, and other authorities, that they were at that time very numerous (though among the lower classes of people) and probably in all parts of the christian world.

When these things are duly considered, it can hardly be imagined but that, let this passage in Justin be construed in any manner that the words can possibly bear, it will be sufficiently to my purpose, and authorize all the use that I have ever made of it. But I can very well spare the passage altogether, thinking that I have evidence enough of my general position without it.

If we consider the time in which Justin wrote, viz. about A. D. 140, that is, about eighty years after the time of the apostles, and compare it with the account that Tertullian and others give of the state of opinions among the Jews and Gentiles in their time, we can hardly doubt (whether Justin confesses it or not) that the doctrine of the simple humanity of Christ must

must have been the prevailing one in his time. According to the ancient Fathers, the Jews, meaning the Jewish christians, were so fully persuaded concerning the simple humanity of their Messiah, that the apostles did not chuse to inform them, except in an indirect manner, that Christ was any thing more than a man, and the Gentiles were drawn by the Jews into the same opinion; and though John was supposed to speak more plainly, we find no effect from it.

Since, therefore, it was only an indirect evidence of the divine or super-angelic nature of Christ, that the Jewish christians (by whom the gospel was communicated to the Gentiles) were ever favoured with; can it be thought probable, so highly averse as the account itself states the Jews to have been to the idea of any super-human nature in Christ, that they should, by their own reasoning alone on the subject, have generally abandoned their favourite doctrine in so short a time as fourscore years? Or, if from some most unaccountable cause, and without any person of great authority to lead them,

CHAP. XIV. *originally Unitarians.* 289

them to it (for no such authority can we trace) they should have abandoned their original and favourite doctrine, is it probable that they would have been so extremely active and successful in the propagation of their new opinion, and withal have found the Gentiles so very pliant as to have been able to induce the generality of them to make the same change, when at the same time they are known to have had but little connexion, and indeed but little respect for each other? Is a period of eighty years naturally sufficient for these two successive changes?

But if we take another well authenticated circumstance, we shall be obliged to reduce this short space (too short as it already is for the purpose) to one still shorter. Hegesippus, as explained by Valesius, in his notes on Eusebius's ecclesiastical history, says, that the church of Jerusalem continued a virgin, or free from heresy, till the death of Simeon, who succeeded James the Just, that is, till the time of Trajan, or about the year 100, or perhaps 110, for his reign began A. D. 98, and ended A. D.

117. Knowing, therefore, from other circumstances, what this purity of chriſtian faith was, and what Hegeſippus muſt have known it to be, we have only the ſpace of forty, or perhaps, thirty years for ſo great a change. So rapid at that particular period muſt have been that movement, which we find by experience to be naturally one of the very ſloweſt in the whole ſyſtem of nature, viz. the revolution of opinions in great bodies of men. Can it then be thought probable that, conſidering the Jewiſh and Gentile chriſtians as one body, the generality of them ſhould have abandoned the doctrine of the ſimple humanity of Chriſt, in the time of Juſtin Martyr.

On the contrary, it is certainly not at all improbable, that the more learned and philoſophical of the chriſtians, beginning to be aſhamed of *a crucified man* for their ſaviour, and firmly believing the doctrine of the pre-exiſtence of *all ſouls*, and of their deſcent into human bodies, ſhould have begun to fancy that Chriſt muſt have had ſome origin ſuperior to that of other men, that this ſhould firſt of all produce the

the opinions of the Gnostics, who thought that *the Christ,* who came down from heaven, was quite distinct from the man *Jesus,* and felt nothing of his pains or sorrows; or that these opinions being rejected through the authority of the apostles, the generality of christian teachers or bishops (many of whom were educated in the Platonic school at Alexandria) should afterwards apply the Platonic doctrine of the *logos* to the same subject, and that by their influence, opinions leading to the *deification of Christ* should gradually gain ground among the common people. But this must have been a work of *time,* so that the majority of christians could hardly have been infected with these principles so early as the time of Justin Martyr.

Irenæus, who wrote forty years after Justin, makes no mention of any Gentile unitarians, in his works against heresy, but only of the Ebionites; and what he says of them is a very small proportion of the whole of his work. And almost all the orthodox Fathers, both before and after the council of of Nice, make laboured apologies for their seeming to teach the doctrine of *more Gods than one*. This circumstance is a sufficient indication that the trinitarians were then the minority, as their violence and insolence afterwards shows, that if they were not the majority, at least they had the advantage of *power* in their favour.

As the advocates for the doctrines of the pre-existence and divinity of Christ, advanced it with caution and with apology, as being sensible that they were not likely to be well received; so, on the other hand, it appears that the unitarians did express the greatest *dread* of them, as the introduction of *polytheism*. Several instances of this have been produced already, and others will appear in different connexions, especially when I shall show the zeal with which the ancient unitarians defended their tenets. But I shall in this place introduce a few others.

Origen says, " Because it is probable that
" some will be *offended* with our saying, that
" the Father being called the only true God,
" there are other gods besides him partaking
" of

"of his divinity *." Novatian speaks of the unitarians as *scandalized* at the doctrine of the divinity of Christ †." And the state of things was not different about the time of the council of Nice. Eusebius, in his controversy with Marcellus, says, " If " they are *afraid* of making two Gods ‡." " Some for *fear* of introducing a second " God, make the Father and the Son the " same ‖." " Marcellus, for fear of saying " there are two Gods, denies the Son to be a " separate person §." And again, " But you

* Αλλ' επει εικος προσκοψειν τινας τοις ειρημενοις, ενος μεν αληθινε θευ-τε πατρος απεγγελλομενε, παρα δε τον αληθινον θεον θεων πλειονων τη μετοχη τε θεε γινομενων. Comment. vol. 2. p. 47.

† Sed quia obluctantes adversus veritatem semper hæretici sinceræ traditionis, et catholicæ fidei controversiam solent trahere, scandalizati in christum quod etiam deus et per scripturas adseratur, et a nobis hoc esse credatur, merito a nobis, ut omnis a fide nostra auferri possit hæretica calumnia, de eo quod et deus sit Christus, sic est disputandum, ut non impediat scriptura veritatem Cap. 30. p. 115.

‡ Ει δε φοβον αυτοις εμποιει, μη πη αρα δυο θεες αναγορευειν δοξαι. Ec. Theol. lib. 1. cap. 11. p. 69.

‖ Οι δε, φοβω τε δοκειν δευτερον εισηγεισθαι θεον, τον αυτον ειναι πατερα κ῀ υιον ορισαμενοι. Ibid. cap. 3. p. 62.

§ Ο μεν γαρ, δεει τε μη δυο θεες ειπειν, την αρνησιν τε υιε πα-βαλλετο, την υποστασιν αθετων αυτε. Ibid. cap. 10. p. 69.

"are *dreadfully afraid* left you should be obliged to acknowledge two hypostases of the Father and Son *."

In short, it appears that the ancient unitarians entertained the same *dread* of the doctrine of the divinity of Christ, that the trinitarians of this day do of that of his simple humanity; a proof that each of them had been brought up in the persuasion of the opinions they held, being the doctrine of their ancestors, and of the apostles. In this the ancient unitarians could not be mistaken, but the trinitarians of the present age may very well be so. Whether, therefore, we consider the feelings of the unitarians, or those of the trinitarians of the early ages, we perceive evident traces of the former maintaining an *old* opinion, and the latter a *new* one.

* Αλλα αγωνιας μη δυο θεες αναγκη παραδεξασθαι τον δυο υποστασεις πατρος ϗ υιν ειναι ομολογενϊα, Ec. Theol. lib. 2. cap. 7. p. 109.

CHAP-

CHAPTER XV.

Objections to the preceding State of Things considered.

THAT I may conceal nothing from my readers that can tend to throw any light on this subject, I shall fairly state every objection that I have yet met with, to any part of the evidence that I have produced.

SECTION I.

Of the Testimony of Eusebius to the Novelty of the Unitarian Doctrine.

IT is alledged by Eusebius, the historian, or rather Caius (who is supposed to be the author that he quotes, and who, Photius says*, wrote *The Little Labyrinth*,

---

* Γαιȣ τινος πρεσϐυτερȣ εν Ρωμη διατριϐοντ۞ ου φασι συντάξαι κ̉ τον λαϐυρινθον.—Τον λαϐυρινθον τινες επιγραψαν Ωριγενȣς, επει Γαιȣ ετι ποιημα. Bib. sect. 48. p. 35.

which is thought to be the work that Eusebius copied from) is so far from confirming this account of the great antiquity of the unitarians, that he expressly asserts that they were a modern sect. That this charge, with the evidence, may be fairly before the reader, I shall quote the passage in which it is contained at full length.

"Artemon made Christ a mere man. They who hold this doctrine pretend that it is very ancient; for they say that all the primitive christians, and the apostles themselves, received and taught it, and that the truth was preserved till the time of Victor, the thirteenth bishop of Rome from Peter, but that it was corrupted in the time of his successor Victorinus. This might appear probable, if, in the first place, the sacred scriptures were not against it; and if there were not writings of christians now extant, older than the time of Victor, which they wrote against the heathens and against heresies. I mean those of Justin, Miltiades, Tatian, Clemens, and many others, in all of which Christ is spoken of as a God. Who is unacquainted with

" with the writings of Irenæus, Melito, and
" others, speaking of Christ as God and
" man? How many psalms and hymns also
" are there, written by christians from the
" beginning, in which Christ is celebrated
" as a God——How were they not ashamed
" to speak thus falsely of Victor, knowing
" very well that Victor excommunicated
" Theodotus, the leader and father of that
" God-denying heresy, who first said, that
" Christ was a mere man *."

* Τὴν γάρ τοι δεδηλωμένην αἵρεσιν ψιλὸν ἄνθρωπον γίνεσθαι τὸν σωτῆρα φάσκουσαν ου πρὸ πολλοῦ νεωτερισθεῖσαν διευθύνων. Ἐπειδὴ σεμνύνειν αὐτὴν ὡς ἂν ἀρχαίαν οἱ ταύτης ἤθελον εἰσηγηταί. Φασὶ γὰρ τοὺς μὲν προτέρους ἅπαντας κ, αὐτοὺς τοὺς ἀποστόλους παρειληφέναι τε κ, δεδιδαχέναι ταῦτα, ἃ νῦν οὗτοι λέγουσι· κ, τετηρῆσθαι τὴν ἀλήθειαν τοῦ κηρύγματος μέχρι τῶν Βίκτορος χρόνων, ὃς ἦν τρισκαιδέκατος ἀπὸ Πέτρου ἐν Ῥώμῃ ἐπίσκοπος. ἀπὸ δὲ τοῦ διαδόχου αὐτοῦ Ζεφυρίνου, παρακεχαράχθαι τὴν ἀλήθειαν. ἦν δ᾽ ἂν τυχὸν πιθανὸν τὸ λεγόμενον, εἰ μὴ πρῶτον μὲν ἀντέπιπτον αὐτοῖς αἱ θεῖαι γραφαί· κ, ἀδελφῶν δέ τινων ἔστι γράμματα πρεσβύτερα τῶν Βίκτορος χρόνων, ἃ ἐκεῖνοι πρὸς τὰ ἔθνη ὑπὲρ τῆς ἀληθείας, κ, πρὸς τὰς τότε αἱρέσεις ἔγραψαν. λέγω δὲ Ἰουστίνου κ, Μιλτιάδου κ, Τατιανοῦ κ, Κλήμεντος κ, ἑτέρων πλειόνων ἐν οἷς ἅπασι θεολογεῖται ὁ χριστός. τὰ γὰρ Εἰρηναίου τε κ, Μελίτωνος κ, τῶν λοιπῶν τίς ἀγνοεῖ βιβλία, θεὸν κ, ἄνθρωπον καταγγέλλοντα τὸν χριστόν; ψαλμοὶ δὲ ὅσοι κ, ᾠδαὶ ἀδελφῶν ἀπαρχῆς ὑπὸ πιστῶν γραφεῖσαι, τὸν λόγον τοῦ θεοῦ τὸν χριστὸν ὑμνοῦσι θεολογοῦντες. Πῶς δὲ οὐκ αἰδοῦνται ταῦτα Βίκτορος καταψεύδεσθαι, ἀκριβῶς εἰδότες, ὅτι Βίκτωρ τὸν σκυτέα Θεόδοτον τὸν ἀρχηγὸν κ, πατέρα ταύτης τῆς ἀρνησιθέου ἀποστασίας, ἀπεκήρυξε τῆς κοινωνίας, πρῶτον

In these passages we have an account of the claims of the ancient unitarians to the high antiquity of their doctrine. And it has been seen that, by the general acknowledgment of the Fathers, and of Eusebius himself, among the rest, that the first doctrine that was taught by the apostles, was that of the simple humanity of Christ; and that his divinity was very little known till it was published by John, after the death of the other apostles. Eusebius, therefore, denying it in this case, is not at all to be regarded, since it is contrary to all other evidence, and also to the reason of the thing, as I have abundantly proved, unless he had brought some sufficient proof to counteract that evidence. What he has offered of this kind I shall distinctly consider, after I have produced a passage from Theodoret, in which he also mentions the claim of the unitarians to the antiquity of their doctrine. " Artemon," he says, " taught that Christ " was a mere man, born of a virgin, and ex-

πρωίον ειποντα ψιλον ανθρωπον τον χριστον; ει γαρ Βικίωρ κατ' αυτας ιδως εφρονει ως η τειων διδασκει βλασφημια, πως αν απεβαλλε Θεοδοτον τον της αιρεσεως ταυτης ευρετην. Hist. lib. 5. cap. 28. p. 252.

" celling

"celling the prophets in virtue. This, he
"says, the apostles taught, perverting the
"sense of the sacred scriptures, but that
"those who came after them made a God of
"Christ, who was not God*." It appears
also from Eusebius's answer to Marcellus,
that he also charged his opponents with
holding a new doctrine, and scrupled not to
call that doctrine *heresy* †.

The first argument of Eusebius is, that
the sacred scriptures are against the unitarians. This, however, is a matter of *opinion*, in which he might be, and I doubt not
was, mistaken. He then mentions the
writings of some persons who held the doctrines of the pre-existence and divinity of
Christ, viz. Justin, Miltiades, Tatian, and

* Τον δε κυριον Ιησυν χριςον ανθρωπον ειπε ψιλον, εκ παρθενε γεγενημενον, των δε προφητων αρείη κρειτίονα. ταυία δε κ) της αποςολης ελεγε κεκηρυχεναι, παρερμηνευων των θειων γραφων την διανοιαν, της δε μεθ εκεινης θειλογησαι τον χριςον, εκ οντα θεον. Hær. Fab. lib. 2. cap. 4. Opera, vol. 4. p. 220.

† Ψιλον γαρ κ) τω ανθρωπινω λογω ομοιον, εχι δε υιον αληθως ζωντα κ) υφεςωτα, τον χριςον ειναι ομολογειν εθελει. κ) επειδη ταυτην ειπε επινοεισθαι νυν αιρεσιν, &c. Contra Marcellum, lib. 1. p. 19.

Clemens.

Clemens. But of these Justin was the oldest, and it is not denied that he *did* hold those doctrines, being probably the first who advanced them. Who the Clemens is that he mentions, he does not say; but had it been Clemens Romanus, it is probable that he would have placed him first, the rest being named in the order of time in which they flourished; and besides, there is nothing in the epistle of Clemens that is in the least favourable to those doctrines. Consequently, it must have been Clemens Alexandrinus that he intended, and therefore the highest antiquity of the doctrine of the divinity of Christ that Eusebius could prove, is that of Justin.

Pearson makes no difficulty of contradicting Eusebius in this case. His opponent, Mr. Daillé, having said, *if that account be true*, he replies, " He knew very " well that, strictly speaking, it was not " true; for he knew many others, long " before Theodotus, and not a few even " before Ignatius, who taught the same " heresy, a catalogue of whom may be seen " in

CHAP. XV. *originally Unitarians.* 301

" in Epiphanius *," and whom he proceeds to mention.

Eusebius's reply to Marcellus's charge of novelty is equally unsatisfactory, as he only, in a general way, refers to writings older than those of Origen, in all which he says he found the same faith †.

As to the *hymns* used by christians, and said by Eusebius to have been *from the beginning*, no inference can be safely drawn from them, because *divinity* may be ascribed to persons in very different senses, and some of them very innocent ones, especially in

---

* Theodotum novisse rursus pernego. Dallæus ipse dubitanter hæc proponit, si vera sunt, inquit, quæ Caius, sive alius apud Eusebium scriptor vetustissimus dicit, Theodotum scilicet primum asseruisse Christum fuisse nudum hominem; ipse enim optime novit hæc, si stricte sumantur, vera non esse: novit alios quamplurimos diu ante Theodotum, non paucos etiam ante Ignatium, eandem hæresin promulgasse, quorum catalogus apud Epiphanium legitur. Vindiciæ, lib. 2. cap. 2. p. 24.

† Εγω δε και Ωριγενες παλαιοτερων ανδρων, πλειτοις οσοις εκκλησιαστικοις συγγραμασιν εντετυχηκα, επισκοπων τε και συνοδων επιστολαις, προπαλαι γραφεισαις, δι ων εις και αυτος ο της πιστεως χαρακτηρ αποδεικνυται. εκ ορθως αρα διαβεβληκεν ειπων επινοεισθαι την νυν αιρεσιν υπο των διαβαλλομενων. Contra Marcellum, lib. 1. p. 20.

the language of poetry; and as to the antiquity of these hymns, as the historian has not mentioned the age of them, it is very possible, for any thing that appears to the contrary, that they might have been those very hymns which were rejected by Paulus Samosatensis on account of their novelty.

It is likewise alledged, that Pliny says, that " the christians on a certain day, before " it was light, met to sing a hymn to Christ " as to God (or a God) *." But as to this writer, if he had been told that hymns were sung by christians in honour of Christ, being himself a heathen, he would naturally imagine that they were such hymns as had been composed in honour of the heathen gods, who had been men. He would be far from concluding from that circumstance, that Christ was considered by his followers either as the supreme God, or as a pre-existent spirit, the maker of the world under God.

* Affirmabant autem hanc fuisse summam vel culpæ suæ, vel erroris, quod essent soliti stato die, ante lucem convenire; carmenque Christo, quasi deo, dicere. Epist. 97.

SECTION II.

Of the Excommunication of Theodotus by Victor.

THE argument that is urged with the most plausibility against the antiquity of the unitarian doctrine, is that which is drawn from the excommunication of Theodotus, by Victor, bishop of Rome, about the year 200; as it may be said, that this bishop, violent as he was, would not have proceeded to the public excommunication of a man whose opinions were not generally obnoxious.

I wish that we had a few more particulars concerning this excommunication of Theodotus, as it is the first of the kind that is mentioned in history. It is to be observed, that it is not Caius, the writer quoted by Eusebius, who says that he was excommunicated on account of his being an unitarian, but Eusebius himself*; so that,

* Ησαν δε ητοι αμφω Θεοδοτε τε σκευεως μαθηται, τε πρωτε επι ταυτη τη φρονησει, μαλλον δε αφροσυνη, αφορισθεντος της κοινωνιας υπο βικτορος ως εφην, τε τοις επισκοπε. Hist. lib. 5. cap. 21. p. 253.

considering the writer's prejudices, there may be some room to doubt, whether he *was* excommunicated on that account.

The unitarians, it has been seen, said that Victor favoured their doctrine, and this we find asserted in the Appendix to Tertullian's Treatise, *De Præscriptione*, which, whether written by Tertullian himself, or not, is probably as good an authority as that of Eusebius. He says that, after the two Theodotus's, "Praxeas introduced his "heresy into Rome, which Victorinus en- "deavoured to strengthen. He said that "Jesus Christ was God the Father omni- "potent, that he was crucified, suffered, "and died, &c.*" Victorinus, in this passage, Beausobre says †, it is agreed, should be Victor, and it cannot be supposed, that he would have patronized in Praxeas the same doctrine for which he had before excommunicated Theodotus. The probabi-

* Sed post hos omnes etiam Praxeas quidam hæresim introduxit, quam Victorinus corroborare curavit. Hic deum patrem omnipotentem Jesum Christum esse dicit; hunc crucifixum passumque contendit et mortuum. Ad Finem, p. 223.

† Histoire de Manicheisme, vol. 1. p. 533.

CHAP. XV. *originally Unitarian.* 305

lity, therefore, is, that Theodotus was excommunicated on some other account than that of his being an unitarian.

Theodotus having been excommunicated as an unitarian, is not consistent with that general prevalence of the unitarian doctrine in the time of Tertullian (which was also that of Victor) which we have seen that Tertullian expressly asserts. However, the account of Eusebius, though improbable, may be admitted without denying that of Tertullian, when the circumstances attending them are duly considered.

Tertullian lived in Africa, where there seems to have been a greater inclination for the unitarian doctrine than there was at Rome; as we may collect from the remarkable popularity of Sabellius in that country, and other circumstances. Athanasius also, who complains of many persons of low understanding favouring the same principle, was of the same country, residing chiefly in Egypt; though he had seen a great part of the christian world, and was, no doubt, well acquainted with the state of it.

We should likewise confider the peculiarly violent character of Victor, who was capable of doing what few other persons would have attempted; being the same person who excommunicated all the eastern churches, because they did not observe Easter at the same time that the western churches did, for which he was much censured by many bishops, even in the west.

Such an excommunication as this of Theodotus was by no means the same thing with cutting a person off from communion with any particular church, with which he had been used to communicate. Theodotus was a stranger at Rome, and it is very possible that the body of the christian church in that city did not interest themselves in the affair; the bishop and his clergy only approving of it. For I readily grant that, though there were some learned unitarians in all the early ages of christianity, the majority of the clergy were not so.

Theodotus, besides being a stranger at Rome, was a man of science, and is said by the unitarians to have been well received by Victor at first; so that it is very possible

possible that the latter might have been instigated to what he did by some quarrel between them, of which we have no account.

Upon the whole, therefore, though Victor excommunicated this Theodotus, who was a stranger, and had, perhaps, made himself conspicuous, so as to have given some cause of umbrage or jealousy to him, it is very possible that a great proportion of the lower kind of people, who made no noise or disturbance, might continue in communion with that church, though they were known to be unitarians.

There is no instance, I believe, of any person having been excommunicated for being an unitarian before Theodotus.— Whereas, had the universal church been trinitarian from the beginning, would not the first unitarians, the first broachers of a doctrine so exceedingly offensive to them, as in all ages it has ever been, have experienced their utmost indignation, and have been expelled from all christian societies with horror.

SECTION III.

Of the Part taken by the Laity in the Excommunication of the early Unitarians, and other Considerations relating to the Subject.

IT is particularly remarkable, that we read of none of the *laity* having been excommunicated on account of their unitarian principles, which they were well known to hold. And whenever any of the bishops were deposed on this account, it is also remarkable, that the common people appear to have been their friends. None of the laity were excommunicated along with Noetus, about A. D. 220, with Sabellius, about A. D. 255. (See Lardner's Credibility, vol. 4. p. 593.) Paulus Samosatensis, A. D. 269, or Photinus, A. D. 344, &c. After the bishops had deposed Paulus Samosatensis, it is observable, that only sixteen signed the condemnation (Eusebii, Hist. lib. 7. cap. 30. p. 359) and he could not be expelled from the episcopal house till

CHAP. XV.   *originally Unitarians.*   309

till the aid of the emperor Aurelian was called in; and *he* may be supposed to have been offended at him for his having been in the interest of his rival Zenobia. This could not have been necessary, if the majority of his people had not been with him, and therefore, if his deposition had not, in fact, been unjust.

Besides, the prosecution of Paulus Samosatensis, as Dr. Lardner has observed, was vehemently urged by his presbyter Malchion, who had a quarrel with him. Having been disobliged, he could not be satisfied till he was deposed. Credibility, vol. 4. p. 624. " He wrote, says Jerom, the " large epistle in the name of the coun- " cil. Paul had many friends and admi- " rers among the bishops and presbyters " of the neighbouring churches and vil- " lages, and was much beloved and ad- " mired by others." Ibid. p. 640. He could not be expelled in the first council, in 264, when Firmilian of Cappadocia and Gregory of Neocæsarea were present; and Firmilian was dead at the time of the second council, in 269 or 270. Ibid. p. 534.

Dr. Lardner's account of Paulus Samosatenfis, is as follows:

"As we have not now before us any of Paul's writings, and have his history from adversaries only, we cannot propose to judge distinctly of his talents, nor draw his character at length. However, from the several particulars before put down, and collected from divers authors, some things may be concluded. And I apprehend that, laying aside for the present the consideration of his heterodoxy, we shall not mistake much if we conceive of him after this manner. He had a great mind, with a mixture of haughtiness, and too much affection for human applause. He was generally well respected in his diocese, and by the neighbouring bishops, in esteem with the great, and beloved by the common people. He preached frequently, and was a good speaker. And from what is said by the Fathers of the council, of his rejecting, or laying aside, some hymns, as modern, and composed by moderns, it may be argued, that he was a critic, which is a valuable accomplishment

"ment at all times, especially when un-
"common." Ibid. p. 644.

He adds, in a note, "A learned writer
"among the moderns (viz. Garnier) whom
"I did not think of when I drew the above
"character, confirms almost every part of it.
"For he allows Paul to have possessed the
"third see in the church, and to have had
"the patronage of a great princess, an ap-
"pearance of piety, reputation for learning,
"flowing eloquence, and the favour of the
"multitude."

As to Photinus, he was so popular in his
diocese, that his solemn deposition by two
councils, could not remove him from his
see. "He defended himself," says Tele-
mont (Hist. of the Arians, vol. 1. p. 116.)
"against the authority of the church, by
"the affection which his people had for
"him, even to the year 351, though his
"heresy began to appear as early as 342, or
"343, according to Socrates; and the Eu-
"sebians condemned it in one of their con-
"fessions of faith, in 345." At length the
Emperor Constantius, a zealous Arian,
thought it necessary to interfere, and to get

him banished, in a council held at Sirmium itself. Had the body of christians in those times been generally trinitarians, the common people would, no doubt, have been ready enough to take an active part against their heretical bishops.

As to Eusebius charging heretics with teaching *new doctrines*, he is remarkably inaccurate and inconsistent with himself in that respect, and so, indeed, are all the other ecclesiastical historians. No unitarian is mentioned, but he is said to have been the *first* to have taught the unitarian doctrine. This language is held even with respect to Photinus, the very last of the celebrated unitarians. But it is possible, as I have observed before, that by *novelty* these writers might sometimes mean nothing more than *heresy*.

The charge of teaching the unitarian doctrine as a novelty, is first advanced against Beryllus, bishop of Bostra in Arabia, who, perhaps, was the first who *wrote* in defence of the doctrine, that of the divinity of Christ beginning at that time to be prevalent. Eusebius says of him, that
" he

CHAP. XV.   *originally Unitarians.*   313

" he introduced things *new and strange* to
" the catholic faith; having dared to assert,
" that 'our Lord and Saviour did not pre-
" exist in his own distinct person before his
" incarnation, that he had no proper divi-
" nity of his own, but that of the Father
" only abiding in him *."

Sozomen also says, that Marcellus introduced a new doctrine, that " the Son of
" God had his beginning with his birth of
" Mary;" and yet, in the same section, he
says of him, that he adopted the opinion of
Paulus Samosatensis †.

The same writer calls Photinus the introducer of a new heresy, when, in the same
chapter, he says, that he held the same opi-

---

* Βηρυλλ۞ ο μικρω προσθεν δεδηλωμεν۞ Βοςρων της Αραϐιας επισκοπ۞, τον εκκλησιαςικον παρεκτρεπων κανονα, ξενα τινα της πιςεως παρεισφερειν επειρατο · τον σωτηρα κȝ κυριον ημων λεγειν τολμων μη προϋφεςαναι και, ιδιαν ουσιας περιγραφην, προ της εις ανθρωπους επιδημιας, μηδε μην θεοτητα ιδιαν εχειν, αλλ' εμπολιτευομενην αυτω μονην την πατρικην. Hist. lib. 6. cap. 33. p. 297.

† Εν δε τω τοτε κȝ Μαρκελλον Αγκυρας επισκοπον της Γαλατων, ως καινων δογματων εισηγητην, κȝ τον υιον τȣ θεος λεγοντα εκ Μαριας την αρχην ειληφεναι.—Εις την Παυλȣ τȣ Σαμοσατεως εξεκυλισθη δοξαν. Hist. lib. 2. cap. 33. p. 91, 92.

nion

nion with Sabellius and Paulus Samosatensis *.

Photinus is also charged with being the author of his own opinion by Socrates †; and yet he had before mentioned him as a disciple of Marcellus ‡.

As to the general testimony of Eusebius, and other writers, who were themselves believers in the pre-existence and divinity of Christ, that the primitive church was orthodox in their sense of the word, it is not, as I said, to be regarded, unless they bring some sufficient proofs of their assertion. They were, no doubt, willing to have it thought so, and, without considering it very particularly, might presume that it was so. But the facts which they them-

---

* Ηδη προτερον καινης αιρεσεως εισηγητης γενομενος.—Ως τα Σαβελλιε κ) Παυλε τε Σαμοσαλεως φρονεντα. Hist. lib. 4. cap. 6. p. 135.

† Τοτε δη κ) Φωτεινος ο της εκει εκκλησιας προεσεως, το παρευρεθεν αυτω δογμα φανερωτερον εξεθρυλλει. Hist. vol. 2. p. 123.

‡ Φωτεινος γαρ των εκει εκκλησιων προεσως, γενος της μικρας Γαλατιας, Μαρκελλε τε τε καθηρημενε μαθητης, ακολεθων τω διδασκαλω, ψιλον ανθρωπον, τον υιον εδογματισε. Hist. lib. 2. cap. 29. p. 98.

selves record, and the account which they give of the apoſtles in divulging the orthodox doctrine with ſo much caution, make it impoſſible to have been as, in general terms, they aſſert. I am even ſurprized that any perſon ſhould lay the leaſt ſtreſs on the mere aſſertion of a writer in this caſe, when it is ſo common for men to repreſent the opinions of thoſe whoſe authority they know to be great, as being the ſame with their own. Every man ſhould be heard with caution in ſuch a caſe, and what he ſays on one occaſion, ſhould be compared with what he ſays on another, and eſpecially with what he drops, as it were, accidently, and when he was off his guard.

This may certainly be ſaid in favour of the unitarians, that they did not contradict themſelves on this ſubject, but uniformly maintained, that theirs was the ancient doctrine, tranſmitted to them from the apoſtles; whereas Euſebius manifeſtly contradicts himſelf. He certainly knew that Juſtin Martyr had not only mentioned unitarians, as exiſting in his time, but had alſo treated them with much reſpect; and

to

to say nothing of his own testimony, to the apostle John having been the first who taught with clearness, and consequently with effect, the doctrine of the divinity of Christ; he himself speaks of the Ebionites as cotemporary with Cerinthus, who by his own account lived in the time of the apostle John*.

That Eusebius should take so violent a part, as he always does, against the ancient unitarians, is not difficult to be accounted for. He was himself strongly suspected of Arianism, at a time in which the Athanasian doctrine was prevalent, and though a learned man, he was not of the firmest tone of mind. In these circumstances, he would naturally make the most of such pretensions to orthodoxy as he had, and would be inclined to shew his zeal by invectives against those who were more heretical than himself. This we see illustrated every day. This was the cause why many of the reformers from popery joined with the papists, in the persecution of those who were desirous of carrying the reformation farther than them-

---

* Hist. lib. 3. cap. 27, 28, p. 121, &c.

selves,

selves. This might, in some measure, contribute to produce the zeal of the Calvinists against the Arminians, that of the Arminians against the Arians, that of the Arians against the Socinians, and that of Socinus himself against Francis David.

It may be said, that if the great majority of christians in early times were unitarians, why did they not excommunicate the innovating trinitarians. I answer, that the doctrine of the trinity, was not, in its origin, such as could give much alarm, as I have already explained; and it was not obtruded upon the common people as an article of faith necessary to their salvation, or indeed as a thing which they were at all concerned to know. And before it became very formidable, there was a great majority of the learned and philosophizing clergy on its side. However, that it did give very great alarm, as it began to unfold itself, I have produced the most undeniable evidence.

CHAPTER XVI.

Of the State of the Unitarian Doctrine after the Council of Nice.

THAT the unitarians constituted the great body of christians till the time of Justin Martyr, and that they were the majority at least of the common people till about the time of the council of Nice, has, I presume, been proved to as much satisfaction as the circumstances of the case could be expected to admit. There is every reason to believe that it was so *a priori*, a great number of circumstances, applied by the clearest axioms of historical criticism, shew that it *must* have been so. And there is likewise the strongest *positive testimony* to the fact, from some of the most considerable christian writers. The unitarians were the *major pars credentium*, in the

the time of Tertullian, they were the το πληθος, *the multitude*, and the τα πληθη, *the multitudes* of Origen, and the οι πολλοι, *the many* of Athanasius.

According to Eutychius, who is said to have compiled his annals from the archives of the church of Alexandria, there must have been more unitarian bishops than the Greek historians give us any account of. He says, that "there were two thousand and forty "eight bishops assembled at the council "of Nice, some of whom were Sabellians, "who believed that Christ had no being "before he was born of the virgin; others "saying that God was one substance called "by three names, but not believing in the "word, or the Holy Spirit, which," he says, " was the opinion of Paulus Samosa- "tensis; and that Constantine having heard "their opinions, but approving of that of "three hundred and eighteen, who held "the same doctrine, he appointed them to "meet in a large room, and gave them "power to make decrees." The same account Selden, the publisher of Eutychius,

chius, found in an Arabian and christian writer, named Joseph, and also in a celebrated Mahometan historian, Ismael Ebn Ali.

This account, though seemingly very different from that of the other ecclesiastical historians, Beausobre thinks may be reconciled with it, if it be supposed that the bishops of villages, presbyters, and those who were deemed heretical, were not allowed to have a seat with the rest *. Wormius, he observes, says that no sectary was allowed to give his opinion in that council †.

* Histoire de Manicheisme, vol. 1. p. 531.

† Mittens ergo Constantinus rex in omnes passim regiones patriarchas et episcopos convocavit, adeo ut post annum et duos menses, Niceæ convenirent bis mille quadraginta octo episcopi, sententiis et religionibus inter se discrepantes.——Erant qui dicerent christum a patre esse, instar flammæ ignis quæ ab igne flammante dependeret, nec priorem diminuere posterioris ab ipso derivationem. Erat que hæc Sabellii et assectarum ipsius sententia.——Alii christum hominem fuisse a divinitate creatum ejusdem cum nostrum aliquo substantiæ, filiique principium a Maria fuisse, ipsumque electum qui substantiæ humanæ liberator esset, comitante ipsum gratia divina, et in ipso

per

That the unitarians were exceedingly numerous in the time of Athanasius, or not long before it, especially in Africa, is evident from his complaints on the subject. He says that " in Pentapolis of Upper Lybia,

per amorem et voluntatem habitante, ideoque appellatum fuisse filium dei. Dicentes etiam deum substantiam unam esse, et personam unam quæ tribus nominibus appellatur, nec in verbum, nec in spiritum sanctum credentes: erat hæc sententia Pauli Samosateni patriarchæ Antiochæni, ejusque sectatorum qui Pauliciani audiunt.—Alii (denique) asseruerunt divinitatem Christi; quæ Pauli apostoli sententia est, nec non episcoporum trecentorum et octodecim. auditis ipsorum sententiis miratus est Constantinus rex hanc discrepantiam, domoque ipsis seposita in qua loca ipsis paravit, disputationes ipsos habere jussit, ut perspecto apud quem vera esset fides, ipsum sequeretur. Illi ergo tercentum et octodecim in unam fidem, unamque sententiam consenserunt, cumque reliquis qui litem ipsis moverunt disputantes, illis argumentis suis superiores evaserunt fidemque veram declararunt: reliqui autem episcopi sententiis et religionibus inter se diversi fuerunt: Rex ergo trecentis et octodecim episcopis istis loco quodam proprio et amplo parato, ipse in eorum medio consedit, acceptaque, annulum, gladium et sceptrum suum ipsis tradidit, dicens ipsis, vobis hodie in imperium meum potestatem concessi, ut in eo faciatis quicquid facere vobis expedit eorum quæ ad religionem rite stabiliendam et fidelium commodum spectant. Selden's Eutychius, p. 439, 440. 443, 444.

"some of the bishops embraced the doc-
"trine of Sabellius, and prevailed so much,
"that the Son of God was hardly preached
"in the churches *."

SECTION I.

Of the State of the Unitarians from the Time of the Council of Nice, to the Sixth Century.

I NOW proceed to mention the traces I have found of unitarians after the council of Nice. And notwithstanding their numbers certainly kept decreasing, owing to the prevalence of the trinitarian and Arian doctrines, each in their turns favoured by the civil powers (which it is remarkable, the unitarian doctrine never was in any age or country) it appears from circumstances, that the unitarians were in considerable numbers, some holding separate assemblies, but

* Εν Πενταπολει της ανω Διβυης τηνικαυτα τινες των επισκοπων εφρονησαν τα Σαβελλιε· κ̓ τοσετον ισχυσαν ταις επινοιαις, ως ολιγε δειν μηκετι εν ταις εκκλησιαις κηρυτ[τ]εσθαι τον υιον τε θευ. De Sententia Dionysii, Opera, vol. I. p. 552.

many

many more concealed in the great body of christians, and joining their public worship.

It is highly probable that, even long after the doctrine of the divinity of Christ was established by councils, and the decrees of emperors, many of the common people were well known to believe nothing of the matter; and yet, if they made no disturbance, and did not think proper to separate themselves from the communion of the orthodox bishops, who were not authorized to propose any test to them, they were not excommunicated. In fact, they were considered by the more learned as simple ignorant people, who acquiesced in the doctrine of the humanity of Christ, because they were incapable of comprehending that of his divinity, and the sublime doctrine of *three persons in one God*. This circumstance, together with there being no distinguished writers among them, and also their being mixed and confounded with other sects, accounts for our hearing so little of them.

Many of the Montanists, besides Praxeas, against whom Tertullian wrote, were probably unitarians. Jerom represents the

Montanists in general, as " differing from " the orthodox in the rule of faith, and " agreeing with the Sabellians *."

Sandius says, that Noetus was said by some to have been the disciple of the Montanists †. According to Socrates, Eusebius said that they who disliked the term *consubstantial* at the council of Nice, charged their adversaries with favouring the sentiments of Sabellius and Montanus ‡."

Nicephorus observes, that " Some Mon- " tanists were Sabellians." He also expresly says, that " they denied the per- " sonal existence of the Son, and that he " was consubstantial with the Father ‖."

---

* Primum in fidei regula discrepamus. Nos patrem, et filium, et spiritum sanctum in sua unumquemque persona ponimus, licet substantia copulemus: illi, Sabellii dogma sectantes, trinitatem in unius personæ angustias cogunt. Ad Marcellum, Opera, vol. I. p. 414.

† Hist. p. 97.

‡ Οι μεν γαρ τε ομοεσιε την λεξιν εκκλινοντες την Σαβελλιε κỳ Μοντανε δοξαν εισηγεισθαι αυτην τες προσδεχομενες ενομιζον · κỳ δια τετο τες βλασφημες, εκαλεν, ως αναιρεντας την υπαρξιν τε υιε το Θεε · οι δε παλιν τω ομοεσιω προσκειμενοι πολυθειαν εισαγειν τες ετερες νομιζοντες, ως ελληνισμον εισαγοντας, εξετρεποντο. Hist. lib. I. cap. 23. p. 57.

‖ Οι μεν γαρ το ομοεσιον μη προσιεμενοι, δοξαν εσχον τα Μοντανε κỳ Σαβελλιε φρονειν", τες αυτο παραδεχομενες · κỳ βλασφημες ελαλων

Zonaras also says, that " Montanus, besides
" maintaining that himself was the para-
" clete, confounded the whole trinity, con-
" tracting it into one person *." Lastly,
Harmenopulus, in his account of sects, says
expressly, that the disciples of Montanus
reduced the holy trinity to one person †.

Upon the whole, therefore, though Tertullian was a Montanist, and no unitarian, it may be concluded, that the prevailing sentiments of those who went by that name were unitarian. Sabellius himself is said by Nicephorus, to have learned his doctrine from some of the Montanists ‡. According to the author of the Appendix to to Tertullian's Treatise De Præscriptione, they were only those Montanists who fol-

---

ελαλων ως την τυ υιυ υπαρξιν αναιρετοιίας. Hist. lib. 8. cap. 45. p. 637.

* Και εις εν προσωπον την αγιαν τριαδα συνηρεν κ̀ συνεχεον. Canones, p. 78.

† Οι περι τον Μονλανον —— εις εν προσωπον την αγιαν συναιρενλες τριαδα κ̀ το πασχα διεςρεφον. Harmenopulus de Sectis.

‡ Τινες δε των εξ αυλα, ες υςερον τας τρεις της θεολητος υποςασεις εν ειναι εδοξασαν · τον αυλον λεγονλες ειναι κ̀ παλερα κ̀ υιον κ̀ αγιον πνευμα · εξ ων φασι και τον Λιβυν Σαβελλιον, τας της αιρεσεως αρχας εκπορισασθαι. Hist. vol. 1. p. 319.

lowed Æschines, who were unitarians, while those who followed Proclus were not so*.

The Donatists, also, who did not separate from the church on this subject, are yet said to have been afterwards heretical with respect to the trinity †.

Jerom says, that Donatus himself wrote a book concerning the Holy Spirit agreeable to the Arian doctrine ‡, which in this respect was the same as the unitarian. Austin also says, that he did not hold the catholic doctrine of the trinity, but that he was not generally followed by those who bore his name. Theodoret says, that the Donatists agree with the Arians ||. The probability

---

* Sunt etiam qui κατα Proclum dicuntur. Sunt qui secundum Æschinem pronunciantur——Privatam autem blasphemiam illi qui sunt κατα Æschinem hanc habent, qua adjiciunt etiam hoc, ut dicant Christum ipsum esse filium et patrem. Sect. 52. p. 223.

† Cur autem solis Donatistis, qui a schismate profluerunt in hæresim, ut postea etiam de baptismate et divina trinitate male sentirent. Facundus contra Mocianum, p. 199.

‡ Extant ejus multa ad suam hæresim pertinentia et de spiritu sancto liber, Ariano dogmati congruens. Catalogus Scriptorum, Opera, vol. 1. p. 311.

|| Ουτοι δε κατα μεν την αιρεσιν τοις Αρειε συμφερουται. Lib. 4. cap. 6. Opera, Ed. Halæ, vol. 4. p. 360.

is, that both Montanus and Donatus, living at a time when the unitarian doctrine was generally received, held it themselves; though their followers, influenced by the same causes that affected other christians, gradually adopted the philosophical opinions.

That the Pelagians should be heretical, with respect to the doctrine of the trinity, will not be wondered at (though Pelagius himself is said to have been orthodox in that respect) as the unitarians of all ages have adopted the sentiments of Pelagius with respect to human nature. Cassian, who met with them in Gaul, evidently considered them in this light. For he censures them as holding that " Christ was a mere man; " and saying that men may live sinless lives, " because Christ, who was a man, did so. " They say, that Jesus became Christ after " his baptism, and God after his resurrec- " tion; the one arising from his unction, " the other from the merit of his passion*."

* Addiderunt quoque dominum, salvatoremque nostrum post baptisma factum esse Christum, post resurrectionem deum: alterum adsignantes unctionem mysterio, alterum

"Otherwife," he fays, "we come to the Pelagian herefy, and fay that God dwelled in Chrift from a certain time, and came into him, when, by his life and converfation, he deferved that the power of the divinity fhould dwell in him *."

Admitting this to be true to any confiderable extent, it will not be doubted, but that the unitarians muft have been very numerous, becaufe the Pelagians were fo. Perhaps the Pelagians, defcribed by Caffian, might be inclined to the opinion of Neftorius. But this, as I fhall fhew, did not differ from unitarianifm with refpect to the perfon of Chrift.

---

terum merito paffionis: unde advertit novus nunc jam, non novæ hærefeos autor, qui dominum falvatoremque noftrum folitarium hominem natum effe contendit, idem fe omnino dicere quod Pelagianiftæ ante dixerunt ; et confequens errori fuo effe, ut qui utique fine peccato folitarium hominem Jefum Chriftum vixiffe afferit, omnes quoque per fe homnines fine peccato poffe effe blafphemet. De Incarnatione, lib. 1. cap. 3. p. 966. See alfo p. 1017, 1018, 1066.

* Alioquin ad illam Pelagianæ hærefeos impietatem devolvimur: ut dicamus ex certo tempore habitantem in Chrifto deum ; tum in eum fuperveniffe, quando ille vita et converfatione id promeruerit, ut in fe virtus divinitatis habitaret. Hær. lib. 5. cap. 4. p. 1022.

Marius

Marius Mercator says, that Julianus, a Pelagian, adopted the opinion of Theodorus, the master of Nestorius *.

The *simplicity* of the unitarians is a circumstance by which they are generally noted; and by this they were likewise concealed, as giving no umbrage to any. But it does not follow, that because they were styled *simple*, they were persons of low understanding. Tertullian, who gave them that epithet, in answer to the Gnostics, who likewise applied it to the orthodox christians, says, " we are reckoned simple by " them, but we are not therefore sense- " less †." In a treatise ascribed to Athanasius, the more simple are represented as easily taken with the assertion, that God the

---

* Simul admonere volens Julianum exepiscopum oppidi Eclanensis, hæreticum Pelagianum seu cælestianum, hunc secutum esse Theodorum. Opera, p. 40.

† Ideoque simplices notamur apud illos, ut hoc tantum, non etiam sapientes: quasi statim deficere cogatur a simplicitate sapientia, domino utramque jungente: Estote prudentes ut serpentes et simplices ut columbæ. Aut si nos propterea insipientes quia simplices. Adv. Valent. sect. 2. Opera, p. 250.

logos

logos suffered in the flesh*. Basil represents "simplicity of faith as a bait with "which the ignorant are drawn to their de- "struction †." Writing on the subject of the Holy Spirit, he begs that what he wrote "might be concealed from the vulgar, lest "it should be throwing pearls before "swine ‡." Gregory Nazianzen also must have felt himself in the same situation, when he said, "Have we not suffered from the "mad populace §."

The doctrine of the trinity being considered as a sublime doctrine, the common people, who could not comprehend, or relish it, but who at the same time made no disturbance in the church, would naturally

---

* Αλλα ει τι ξενον επινοειν προς απατην των απλυστερων νεωτευονται, οιον η το προκειμενον νυν εις εξετασιν, Επαθεν ο θεος λογος Σαρκι. Opera, vol. 2. p. 311.

† Τϋτο δε παντι γνωριμον, οτι ωσπερ αγκιστρω προς θανατον ελκοντι, τω εαυτϋ φρονηματι το απλϋν της επιστεως, οιον τι δελεαρ, περιβαλλει, ινα τω φαινομενω επιδραμοντες οι απειροτεροι, αφυλακτως τω κακω της ασεβειας περιπαρωσιν. Ad Eunom. lib. 1. Opera, vol. 1. p. 701.

‡ Ουχ ως αξια κατακρυπτεσθαι, αλλ' ωστε μη ριπτεσθαι τοις χοιροις τϋς μαργαριτας. De Sp. S. cap. 30. Opera, vol. 2. p. 366.

§ Ουκ πεπαϋμεν ϋπνον μαινομενων. Or. 32. p. 525.

be

be pitied and overlooked. Athanasius, considering the violence of his character, speaks of the unitarians with a good deal of tenderness, on account of the difficulty of understanding the doctrine of the trinity. I have quoted a passage from him, in which he represents them as (οι πολλοι) *the many*, and persons of a *low understanding*, but by no means as persons out of the church. Contrasting them with the Gnostics and the Arians, he says, " some persons considering
" what is human in Christ, seeing him
" thirsting, labouring, and suffering, and
" degrading him to a mere man, sin indeed
" greatly ; but they may readily obtain for-
" giveness if they repent, alledging the
" weakness of the flesh ; and they have the
" apostle himself administering pardon to
" them, and as it were holding out his hand
" to them, while he says, *Truly great is the*
" *mystery of godliness, God was manifest in the*
" *flesh* *."

* Οταν τινες, εις τα ανθρωπινα βλεποντες, ιδωσι τον κυριον διψωντα, η κοπιωντα, η πασχοντα, ᾗ μονον φλυαρησωσιν ως και ανθρωπε τε σωτηρ⁘, ἁμαρτανεσι μεν μεγαλως. δυναντι δε ομως ταχεως μετεγινωσκοντες λαμβανειν συγγνωμην, εχοντες προφασιν την τε σωματ⁘ ασθενειαν :

According to him many persons within the pale of the church, must either have been unitarians, or have believed the doctrine of the trinity without understanding it, which, in fact, is no belief at all. For, being consulted what was to be done with respect to the spread of the doctrine of Paulus Samosatensis; after acknowledging that persons of low understanding were chiefly infected with it, and quoting what Paul says of *the great mystery of Godliness, God manifest in the flesh*, he says, "those who understand the "subject accurately are few, but all pious "persons may hold the faith delivered to "them *." But what kind of *holding* must it be, when they had no perfect understanding of what they held.

Gregory Nazianzen also represents the common people as excusable for their errors,

---

νειαν· εχυσι γαρ κ̀ αποϛολον συγγνωμην αυτοις νεμοντα, κ̀ οιονει χειρα αυτοις εν τω λεγειν εκλεινοντα, οτι και ομολογυμενως μεγα εϛι το της ευσεβειας μυϛηριον, Θεὸς εφανερωθη εν σαρκι. In illud Evangelii Quicunque dixerit, &c. Opera, vol. 1. p. 975.

* Οτι την μεν ακριβειαν αυτης επιζητειν ολιγων εϛι, την δε πιϛιν κατεχειν απαντων των προς τον Θεον ευπειθων. De Incarnatione contra P. Samosat. Opera, vol. 1. p. 592.

and safe from not being disposed to scrutinize into things *.

Unitarians, however, were far from being all of the common people, and unlearned. There were several considerable writers among them. "Beryllus of Bostra," Nicephorus says, "left elegant writings be-"hind him †." Marcellus and Photinus distinguished themselves as writers, and Gregory Nazianzen says, that the heretics boasted of the number of their books ‡. Unhappily there are none of them now extant.

After the establishment of orthodoxy by Constantine, "all the sects," says Eusebius, "were forbidden to hold separate assem-"blies;" and among the rest the unita-

---

* Τοις μεν γαρ τε λαε ταχα αν και συγγινωσκοιμεν τελο πασχυ-σιν. ες σωζει, πολλακις το αβασανιστον. Oratio 21. Opera, p. 388.

† Εν οις ο, τε της κατα Βοςραν αραβων ην Βερυλλος, φιλοκαλε σποεδης συγγραμματα καταλειψας. Hist. lib. 5. cap. 15. vol. 1. p. 363.

‡ Και τω πληθει των βιβλιων φιλοτιμεμενοι. επειδη δε τω περι τριαδος φυσιωμενοι λογω, καταψευδονται μεν ημων, ως ες υγιως εχοντων περι την πιστιν, δελεαζεσι δε τες πολλες. Or. 50. p. 744.

rians,

rians, called Paulians, are mentioned*. But this did not make them change their opinions. For he says that, after Constantine's edict against heresy, some, terrified with the emperor's threats, came into the church, dissembling on account of the times. " For, the law forbidding the " publication of their books, some who " were taken acting contrary to the law, " on that account, consulted their safety " by every dissimulation †."

This accounts for the great number of unitarians that Facundus mentions, as being *in the church,* in the time of Theodosius. Their opinions must have been well known, or he could not have been acquainted with

---

* Επιγνωτε νυν δια της νομοθεσιας ταυτης ω Ναυατιανοι, Ουαλεντινοι, Μαρκιωνισαι, Παυλιανοι, οι κατα τας Φρυγας επικεκλημενοι, και πανlες απλως οι τας αιρεσεις δια των οικειων πληρυνlες συςημαlων— επειδη τον ολεθρον τυτον της υμετερας εξωλειας επι πλειον φερειν ουκ εςιν οσιον τε δια τε νομη τυτα προαγορευομεν, μηlις υμων συναγειν τε λοπυ τολμηση. De Vita Const. lib. 3. cap. 64. p. 621.

† Οι μεν νοθω φρονηματι, βασιλικης απειλης φοβω, την εκκλησιαν υπεδυονlο, τον καιρον καleιρωνευομενοι. επει δε και διερευνασθαι των ανδρων τας βιβλας διηγορευεν ο νομος · ηλισκονlο τοlε απειρημεναις οι κακοlεχνιας μεlιονlες · ου δη χαριν, πανl επρατlον, ειρωνεια την ζωlηριαν ποριζομενοι. Ibid. p. 622.

them;

them; but they were not molested, while they did not molest others, and wished only to be quiet.

As the passage in his writings, from which I infer this, is a pretty remarkable one, I shall cite it at full length. Speaking of the condemnation of Theodorus (the master of Nestorius, whose system differed very little from that of unitarianism) in whose favour he is writing, he says, that " in condemning him, they condemned all " those who thought as he did, even though " they afterwards changed their opinion. " —What will they do with Martha, and " then with Mary, the sisters of Lazarus, " who were particularly attached to our " Lord, while he was upon earth. And yet " both of them, first Martha, and then Mary, " are said to have spoken to him thus, *Lord,* " *if thou hadst been here, my brother had not* " *died*; who, though they thought that he " was the Son of God, who was to come " into the world, yet could they not have " said, *if thou hadst been here*, if they had " believed him to be God omnipresent. " They therefore only thought as Theo-
" dorus

"dorus is said to have done, and were
"excommunicated along with him. And
"how many of this kind do we know, by
"the writings of the apostles and evange-
"lists, there were at that time; and how
"many even now are there still, in the
"common herd of the faithful, who by
"only partaking in the holy mysteries,
"and by a simple observance of the com-
"mandments, we see pleasing God; when
"even the apostles themselves, the first
"teachers, only thought as those whom we
"see to be included in this condemnation
"of Theodorus *."

* Condemnaverunt omnes ab ipso in quem illum incidisse putant errore conversos.—Ubi quid agent de Martha et Maria, sororibus Lazari, quæ familiari devotione ipsi domino dum hic in carne degerit adhæserunt. Et tamen utraque, id est, prius Martha, ac deinde Maria, legitur illi dixisse, domine si fuisses hic frater meus non fuisset mortuus. Quæ licet crederent quod ipse esset filius dei qui in mundum venisset, tamen non dicerent *si fuisses hic*, si eum cognoscerent sicut deum, ubique esse presentem. Eadem ergo sapuerunt quæ dicitur sapuisse Theodorus, et cum Theodoro simul anathematisatæ sunt. Et quantos vel eo tempore in evangeliis et apostolicis scriptis tales fuisse cognovimus? Quantos etiam nunc tales in grege fidelium, sola sanctorum mysteriorum partic'pitione, et simplici
præceptorum

If this was the case in the time of Theodosius, there can be no doubt of its having been so in the time of Constantine, and that it continued to be so long afterwards. The candour of Facundus towards these simple unitarians is remarkable, and is well illustrated by his account of the state of the christian faith in the time of the apostles. Speaking of those who believed Christ to be a mere man, he says, " The apostles
" themselves were once imperfect in the
" faith, but never heretics. For while
" they believed too little concerning Christ,
" they received power to cast out unclean
" spirits, and to cure diseases, when our
" Lord sent them, and gave them a com-
" mission. If, therefore, the apostles, in
" the very time of their ignorance, were
" not heretics, how can any one call these
" so who died such," &c.*? He says,

præceptorum obedientia, placentes deo vidimus; cum et ipsi primi pastores ejus apostoli sic aliquando sapuerunt, quos omnes cum Theodoro vidimus in hoc anathemate condemnatos. Pro Defensione trium Capitulorum, lib. 10. cap. 7. p. 162.

* Cum ipsi apostoli aliquando fuerint in fide imperfecti, nunquam tamen hæretici. Cumque adhuc parum de Christo

"the woman who touched Christ's gar-
"ment did not take him to be God *."

This testimony of Facundus may teach us, that we are not to take it for granted, that the unitarians were extinct at any particular time, merely because they are by some writers *said* to be so. Epiphanius says, that " the heresy of Artemon was " extinct, when it was revived by Paulus " Samosatensis †." But it could only be that there were few, or none, who went publicly by that name The οι πολλοι, *the many* of Athanasius were, no doubt, unitarians, though they might not be call-

---

Christo crederent, magnam potestatem acceperunt spirituum immundorum, ut ejicerent eos, et curarent omnem languorem et omnem infirmitatem, mittente eos domino, atque mandante, euntes prædicate, dicentes, quia adpropinquavit regnum cœlorum. Infirmos curate, mortuos suscitate, leprosos mundate, dæmones ejicite, gratis accepistis, gratis date. Si vero apostoli nec in ipso ignorantiæ suæ tempore fuerunt hæretici, qua ratione quisquam eos qui tales de hac vita transierunt, affirmare possint hæreticos? Lib. 12. p. 184.

* Ibid. p. 183.

† Αρθεις δε τη διανοια, εξεπεσε της αληθειας, και ανεκαινισε την αιρεσιν τε Αρτεμονθ, τε ποτε οντος εν αρχη προ ετων πολλων και εσ-θεσμεις. Hær. 65. Opera, vol. 1. p. 608.

ed *Artemonites*. On the other hand, we are not to give to particular perfons who diftinguifhed themfelves in the defence of the unitarian doctrine, all the *converts* they are faid to have made. They, no doubt, *found* them unitarians, though they might be more encouraged by thofe leaders to declare themfelves more openly. But we fhall find, that when all their great leaders were gone, they did not want boldnefs in afferting their principles, which is a proof that they did not want numbers.

The number of followers that hiftorians give to Marcellus of Ancyra, the capital of Galatia, and alfo to his difciple Photinus, bifhop of Sirmium, in Pannonia, is prodigious; and the effects of their labours are faid to have remained a long time. The former, though living in troublefome times, and probably being induced to make fome improper compliances, is, notwithftanding, noted for the courage with which he, for fome time at leaft, maintained his opinions. That he was not eafily overborne by authority, Eufebius, his antagonift, teftifies, when he fays, that " he made no ac-

"count of the Fathers of the church*." Alluding to the preaching and writings of of Marcellus, Hilary says, " Galatia has "brought up many to the profession of "one God; and," alluding to Photinus, "Pannonia wickedly maintains that Jesus "Christ was born of Mary," i. e. that he did not exist before his birth †. This writer complains heavily of the distressed situation of the truth among so many heresies, and more than intimates, that the followers of Photinus, though often condemned, were not sufficiently separated from the church. The mischief, he says, was *within* ‡.

* Ομε τε παντας τες Εκκλησιαστικες πατερας αθετει. Contra Marcellum, lib. 1. p. 19.

† Impie multos ad unius dei professionem Galatia nutrivit—Pestifere natum Jesum Christum ex Maria Pannonia defendit. Lib. 7. p. 131.

‡ Nihil solicitudini meæ, nihil conscientiæ vacat. Sub specula enim omnium hæreticorum ad occasiones singulorum verborum in os meum pendentium loquor, et omnis, sermonis mei iter aut angustiis præruptum, aut foveis incisum, aut laqueis prætensum est. Jam quod arduum aut difficile sit minus conqueror; non meis enim, sed apostolicis scando gradibus. Mihi vero aut in angustias decidere, aut in defossa incidere, aut plagis illaqueari, semper in periculo,

Photinus, though violently opposed by the Arian emperor Constantius (Hilarius Contra Constantium, p. 332) was remarkably popular in his see, and elsewhere; for an account of which see Sozomen, lib. 4. cap. 6. p. 135; and " though excommuni-" cated and condemned, he could not be re-" moved," says Hilary, " on account of the " affection that the people had for him*," as his language ought to be interpreted. And it is particularly remarkable, that though Photinus was so obnoxious to the

riculo, semper in metu est. Prædicaturo enim, secundum legem, et prophetas, et apostolos, unum deum, adest mihi Sabellius, totum me sub verbi hujus professione, tanquam desideratum cibum, morsu sævissimo transvorans. Negantem me rursum, contra Sabellium, unum deum, et confitentem verum deum dei filium, expectat nova hæresis, et a me duos deos arguat prædicari. Natum quoque dei filium ex Maria, dicturo, Hebion, qui et Photinus assistit; auctoritatem mendacii sui, ex professione veritatis, sumpturus. De cæteris taceo, qui ab omnibus extra ecclesiam esse non ignorantur. Hoc vero damnatum, et abjectum licet frequentur, sed internum hodie adhuc malum est. Lib. 7. p. 131.

* Fotinus hæreticus comprehensus, olim reus pronunciatus, et a communione jampridem unitatis abscissus, nec tum quidem per factionem populi potuit admoveri. Fragmenta, p. 444.

orthodox

orthodox, on account of his principles, his moral character was never impeached. A high encomium on him may be seen in Philaster *. And when he was expelled from his see by the arm of power, he enjoyed an honourable retirement, and employed himself in writing books, in which, besides promoting the cause of christianity in general, he boldly maintained his peculiar opinions. " Photinus," says Jerom, " endeavoured to revive the heresy of the " Ebionites, and wrote many volumes, the " chief of which are against the heathens, " and the books to Valentinian †." Socrates says, that " he wrote against all here-

---

* Nam erat et ingenii viribus valens, et doctrinæ opibus excellens, et eloquio præpotens: quippe qui utroque sermone copiose, et graviter disputaret et scriberet: ut monumentis librorum suorum manifestatur, quos idem partim Græco, partim Latino sermone composuit, Cap. 16. Bib. Pat. vol. 5. p. 71.

† Photinus de Gallogræcia, Marcelli discipulus, Sirmii episcopus ordinatus, Hebionis hæresim instaurare conatus est: postea, a Valentiniano principe pulsus ecclesia, plura scripsit volumina, in quibus vel præcipui sunt, contra gentes, et ad Valentinianum libri. Catalogus, Opera, vol. 1. p. 316.

" sies,

"fies, propofing only his own opinion *."
" Though banifhed," fays Sozomen, " he
" continued to defend his opinion, and
" wrote books in the Greek and Latin
" tongues, in which he endeavoured to
" fhew that all opinions were falfe except
" his own †." That he continued ftrenuoufly to maintain his opinions, notwithftanding his perfecution and banifhment, is evident from all the accounts we have had of him. Nicephorus fays, that " what
" Photinus laboured in all his writings
" was, that all opinions befides his own
" were nothing ‡."

Of all the theological works of the ancients, I own that I regret moft of all the lofs of thofe of Photinus, and especially his *treatife againft herefies*. An impartial ac-

* Εγραφε δε κατα πασων αιρεσεων, το οικειον μονον δογμα παρατιθεμενος. Lib. 2. cap. 30. p. 129.

† Φωτεινος δε φευγειν καταδικασθεις, ȣδε ȣτως επαυσατο το οικειον συγκροτων δογμα· λογȣς τε τη Ρωμαιων και Ελληνων φωνη συγγραφων εξεδιδȣ, δι ων επειρατο, πλην της αυτȣ, τας των αλλων δοξας ψευδεις αποφαινειν. Lib 4. cap. 6. p. 137.

‡ Ο δ' εσπȣδαζετο ταις γραφαις ην, πλην της οικειας, τας των αλλων δοξας μηδεν ȣσας απρεπως εξελεγχειν. Lib. 9. cap. 31. p. 755.

account of his conference with Baſil of Ancyra, would be exceedingly valuable. A few things that are quoted from him I ſhall produce in my account of the arguments uſed by the ancient unitarians in defence of their principles. That his writings were not thought meanly of by his adverſaries, appears by their frequent notice of them, and the anſwers that were written to them long after his death. Among others, Vigilius Martyr, about the year 500, wrote againſt Photinus, as well as Sabellius and Arius *.

Both Photinus and Marcellus were obnoxious to the Arians, but Marcellus more particularly, perhaps, for not having approved of the conduct of the Arians with reſpect to Athanaſius, who always ſhewed a kindneſs for him †.

There are ſeveral traces of there being great numbers of unitarians in the time of Auſtin.

* Bib. Pat. vol. 5. p. 546.
† Athanaſii, Opera, vol. 1. p. 813. Nicephori, Hiſt. lib. 8. cap. 53. vol. 1. p. 663.

There

There appears to have been Photinians who even held open assemblies at Sirmium, contrary to a law of the emperor Gratian, A. D. 381; when the bishops the council of Aquileia petitioned the emperors to take farther measures with respect to them *." The words *invisible* and *impassible*, Ruffinus says, were added to the creed in the church of Aquileia, on account of the Sabellian, or patripassian heresy, though they were not in the creed at Rome †. Jerom speaks of Ancyra, the capital of Galatia, as sorely over-run with various heresies in his time ‡; and yet,

* Photinianos quoque quos et superiori lege censuistis, nullos facere debere conventus, profit jam et sacerdotum concilio sententia in eos lata est. Petimus insuper, ut quoniam in Syrmiensi oppido adhuc conventus tentare eos cognovimus, clementia vestra, interdicta hac ejus coitione, reverentiam primum ecclesiæ catholicæ, deinde etiam legibus vestris deferre jubeat. Ambrosii, Opera, vol. 5. p. 167.

† His additur invisibilem et impassibilem. Sciendum quod duo isti sermones in ecclesiæ Romanæ symbolo non habentur, constat autem apud nos additos, hæreseos causa Sabellii illius profecto, quæ nostris patripassiana appellatur. In Symbol, p. 173.

‡ Scit mecum qui vidit Ancyram metropolim Galatiæ, civitatem, quod nunc usque scismatibus dilacerata sit.

quod

Ambrose, his cotemporary, speaks of the heresies of Photinus, Arius, and Sabellius, as being extinct, but says that, that of the Manicheans prevailed*. But as it is well known that the heresy of Arius was far from being extinct at that time, so it is no less evident that that of Photinus had many adherents.

Sabellianism was one of the *five heresies*, as he calls them, against which Austin thought it more particularly necessary to write. The other four were those of the Pagans, the Jews, the Manicheans, and the Arians †. It is also to the unitarians that he refers in the following passage, " Let " us not," says he, " hear those who say " there is only the Father, and that he has " no son, nor that there is a Holy Spirit, " but that the Father himself is sometimes " called the Son, and sometimes the Holy

quod dogmatum varietatibus constuprata. In Gal. cap. 2, Opera, vol. 6. p. 134.

* Postea quam Photinus obmutuit, Arius conticuit, Sabellius vocem perdidit, adhuc tamen hæreses diversa contra ecclesiam exerentes ora conspicio. Apologia, David cap. 4. p. 508.

† De Quinque Hæresibus, Opera, vol. 6. p. 35.

" Spirit."

" Spirit *." Lardner says, that the frequent notice which Austin takes of the Sabellians, in his tracts and sermons to the people, is an argument that in his time there was some considerable number of persons who maintained his opinion †. Paulinus of the same age, speaks of heretics in his time, who said, that " Christ was " God by adoption," from which he infers, that " they must think him to be a " mere man ‡."

If we look towards the east, where Basil and the two Gregories were then flourishing, we shall find still louder complaints of the prevalence of heresy, and especially that of the unitarians. For it is to be observed that, as it was some time before the

* Nec eos audiamus qui dicunt patrem tantummodo esse, nec habere filium, nec esse cum eo spiritum sanctum: sed ipsum patrem aliquando appellari filium, aliquando spiritum sanctum. De Agen. Christ. cap. 13. Opera, vol. 3. p. 268.

† Credibility, vol. 4. p. 606.

‡ Aut certe purum eum hominem sine deo natum (quod cogitare impium est) necesse est fateantur, ac per hoc quasi eguerit adoptione a patre in filium sit adoptatus. Adv. Felicem, Bib. Pat. vol. 5. p. 435.

gospel

gospel was propagated with success in the western parts of the Roman empire, not till the doctrine of the divinity of Christ had made considerable progress, the christianity of those parts was always what was called more *orthodox* than that of the east, where the gospel was first preached, and consequently, where the prejudices of christians in favour of the old unitarian doctrine were stronger than in other places.

Cyril of Jerusalem complains of heretics, both Arians and unitarians, as in the bosom of the church. "Now," says he, "there is an apostacy; for men have departed from the right faith, some confounding the Son with the Father," meaning the unitarians, "others daring to say that Christ was created out of nothing," meaning the Arians. "Formerly heretics were open, but now the church is full of concealed heretics *."

---

* Νυν δε εςιν αποςασια: απεςησαν γαρ οι ανθρωποι της ορθης πιςεως. και οι μεν υιοπατοριαν καταγγελλουσιν, οι δε τον χριςον εξ ουκ οντων εις το ειναι παρενεχθεντα λεγειν τολμωσιν. και προτερον μεν ησαν φανεροι αιρετικοι, νυν δε πεπληρωται η εκκλησια κεκρυμμενων αιρετικων. Cyrilli, Catech. 15. p. 209. See also p. 5.

Complaints

Complaints of the spread of heresy, both that of the unitarians, and that of the Arians, by Basil himself, and his cotempories, are particularly loud and incessant. The opinions he most complains of were such as were held by the common people, though many of the clergy were also infected; and what is remarkable, the malecontents complained loudly of Basil's *innovations*, both with respect to doctrines, and practices. For some time Basil, though surnamed the *Great*, was obliged to give way to the storm, and to retire from his diocese; and yet, this it seems was a dangerous step. For according to him, the most unremitted assiduity was necessary to guard their flocks from seduction. " If " any person," says he, " leave his diocese " for the shortest time, he leaves the com- " mon people exposed *."

To give my readers a clear idea of Basil's situation, I shall select from his writings a few passages, which will give us a suffi-

† Ει γαρ τις και προς το βραχυτατον της εκκλησιας αυτα αποστη εκδοτας αφησει τας λαας τοις εφεδρευσσι. Basilii Epist. lxx. Opera, vol. 3. p. 114.

cient infight into it; and the cafe appears to have been the fame through the whole of Afia Minor, but more efpecially in Galatia, which had been the diocefe of Marcellus. "Groan with us," fays Bafil, "the only "begotten is blafphemed, and there is no "one to contradict it *." Gregory Nazianzen reprefents him as abfolutely banifhed for holding opinions different from thofe of his people †.

The difficulties of Bafil were occafioned both by the Arians, and the unitarians, but chiefly the latter; though they both agreed in decrying the novel doctrine of the divinity of the Holy Spirit, which was the great topic of controverfy, as has been already feen, at that particular time. All the following paffages fhew that his ftrongeft apprehenfions were from the unitarians, the difciples of Sabellius, Marcellus, and Paulus Samofatenfis. "We are torn in "pieces," he fays, "on one fide by the

---

* Στεναξαῖε εφ ημιν ὁτι ὁ μονογενης βλασφημεῖται, και ὁ αντιλεγων ουκ εστι. Epift. 70. Opera, vol. 3. p. 114.

† Ος γε και εξοριαν υπερ της αληθειας καῖακριθεις. Or. 20. p. 364.

"Anomeans,

CHAP. XVI.   *the Council of Nice.*   351

" Anomeans, and on the other by Sabel-
" lius *." " Is not the myſtery of godli-
" neſs every where laughed at; the biſhops
" continuing without people, and without
" clergy, having nothing but an empty
" name, able to do nothing for the ad-
" vancement of the goſpel of peace and
" ſalvation. Are there not diſcords con-
" cerning God, and blaſphemy, from the
" old impiety of vain Sabellius †." " You
" know, ſays he, " my dear brethren, that
" the doctrine of Marcellus, overturns all
" our hopes, not acknowledging the Son
" in his proper perſonality ‡."

Baſil's enemies alledged the authority of his predeceſſor, the famous Gregory Thaumaturgus, as he is now generally called, as if

* Ενθευθεν γαρ ημας ο ανωμοιος σπαρασσει, ετερωθεν δε ως εοικεν
ο Σαβελλιος. Epiſt. 64. Opera, vol. 3. p. 100.

† Ουχι γελαται το μεγα της ευσεβειας μυστηριον, ως ανευ λαου και
κληρου επισκοπων περιερχομενων, και ονομα ψιλον περιφεροιτων, ουδεν
δε κατορθουντων εις προκοπην του ευαγγελιου της ειρηνης και σωτηριας; ουχι
οι περι του θεου λογοι παρ' αυτω πληρεις εισιν ασεβων δογματων, της
παλαιας ασεβειας του ματαιοφρονος Σαβελλιου, δι αυτου νυν ανανεωθεισης
εν τοις συνταγμασιν. Epiſt. 293. ibid. p. 284.

‡ Οιδατε, αδελφοι τιμιωτατοι, δι πασης ημων της ελπιδος αθετησιν
εχει το Μαρκελλου δογμα. ὁτε υιον εν ιδια υποστασει ομολογουν.
Epiſt. 74. ibid. p. 126.

he

he had held that "the Father and Son were "two in conception, but one in hypostasis." This he does not absolutely deny, but says, "that it was advanced by him not seriously, "but only in disputation *."

Writing to the clergy of the church of Neocæsarea, he says, that Sabellius the Lybian, and Marcellus of Galatia, were the real authors of the doctrines taught by his opposers. He complains heavily of the violence with which they opposed him, and that they had the assurance to call his doctrines mischievous ones †.

---

* Ως αρα Γρηγοριῳ ειποντος εν εκθεσει πιστεως, πατερα και υιον επινοια μεν ειναι δυο, υποστασει δε εν. τυτο δε, οτι ȣ δογματικως ειρηται, αλλ' αγωνιστικως εν τη προς Αιλιανον διαλεξει. Epist. 64. Opera, vol. 3. p. 101.

† Σαβελλιος α Διβυς, και Μαρκελλος ο Γαλατης μονοι εκ παντων ετολμησαν, και διδαξαι ταυτα και γραψαι, απερ νυν παρ ημιν, ως ιδια εαυτων ευρηματα επιχειρȣσι προσφερειν οι καθηγȣμενοι τȣ λαȣ, βομβαινοντες τη γλωσση, και ȣδε εις πιθανην κατασκευην εξαγαγειν τα σοφισματα ταυτα, και τȣς παραλογισμȣς εξαρκȣντες. ῥητα και αρρητα καθ' ημων δημηγορȣσι, και παντα τροπον τας συντυχιας ημων εκκλινȣσι. τινος ενεκεν; ȣχι τον επι τοις πονηροις εαυτων διδαγμασιν ελεγχον υφορωμενοι; οι γε επι τοσȣτον ημων κατῃναισχυνθησαν, ωστε και ονειρȣς τινας εφ ημας συμπλαται, διαβαλλοντες ημων τας διδασκαλιας, ως βλαβερας. Epist. 63. Opera, vol. 3. p. 95.

It

It is acknowledged that, in general, the unitarians were of the lower sort of people; yet, in Basil's diocese many of them were those of better condition. He complains of the leading men in his own church being addicted to the opinions of Sabellius and Marcellus, and of their being dissatisfied with his psalms, his new mode of singing, and his institution of monks*. He particularly mentions an excellent person, of the name of Terentius, as having joined the Paulians, in a passage in which he makes great complaint of the progress of that sect, of their boldness, the publication of their confessions of faith, and threatening to join his church †. This would not have been thought of, if their number had not been very considerable. Basil himself was charged with having been a favourer of the unitarian doctrine, and even with having writ-

---

* Epist. 63. Ibid. p. 95.

† Και μεγαφρονειν τας ϛασιαϛας τα μερας εκεινα, κ᾽ επαγαλλεσ-θαι, τοις γραμμασιν, ειλα κ᾽ πιϛιν προϊεινεσθαι, κ᾽ επι ταυτη ετοιμως εχειν συναπτεσθαι τη καθ ημας εκκλησια, προς δε τατοις κακεινο ημιν απηγγελη, οτι υπηγαγοντο προς την υπερ αυτων σπαδην, τον παντα αριϛον ανδρα Τερεντιον. Epist. 272. Ibid. p. 263.

ten in defence of it; but this he absolutely denies, appealing to God for the truth of his declaration *.

In this age it was the custom to apply to the church of Rome, in any difficulties from the distant churches of the empire; a circumstance which greatly contributed to advance the power and insolence of that church. And it was chiefly by means of the overbearing influence of this church, that those doctrines, which are generally termed *orthodox*, got established. Basil requested that persons might be sent from Rome to condemn the heresy of Marcellus, saying, that " to this day, in all the letters
" they send, the heresy of Arius is anathe-
" matized, where no fault was found with
" Marcellus, who brought in a contrary he-
" resy, affecting the very being of the deity
" of the only begotten Son, and giving a
" wrong sense to the word logos †."

---

* Ουτε εγραψαμεν εκεινα, ὐτε συντιθεμεθα αυτοις, αλλα, κỳ αναθεμα-τιζομεν τας εχοντας εκεινο το πονηρον φρονημα, το της συγχυσεως των υποςασεων, εν ω η ασεβεσατη αιρεσις τε Σαβελλιε ανενεωθη. τετο μεν εν γνωριμον τω θεω, τω τας καρδιας γινωσκοντι, Epist. 345. Ibid. p. 339.

† Επει μεχρι τε νυν εν πασιν οις επιςελλεσι γραμμασι, τον μεν δυσωνυμον Αρειον ανω κỳ κατω αναθεματιζοντες κỳ των εκκλησιων εξορι-ζοντες

Gregory Nazianzen, who was cotemporary with Basil, complains of the small number of the orthodox, saying, " they " were the smallest of the tribes of Israel*." And yet Optatus, who was cotemporary with him in Africa, speaks of all heretics as extinct, and the Sabellians among the rest, their very names being unknown in Africa †. But if this had been the case, we should never have heard of the complaints

ζουτες ȣ διαλειπȣσι. Μαρκελλω δε, τω καλα διαμέιρον εκεινω την ασε-
βειαν επιδειξαμενω, κ̀ εις αυτην την υπαρξιν της τȣ μονογενȣς θεοληλος
ασεβησανλι, κ̀ κακως την τȣ λογȣ προσηγοριαν εκδεξαμενω, ȣδεμιαν
μεμψιν επενεγκονλες φαινονλαι. Epist. 52. Ibid. p. 80.

* Και ȣ παρησω ταις αριθμȣμεναις των πολεων, ȣδε των ποιμνιων τοις πλαλυλαιοις εχειν τι πλεον ημων, των ολιγων της ελαχιστης φυλης εν υιοις Ισραηλ, των ολιγοσων εν χιλιασιν Ιȣδα, της μικρας Βηθλεεμ εν πολεσιν εν η χριστος γεννάλαι, νυν τε κ̀ απ αρχης καλως κ̀ γινωσκομενος κ̀ σεβομενος, παρ οις ταυτη υφέλαι, κ̀ υιος ισαζέλαι, κ̀ πνευμα αγιον συνδοξαζέλαι. Or. 2. p. 48.

† Hæreticos cum erroribus suis mortuos, et oblivione jam sepultos, quodammodo resuscitare voluisti, quorum per provincias Africanas non solum vitia, sed etiam nomina videbantur ignota. Marcion, Praxeas, Sabellius, Valentinus, et cæteri temporibus suis a Victorino Pictaviensi, et Zepherino Urbico, et Tertulliano Carthaginiensi, usque ad Cataphrygas; et ab aliis adsertoribus ecclesiæ Catholicæ superati sunt. Lib. 1. p. 9.

of Auſtin, who reſided in Africa at the ſame time.

We have likewiſe boaſts of the extinction of hereſy in Chryſoſtom. But, by his own evidence, they may be proved to be premature. He ſpeaks of all heretics by name as extinct; and among the reſt the Arians are mentioned, which is known to have been by no means the caſe*. It may even, with ſome probability, be inferred from this writer himſelf, that notwithſtanding the prohibitions of government, the unitarians of that age had the zeal and courage to hold public aſſemblies. For, ſpeaking of the unitarians, he ſays, " Let us " avoid their aſſemblies, and learning the " eternal exiſtence of the Son, his power as " the maker of the world, &c. let us hold " the truth†," &c.

It appears from the writings of Chryſoſtom, that, in his time, many perſons were much attached to the religion and cuſtoms of the Jews; and it is very probable, that

* De Pſeudoprophetis, Opera, vol. 6. p. 479.

† Φευγωμεν τοινυν αυλων τας συλλογας, κ̀ μαθονίες τα μονογενας προαιωνιον υπαρξιν, την δημιυργικην δυναμιν.—Διαληρωμεν των δογματων την ακριβειαν. In Pſ. 8. Opera, vol. 3. p. 122.

the doctrine of the unity of God, of which the Jews were strenuous assertors, might be a principal inducement to it, especially as some who were fond of the Jews are represented as continuing in the church. " Let " the Jews," says he, " learn this, and " those who rank with us, and yet think as " they do *."

No person speaks with more triumph of the extinction of heresy, especially that of the unitarians, than Theodoret; and yet his account is flatly contradicted by Facundus, in the passage above quoted from him. And as Facundus wrote after Theodoret, it may be taken for granted, that the unitarians were more numerous in the time of Theodoret than they were in his.

Theodoret represents the cities in his neighbourhood as full of heretics when he came into the diocese; mentioning the Arians, Eunomians, Manichæans, Marcionites, Valentinians, and Montanists, and even heathens and Jews; when himself, who

* Μαθέτωσαν και Ιυδαιοι, και οι μεθ ημων μεν τέταχθαι δοκυντες, τα δε εκεινων φρονυντες. Hom. 38. Opera, vol. 1. p. 525.

maintained the evangelical truth was excluded from all cities *. Though he does not mention unitarians, it will appear probable, from what has been seen above, that they were intended by the term Montanists. He boasts, however, of his having purged his diocese of all those heresies, especially that of the Marcionites †. In another place, he particularly speaks of the unitarians as extinct, and as an event produced by that power which rebuked the deep, If. iv. 27. and "dried it up, who says "to the deep, Thou shalt be desolate, and "I will dry up the rivers ‡." He likewise speaks of the doctrine of the trinity as held not only by the teachers in the church, but also by the lowest artificers, several of whom he

---

* Μαλλον δε τοις μεν αλλοις απασι πασα πολις ανεωκῖαι, ε μονον τοις τα Αρειε και Εινομιε φρονεσιν, αλλα και Μανιχαιοις, και Μαρκιωνιςαις, και τοις τα Βαλενῖινε, και Μοῦανε νοσεσι, και μενῖοι και Ελλησι και Ιεδαιοις· εγω δε των ευαγῖελικων υπαραγωνιζομενος δογμαῖων πασης ειργομαι πολεως. Epist. 81. Opera, vol. 3. p. 953.

† Ibid. p. 954.

‡ Ταῦῖας απασας τας αιρεσεις επι αναιρεσεως τε μονογενες Θεοῖηῖος επινενοηκεν ο των ανθρωπων αλαςωρ. αλλ' εσβεσεν απασας ο επιῖιμων αβυσσω, και ξηραινων αυῖην, ο λεγων τῃ αβυσσω ερημωθηση, και τες ποῖαμες σε ξηρανω. Hær. Fab. lib. 2. cap. 11. Opera, vol. 4. p. 224.

enume-

CHAP. XVI. *the Council of Nice.*

enumerates, by women, even of the lowest ranks, and by the inhabitants of villages, as well as those of cities *.

How far this is to be considered as a faithful state of facts, or the flourish of an orator, I leave the reader to determine, by comparing it with the accounts of Facundus and others. Cyril of Alexandria, who was cotemporary with Theodoret, holds a different language. "Some," says he, "are so far seduced, that they cannot "bear any longer to confess that Christ is "God; but that he is rather the organ and "instrument of the deity, and inspired by "God †." In this it is possible, that he alluded to the Sabellian, or Patripassian doctrine, which I shall shew was the language

---

* Και εστιν ιδειν ταυτα ειδοιας τα δογματα, ε μονας γε της εκκλησιας τας διδασκαλας, αλλα και σκυτοτομας, και χαλκοτυπας, και ταλασιεργας και τας αλλας αποχειροβιωτας· και γυναικας ωσαυτως, ε μονον τας λογων μετεσχηκυιας, αλλα και χερνητιδας, και ακεστριδας, και μετιοι και θεραπαινας· και ε μονον ασοι, αλλα και χωρητικοι την δε την γνωσιν εσχηκασι. Serm. 5. Opera, vol. 4. p. 556.

‡ Prope namque usque adeo quidam seducti sunt, ut non sustineant amplius confiteri, quod Deus sit Christus, sed quod sit magis organum et instrumentum divinitatis, et homo numine afflatus. Epist. Opera, vol. 2. p. 14.

of the philosophical unitarians. But it may be inferred, from several passages in the writings of Cyril, that there were unitarians in his time. I shall give one of them in the notes *.

Cyril even speaks of writers in defence of the unitarian doctrine in his time, and such as he thought it worth his while to animadvert upon. "But because a heretic," he says, "famous for his skill in the Jewish "scriptures, in his exposition of this pas-"sage" *(the Father is greater than I)* "has "written intolerable blasphemies against "the only begotten, I thought it my duty "to shew the falsehood of his discourse †."

---

* Obliterant enim quidam, veritatis pulchritudinem, et sicut numisma, adulterant, extollentes in excelsum cornu et injustitiam contra deum loquentes, sicut scriptum est. Imaginantur unigenitum non habere existentiam, et proprie non subsistere, et per se quidem non esse in subsistentia, Verbum autem simpliciter, et sermonem juxta solam pronunciationem a deo factum quemadmodum et in homine inhabitasse dicunt miseri : et componentes sic Jesum, sanctis quidem sanctiorem esse dicunt, attamen non deum. De Recta Fide, vol. 2. p. 686.

† Verum quoniam quidam hæreticorum etiam apud Judæos sacrarum peritia literarum illustris hunc locum exponens intolerabiles in unigenitum scripsit blasphemias,

mei

"He has the arrogance," he says, " to af-
" fert, that the Father is in no fenfe greater
" than the deity of the Son, but only fup-
" pofes that the nature of the Father ex-
" ceeds his humanity *." In this manner
he muft have meant to defcribe the Sabellians.

From thefe circumftances, let the reader
judge, whether the unitarian herefy was
extinct in the *time* of Theodoret, whatever
it might be in his *neighbourhood*. His
great zeal, and his power in his diocefe,
would probably prevent the unitarians from
declaring themfelves, and their acquiefcence
might be called their converfion.

The Pelagians, as I have fhewn, very
generally adopted the unitarian doctrine.
But, befides thefe, Caffian fpeaks of other
unitarians in Gaul, whom he does not clafs
with Pelagians. "There have lately ri-
" fen," he fays, " I mean in our days, a

---

mei officii putavi falfitatem orationis ejus arguere. In
John, lib. 10. cap. 9. Opera, vol. 1. p. 938.

* Ad hoc arrogantiæ quidam procefferunt, inquit, ut
nullo modo audire patiantur patrem, filii deitate majorem
effe, fed fola humanitate naturam patris excedere arbitren-
tur, Cyril. Alex. vol. 1. p. 939.

" poifonous

"poisonous heresy, chiefly in the city of
"Beligæ, of a certain name, but an un-
"certain author, which, with a fresh head,
"rises from the old error of the Ebionites.
"It is doubtful whether it can be called
"old, or new. It is new in the assertors,
"but old in the error, viz. that our Lord
"Jesus Christ is a mere man *."

According to Maxentius, who flourished in the year 520, the unitarians were by no means extinct in his neighbourhood. Speaking of the church as rejecting the doctrine of those who say that " Christ is
"God by favour, and not by nature," he says, " against this all heretics, as well those
"who are manifestly cut off and divided,
"as those who are within the church, and
"spiritually divided from it, whom the

---

* Nuper quoque, id est, in diebus nostris emersisse hæresim venenosam, et maxime Beligarum urbe conspeximus, certi erroris, incerti nominis: quia cum recenti capite ex antiqua Ebionitarum stirpe surrexerit, dubium admodum est antiqua magis dici, an recens debeat. Nova enim assertoribus, sed vetusta erroribus fuit. Solitarium quippe hominem dominum nostrum Jesum Christum natum esse blasphemans. De Incarnatione, lib. 1. cap. 3. p. 962.

"holy

"holy charity of the church bravely tolerates, always take up arms, and cease not to urge it with false charges, and endeavour to excite all they can influence against it. As yet," he adds, "we are in the threshing floor, corn mixed with chaff, good men grieve at the society of the wicked*." This passage is very similar to that of Facundus, and makes it extremely probable, that, in all christian countries, there were great numbers of unitarians, sufficiently known to be so, in communion with the catholic church, without being molested.

* Vera dei ecclesia, cui non sunt hæreticorum ignotæ procellæ, non est illa quæ christum gratia non natura deum confitetur.—Adversus illam omnes hæretici, tam qui ab ea manifeste abscissi atque divisi sunt, quam hi qui intra eam positi, spiritaliter ab ea dissentiunt (quos fortiter sancta fidelium tolerat charitas) semper arma corripiunt, eamque falsis criminationibus infestari non desinunt, atque eos quos suis potuerunt erroribus in ejus nituntur invidiam concitare. ——Adhuc, inquit in area sumus, mixta sunt frumenta cum paleis, gemunt boni consortia malorum : sed superest flamma, non necessariis, et parata sunt horrea jam probati, in his remorari diutius superfluum æstimo. Bib. l'at. vol. 5; p. 499.

SECTION II.

Of the State of the Unitarians after the sixth Century.

WE must not expect to find any distinct account of the unitarians, or the condition they were in, in what are called *the dark ages*. There can be no doubt, however, but that they continued to be in the same state in which they had been in the preceding period, i. e. not very conspicuous, or forming many separate societies, at least, such as the historians of the time had any knowledge of; but mixed with other christians, though without making any secret of their opinions. Of this, though there are no distinct accounts, there are sufficient traces. I have noted only a few, as they happened to fall under my observation, when I was reading for other purposes.

Pope Gregory the Great, who flourished about the close of the sixth century, speaks of heretics who said " they did not envy
" Christ

"Christ being God, because they could be so if they would, considering Christ as a mere man, and made a God by favour*." These must have been unitarians, for it is a language that was never held by Arians.

In Bulgaria Sandius says, that the Photinians remained till the time of Pope Nicholas, about the year 860. Hist. p. 117. Agobard speaks of Avitus having written against them, but at what time does not appear †.

For some time the unitarians were called Bonosians, from Bonosus, bishop of Serdica, in the latter end of the fourth, and the beginning of the fifth century. Mention is made of him as an unitarian, along

---

* Non invideo Christo deo facto, quoniam si volo, et ipse possum fieri. Qui Jesum Christum dominum nostrum, non per mysterium conceptionis, sed per profectum gratiæ deum putavit, perversa allegatione astruens eum purum hominum natum: sed ut deus esset, per meritum profecisse, atque ab hoc æstimans et se quoslibet alios posse ei coequari, qui filii dei per gratiam fiunt. In Job. cap. 35. p. 110. C

† Beatus quoque Avitus, Photinianorum hæreticorum validissimus expugnator. Adv. Fælicem, sect. 41. p. 55.

with

with Photinus, by Marius Mercator*, and also by Justinian, who ranks him with Paulus Samosatensis, Photius (probably Photinus) and Nestorius †. Mention is also made of the Bonosians in a council held at Orleans, A. D. 540 ‡.

Sandius says, that the Bonosians were the same with the *Felicians*, so called from Felix, of Urgella in Spain, who, in conjunction with Elipandus, of Toledo, taught heretical doctrines with respect to the trinity, A. D. 780 (Hist. p. 360) and that this Elipandus held the same opinions with Sabellius, he says, appears from a copy of his confession to Beatus, and Heterius. He adds, that the four preceding bishops of Toledo, who compiled the Toledan Gothic

---

* Hunc itaque Hebionum philosophum secutus Marcellus Galata est, Photinus quoque, et ultimis temporibus Serdicensis Bonosus, qui a Damaso urbis Romæ episcopo prædamnatus est. Opera, p. 165.

† Επειδη Παυλον τον Σαμοσαλεα, και Φωλιον, και Βονοσον, και Νεσοριον αναθεματιζει. Epist. p. 122.

‡ Judex civitatis vel loci, si hæreticum aut Bonosiacum, vel cujuslibet alterius hæresis sacerdotem, quam cunque personam de catholicis rebaptizasse cognoverit. Binii Concilia, vol. 2. pt. 2. p. 29.

liturgy,

liturgy, were of the same opinion with him. Ibid. p. 120.

Elipandus, however, may have been a Nestorian, by his asserting that Jesus Christ was the adopted Son of God, as we learn from the transactions of the council of Frankfort in 794 *.

The Goths and Vandals, and all the other northern nations, which invaded the Roman empire, are generally said to have been Arians. But it is very possible that this may have been said without making proper distinctions, and that many of them were unitarians. Chilperic, king of the Franks, was probably one, at least so was Leovigild of Spain, who sent ambassadors to Chilperic in 585, as may be inferred

---

* Adserunt igitur, sed falsis adsertionibus irretiti, dominum nostrum Jesum Christum, adoptivum dei filium de virgine natum ; quod divinis nequeunt adprobare documentis. Hæc igitur dicentes, aut in utero virginis eum suspicantur adoptatum : quod dici nefas est, quia de beata virgine inerarrabiliter sumpsit, non adoptavit, carnem ; aut certe purum eum hominem sine deo natum, quod cogitare impium est, necesse est fateantur. Binni Concilia, vol. 3. pt. 2. p. 140.

from what Sandius says of him, and his ambassadors*.

Some Sabellians, as well as Arians, were condemned at a council held at Toledo, A. D. 400 †. Also unitarians, or Nestorians, seem to be alluded to in a council held in the same city, A. D. 684 ‡.

The Albigenses, at least many of them, appear pretty clearly not to have been orthodox with respect to the trinity; but whether they were more generally Arians, or unitarians, I have not been able to determine.

* Hist. p. 337, 338.

† Si quis dixerit atque crediderit, deum patrem eundem esse filium vel paracletum, anathema sit. Si quis dixerit vel crediderit filium eundum esse patrem vel paracletum, anathema sit. Si quis dixerit vel crediderit paracletum esse vel patrem vel filium, anathema sit. Si quis crediderit vel dixerit, carnem tantum sine anima a filio dei fuisse susceptam anathema sit. Binnii Concilia, vol. 1. p. 60.

‡ Si quis igitur Jesu Christo dei filio, ex utero Mariæ virginis nato, aliquid aut divinitatis imminuit, aut de suscepta humanitate subducit, excepta sola lege peccati; et non eum verum deum, hominemque perfectum in una persona subsistentem sinceriffime credit, anathema sit. Binnii Concilia, vol. 3. p. 297.

Of these Albigenses, Lisoius and Herebert are particularly mentioned, as men of excellent moral characters, who were accused of Manicheisme. However, when they were interrogated at Orleans, in 1017, it appeared that they did not hold the doctrine of the trinity*.

In the same uncertainty are the opinions of Peter Abelard, and those of his disciple, as he is called, Arnold of Brescia. But it is no uncommon thing for the same person

---

* Facta igitur perscrutatione inter clericos, quomodo unusquisque sentiret, et crederet ea, quæ fides catholica per doctrinam apostolicam incommutabiliter servat et prædicat: illi duo, videlicet Lisoius, et Heribertus statim se aliter sentire non negantes, quales diu latuerant, manifestaverunt. Deinde vero plures post illos se parti istorum profitebantur hærere, nec ulla ratione se posse affirmabant ab illorum segregare consortio. Quibus compertis, tam rex, quam Pontifices tristiores effecti interrogaverunt illos secretius, utpote viros hactenus in omni morum probitate perutilissimos, quorum unus Lisoius in monasterio sanctæ crucis clericorum clarissimus habebatur: alter item Heribertus sancti Petri ecclesiæ, cognomento Puellarius capitalæ scholæ tenebat dominium.—— Dicebant enim deliramenta esse, quidquid in veteri ac novo canone certis signis ac prodigiis, veteribusque testatoribus de trinitate unaque deitate beata confirmat auctoritas. Binnii Concilia, vol. 3. pt. 2. p. 176.

to be called an Arian by one writer, and an unitarian by another. Thus Lewis Hetzer is called an Arian by Sandius, who was himself an Arian (Hift. p. 424.) whereas Mosheim (Hift. vol. 4. p. 183) represents him as having been of the fame opinion with Socinus.

Abelard, however, was most probably a Sabellian, as may be inferred from his comparison of the unity of the three persons in the trinity to the unity of the *proposition, assumption,* and *conclusion,* of an oration. At least it was so understood at a council held in 1136*. What is said of him on the occasion of another council, in 1140, may perhaps shew that, with respect to the trinity,

---

* Quare de S. trinitate docens et scribens, tres personas, quas sancta ecclesia non vacua nomina tantum, sed res distinctas, suisque proprietatibus discretis, hactenus et pie credidit, et fideliter docuit, nimis attenuans, non bonis usus exemplis, inter caetera dixit: sicut eadem oratio est propositio assumptio, et conclusio, ita eadem essentia est pater, et filius, et spiritus sanctus. Ob hoc Suessionis provinciali contra eum synodo sub praesentia Romanae sedis legati congregata, ab egregiis viris, et nominatis magistris, Elberico Rhemense, et Leutaldo Novariense, Sabellianus haereticus judicatus. Binnii Concilia, vol. 3. pt. 2. p. 492.

he

he was an Arian, with respect to the doctrine of grace a Pelagian, and with respect to the person of Christ, a Nestorian *.

It appears then, that, in all the periods of antiquity, there were considerable numbers of unitarians, either avowed or concealed; and especially among the Albigenses, who bore so noble a testimony against the errors of the church of Rome. Unitarians also appeared in great numbers about the time of the reformation by Luther. But he and Calvin, not going so far, but retaining more fundamental corruptions of christianity than any that they abolished, employed all their influence to bear down those who did not exactly agree with them, and stop where they did.

The truth has never, however, been without its witnesses, perhaps, even in no age or country; and providence seems now to be opening a way for the much wider spread, and the firmer establishment of the truth, especially in this country.

* Cum de trinitate loquitur, sapit Arrium: cum de gratia, sapit Pelagium: cum de persona Christi, sapit Nestorium. Binnii Concilia, vol. 3. pt. 2. p. 494.

That it is not improbable, but that, even in times of pretty great rigour, quiet people, who wrote nothing, and collected no disciples, would be permitted to continue in communion with the catholic church, notwithstanding their opinions were suspected, or known, to be heretical, may appear from the state of things at home, in the last, and the present age.

Is it not well known that there are both Arians and Socinians members of the church of England, and even among the clergy themselves, and yet, if they can reconcile it to their own minds to keep in communion with a trinitarian church, there are no attempts made to molest them. Zealous as the heads of the church may be for the purity of its tenets, they think proper to connive at these things, and so they did in an age more zealous than this. The excellent Mr. Firmin was not only an avowed Socinian, and in communion with the church of England, but in habits of intimacy with Tillotson, and some of the most distinguished churchmen of his time.

At

At present there are Arian and Socinian writers within the pale of the church, and yet they are not excommunicated. Such a thing as this might not have passed so easily in the time of Theodosius. But even then I make no doubt, but that persons who could content themselves without disturbing others, would not have been molested.

Persons who do not *bona fide* hold the acknowledged tenets of any church (I mean such great and distinguished ones as those relating to the object of worship) ought to withdraw themselves from it, and not, by continuing in communion with it, to countenance its errors. But how many are there who do not see the thing in this light, or whose habits and prejudices are such, that they cannot bring themselves to act as I think every principle of honour, as well as of religion, dictates; and yet I cannot call all such persons hypocrites, doing what they themselves know and feel to be wrong. They have excuses, which I doubt not, satisfy their own minds, though they do not satisfy me. Great allowance is also to be made for the force of habit, and even for a natural timidity. There are many Erasmus's for one Luther, many Dr. Clarke's for one Whiston, a name, which notwithstanding the weakness of his judgment in some things, ought never to be mentioned without respect, on account of his almost singular and unparalelled uprightness.

As to the common people, the *idiotæ* of Tertullian, we generally see that, as they are not innovators in doctrine, they go to public worship where they have been used to do, without any nice discrimination of what is transacted there; and the observation will generally apply to the bulk of the inferior clergy. When Henry VIII. reformed the church of England, how many joined him in it, who would never have declared themselves dissenters from the established church?

These considerations, which are founded on such a knowledge of human nature as we may learn from all history, and our own daily observation, may render it credible, that the majority of the common people, might be unitarians, and yet continue in communion

nion with the church, after its forms became trinitarian, especially as they would not become so all at once. In the most ancient liturgies, there were no prayers addressed to Christ; and as the members of christian societies were not required to *subscribe* to any thing, there was nothing that they were expected to bear a part in, concerning which they might not be able to satisfy themselves.

The case is the same, in a greater or less degree, at all times, and in all churches. Quiet people will generally be indulged in their own way of thinking, and they are only those who disturb others that are themselves disturbed.

CHAPTER XVII.

Of Philosophical Unitarianism.

BESIDES the *simple unitarianism* above described, or the doctrine of Christ being a mere man, inspired by God, which was the belief of the generality of christians of lower rank, there was likewise, in early times, what may be called a *philosophical unitarianism,* or an explanation of the doctrine concerning Christ on the principles of the philosophy of those times. And this deserves the more notice, as it probably gave occasion to what is commonly called the *patripassian* doctrine, if such a doctrine was ever really maintained.

As the sun was supposed to emit rays, and draw them into himself again, so the Divine Being, of whom they imagined the sun to be an image, they likewise supposed, emitted

emitted a kind of *efflux*, or *divine ray*, to which they sometimes gave the name of *logos*, which might be attached to any particular substance, or person, and then be drawn into the Divine Being again. Such a divine efflux was imagined to have been the cause of the appearances of God in the Old Testament, and likewise to have been imparted to Jesus Christ; who, nevertheless, was a mere man. For before his baptism they supposed that he had not this divine ray, and that it would leave him when it had enabled him to act the part assigned to him.

This doctrine preceded that of the *permanent personification of the logos*. It is particularly described by Justin Martyr, and it is remarkable, that, though he does not adopt it, he passes no censure upon it, which is a proof that, in his opinion, it was not heretical.

"There are," he says, "some I know, "who say that the divine power which "appeared to Moses, and Abraham, and "Jacob, was called *an angel*, from his de-
"livering

" livering the will of God to men, and *a*
" *glory*, when he appeared in an ineffable
" manner, and *a man*, when, at the will of
" the Father, he appeared in that form;
" and *logos*, when he brought the will of
" God to man; but that this power is in-
" separable from the Father; as a beam of
" light is from the sun, since, when he
" sets, he takes his beams with him. Thus
" they say the Father, when he pleases,
" makes this power to go out of him, and
" when he pleases, takes it into him again.
" In the same manner, they say, angels
" exist. But that angels are permanent be-
" ings, and do not return into that from
" which they had their origin, I have
" shewn. And that this power, which the
" prophets call *God*, and *angel*, is not like
" a beam of the sun, but numerically dif-
" ferent from it, I have briefly shewn
" above; when I proved that this power
" is produced by the Father's power, and
" at his will, but yet not a thing cut
" off from him, so as to diminish his
" essence, but like the lighting of one
" fire

"fire from another, which is not thereby lessened.*"

Whitby says that Clemens Alexandrinus speaks of this doctrine with approbation.

* Αλλα επει γινωσκω κỳ τινας προλεγειν ταυτα βυλομενυς, κỳ φασκειν την δυναμιν την παρα τυ πατρος των ολων φανεισαν τω Μωσει η τω Αβρααμ, η τω Ιακωβ, αγγελον καλεισθαι εν τη προς ανθρωπυς προοδω, επειδη δι αυτης τα παρα τυ πατρος τοις ανθρωποις αγγελλεται, δοξαν δε επειδη εν αχωρητω ποτε φαντασια φαινεται, ανδρα δε ποτε και ανθρωπον καλεισθαι, επειδη εν μορφαις τοιαυταις σχηματιζομενος φαινεται αισπερ βυλεται ο πατηρ, και λογον καλυσιν επειδη και τας παρα τυ πατρος ομιλιας φερει τοις ανθρωποις. Αμητον δε και αχωριστον τυ πατρος ταυτην την δυναμιν υπαρχειν, ονπερ τροπον το τυ ηλιυ φασι φως επι γης ειναι αμητον και αχωριστον οντος τυ ηλιυ εν τω ορανω, και οταν δυση, συναποφερεται το φως, ετως ο πατηρ οταν βυληται, λεγυσι, δυναμιν αυτυ προπηδαν ποιει, και οταν βυληται παλιν αναστελλει εις εαυτον. Κατα τυτον τον τροπον και τυς αγγελυς ποιειν αυτον διδασκυσιν. Αλλ' οτι μεν υν εισιν αγγελοι, και αει μενοντες, και μη αναλυομενοι εις εκεινο εξ υπερ γεγονασιν, αποδεδεικται. Και οτι δυναμις αυτη ην και Θεον καλει ο προφητικος λογος, δια πολλων ωσαυτως αποδεδεικται, και αγγελον, υχ. ως το τυ ηλιυ φως ονοματι μονον αριθμειται, αλλα και αριθμω ετερον τι εστι, και εν τοις προειρημενοις δια βραχεων τον λογον εξητασα, ειπων την δυναμιν ταυτην γεγεννησθαι απο τυ πατρος δυναμει και βυλη αυτυ, αλλ' υ κατα αποτομην, ως απομεριζομενης της τυ πατρος υσιας, οποια τα αλλα παντα μεριζομενα και τεμνομενα υ τα αυτα εστιν α και πριν τμηθηναι. Και παραδειγματος χαριν παρειληφειν τα ως απο πυρος αναπτομενα πυρα ετερα ορωμεν, υδεν ελαττυμενυ εκεινυ, εξ υ αναφθηναι πολλα δυναται, αλλα ταυτα μενοντος. Dial. p. 412.

He

He also says, " it is particularly remark-
" able, that Justin Martyr, though he did
" not approve of this doctrine, passes it
" without any censure, or mark of heresy *."

They who adopted this notion would naturally say, that the divinity of Christ was only that of the Father residing in him; and it is not impossible but that, as they are charged by their adversaries, they might, on this principle, say, that Christ was God; and the divinity being the same in both, that he was the very same with the Father. The Holy Spirit being another divine efflux, they might also say, that all the three persons were one. Farther, though the thing is hardly probable, especially as it is, in a manner, given up by some of their antagonists, they might say, that since Christ suf-

* Ubi præcipue notandum est, Justinum quidem sententiam hance improbare, eam vero sine censura aut hæreseos nota dimittere. Sententiam hancce, quam post Noetum et Praxeam, Sabellius propugnavit, Clementi Alexandrino ex Pædagogia sua placuisse non sine ratione existimo; eamque postea renovabat, et pro ea acriter contendebat, Marcellus Ancyræ episcopus. Disquisitiones Modestæ, p. 173.

fered

fered while this divine ray, or logos, was in him, it also suffered along with him. For, according to the philosophy of those times, though the supreme being himself was incapable either of evil or of passion, yet other beings, derived even from his substance, were capable of those affections. They might therefore imagine, that the logos, while *out of the deity*, might suffer together with the person to whom it was attached; and hence they might get the name of *patripassians*. This, however, would never apply to any but philosophers. The common people are described as simple unitarians, without having any such whimsical hypothesis as this.

This opinion of the *logos* being something like a *divine ray*, emitted from the Father, and properly belonging to him, though for a time attached to the person of Christ, may be traced in Origen and others; and it is ascribed to almost all the eminent men among the unitarians, as late as Marcellus. For it does not appear that his disciple Photinus was ever charged with it.

Origen,

Origen, after saying that Christ is the God of the dead as well as of the living, says, that "perhaps God the logos is God to those who place every thing in him, thinking him to be the same with the Father *." Celsus objecting to christians that, "while they exclaimed against polytheism, think they do not offend by worshipping his servant." Origen replies, "that he would not have made this objection, if he had understood what our Saviour says, that he and his Father were one," which union he explains by the union of christians, who had one heart and one mind. "This," he says, "is a sufficient argument, without having recourse to the sentiments of those who maintain, that the Father and the Son are not two hypostases †;" by which he must have

---

* Ο δε Θεος λογος ταχα των εν αυτω ιταντων το παν. κ͟ των πατερα αυτον νομιζοντων εστι Θεος. Comment. vol. 2. p. 48.

† Οτι ειπερ νενοηκει ο Κελσος το, εγω ꞇ ο πατηρ εν εσμεν· και το εν ευχη ειρημενον υπο τε υιε τε Θεε εν τω. Ως εγω και συ εν εσμεν, εκ αν αξιο ημας κ͟ αλλον θεραπευειν παρα τον επι πασι Θεον. Ο γαρ πατηρ, φησιν, εν εμοι, καγω εν τω πατρι. ει δε . τις εκ τετων περισπασθησεται, μη πη αυτομολωμεν προς τας αναιςετεας δυο τιναι υποτασεις πατερα

meant the Sabellians, whose doctrine, as far as it may be said to have differed from that of the simple unitarians, was the philosophical unitarianism described above. " The Sabel- " lians," says, Novatian, " while they say " that Christ is a mere man, yet, in a man- " ner, make him to be not the Son, but the " Father, and the Father omnipotent *."

Origen well describes the different classes of unitarians of his time in the following passage: " Hence may be solved the doubts which " disturb many, who alledge a principle of " piety, and a fear of making two Gods, " and by this means fall into false and im- " pious opinions; either denying that the " identity of the Son differs from that of " the Father; saying, that the Son is God " only in name, or denying the divinity of " the Son, while they allow his identity,

πατερα κ̃ υιον · επιςησαlω τω, ην δε παντων των πιςευσαντων η καρδια κ̃ η ψυχη μια, ινα θεωρηση το, εγω κ̃ ο πατηρ εν εσμεν. Ad Celsum, lib. 8. p. 385.

* Siquidem Christus non filius, sed pater creditur, et novo more dum ab istis destricte homo nudus adseritur, per eos, rursum Christus pater deus omnipotens comprobatur. Cap. 12. p. 40.

" and

" and that he is a different person from the
" Father, &c*." The first that he describes
were the philosophical unitarians, who allowed the divinity of the Son, but said it
was the same with that of the Father;
whereas the latter (probably the common
people) denied the divinity of the Son altogether. It is evident from this passage, that
the unitarians, in the time of Origen, were
numerous; for he calls them *many*, which
he would not have done unnecessarily. The
argument by which he solves their doubts
has been mentioned before, viz. that the
Father is God, *with the article* prefixed, and
the Son without it.

* Και το πολλες φιλοθεες ειναι ευχομενες ταρασσον, ευλαβεμενες δυο αναγορευσαι θεες, και παρα τετο περιπιπτοντας ψευδεσι και ασεβεσι δογμασιν, ητοι αρνεμενες ιδιοτητα υιε ετεραν παρα την τε πατρος ομολογεντας θεον ειναι τον μεχρι ονοματος παρ αυτοις υιον προσαγορευομενοι. Η αρνεμενες την θεοτητα τε υιου, τιθεντας δε αυτε την ιδιοτητα, και την εσιαν κατα περιγραφην τυγχανεσαν ετεραν τε πατρος, εντευθεν λυεσθαι δυναται. λεκτεον γαρ αυτοις οτι τοτε μεν αυτοθεος ο θεος εστι, διοπερ και ο Σωτηρ φησιν εν τη προς τον πατερα ευχη. ινα γινωσκωσι σε τον μονον αληθινον θεον; παν δε το παρα το αυτοθεος μετοχη της εκεινε θεοτητος θεοποιεμενον, εκ ο θεος, αλλα θεος κυριωτερον αν λεγοιτο ω παντως ο πρωτοτοκος πασης κτισεως, ατε πρωτος τω προς τον θεον ειναι. In Johan. Comment. vol. 2. p. 46.

It

It does not appear that the persons to whom Origen refers were charged with saying that the Father suffered; but this is expressly alledged against Noetus, who, as Epiphanius says, "scrupled not to say as "much." Being interrogated concerning his doctrine, he said, "What evil have I done? "I honour one God. I know but one, and "no other, besides him who was born, "suffered and died*.

This writer acquits the Sabellians of this charge. For he says that " the Sabellians "agree in every thing with the Noetians, "except that they deny that the Father "suffered †." But Austin blames him for making that difference ‡. And Epiphanius

---

* Τι γαρ κακον πεποιηκα; ενα θεον δοξαζω, ενα επιςαμαι, κ̓ ȣκ αλλον πλην αῦτȣ, γεννηθεντα, πεπονθότα, αποθανοντα. Hær. 57. Opera, vol. 1. p. 480.

† Σαϐελλιανοι, οι τα ομοια Νοητιων δοξαζοντες, παρα τȣ̓το μονον λεγȣσι γαρ μη πεπονθεναι τον πατερα. Anacephalosis, Opera, vol. 2. p. 146.

‡ Unde vero sit factum, et Noetianos ut Sabellianos non unius hæresis duo nomina, sed tanquam duas hæreses supradictus episcopus poneret, liquido invenire non potui; quia si quid inter se differunt, tam obscure dixit, studio forsitan

ascribes to them the proper principle of philosophical unitarianism in the following passage. "The Sabellians say that the Son was sent from the Father, as a beam of light from the sun, to administer every thing relating to the gospel dispensation, and the salvation of men, and was then drawn up into heaven, like a beam of light, which returns to the sun*." In another description of their principles, he is, perhaps, not quite so accurate. "Sabellius said, there was but one hypostasis, and the Father, Son, and Spirit, three names of it; or, as in man, there are the body, soul, and spirit; the body

---

forsitan brevitatis, ut non intelligam. Loco quippe isto, quo et non tam longe a Noetianis, Sabellianos commemorans, Sabelliani inquit similia Noeto dogmatizantes, præter hoc, quod dicunt patrem non esse passum, quomodo de Sabellianis intelligi potest, cum sic innotuerint dicere patrem passum, ut Patripassiani quam Sabelliani crebrius nuncupentur. De Hæresibus, lib. 1. Opera, vol. 6. p. 91.

* Πεμφθεντα δε τον υιον καιρω τοδε, ωσπερ ακτινα, και εργασαμενον τα παντα εν τω κοσμω τα της οικονομιας της ευαγγελικης, και σωτεριας των ανθρωπων, αναληφθεντα δε αυθις εις ουρανον, ως υπο ηλιε πεμφθεισαν ακτινα, και παλιν εις τον ηλιον αναδραμουσαν. Hær. 62. Opera, vol. 1. p. 513.

"being

" being the Father, the foul the Son, and
" the fpirit the Holy Spirit *."

This philofophical unitarianifm is the doctrine afcribed by Tertullian to Praxeas, though he fpeaks of the common people as fimple unitarians. " He fays, that the Father, Son, and Holy Spirit are the fame †." He likewife calls him a *Patripaffian*, and fays, that " he firft carried the Patripaffian " doctrine into Rome ‡." They are Patripaffians alfo whom Cyprian enumerates among heretics. Epift. Opera, p. 200.

Beaufobre thinks that the charge of Patripaffianifm was entirely founded on a miftake, and as Lardner obferves, Auftin only *inferred* that the Sabellians held that doc-

---

* Τον αυτον ειναι πατερα, τον αυτον υιον, τον αυτον ειναι αγιον πνευμα· ως ειναι εν μια υποϛασει τρεις ονομασιας, η ως εν ανθρωπω σωμα, και ψυχη, και πνευμα. Και ειναι μεν το σωμα, ως ειπειν τον πατερα, ψυχην δε ως ειπειν τον υιον, το πνευμα δε ως ανθρωπε, ὁιως και το αγιον πνευμα εν τη θεοτητι. Hær. 62. Opera, vol. 1. p. 513.

† Dum unicum deum non alias putat credendum, quam fi ipfum eundemque et patrem, filium, et fpiritum fanctum dicat.—— Itaque poft tempus pater natus, et pater paffus: ipfe deus, dominus omnipotens, Jefus Chriftus prædicatur. Adv. Praxeam, fect. 2. Opera, p. 501.

‡ Ibid. fect. 1. p. 500.

trine (Credibility, vol. 4. p. 450). Beaufobre accounts for the mifreprefentation of the ancients, by fuppofing that they confounded the terms *word* of God and *Son* of God, becaufe in the theology of the church they were the fame, though in the mind of a Sabellian they were very different. Hiftoire de Manicheifme, vol. 1. p. 539.

It is very poffible that Tertullian and others might give the epithet of *heretical* to the unitarian doctrine in this obnoxious form only. For it is evident that he did not confider the fimple unitarians as heretics, for he fays they were the *major pars credentium*, the majority of the believers.

Marcellus is generally defcribed as being what I call a philofophical unitarian, but he is not faid to have been a Patripaffian. According to Theodoret, he held that " Chrift came as an extenfion of the Fa- " ther's divinity. This he called God the " logos; but after all the œconomy" (that is, when the gofpel difpenfation fhall be accomplifhed) " it will be again drawn into " him, and centered in God, from whom " it had been extended. He called the Holy " Spirit

"Spirit an extension of an extension, and
"said that this was given to the apostles *."

Beryllus, one of the first who is noticed as an unitarian, though celebrated for the elegance of his writings, is not said to have been a Patripassian. He only held that "Christ had no proper subsistence till he "came into this world, and had no divinity "of his own, but only that of the Father "residing in him †."

It is allowed by Tertullian, that the Patripassians, as well as the orthodox, said that the Father himself was impassible. That was an universal maxim concerning the *divine nature*; but they said that the Father had *compassion* for the Son. Whether this compassion was ascribed by them

---

* Εκλασιν δε τινα της τε πατρος θεοτητος ερησεν εις τον χριστον εληλυθεναι, και ταυτην θεον λογον εκαλεσε. μεια δε την συμπασαν οικονομιαν παλιν ανασπασθηναι. και συγαληναι προς τον θεον, εξ ὑπερ εξελαθη. το δε παναγιον πνευμα παρεκλασιν της εκτασεως λεγει, και ταυτην τοις αποστολοις παρασχεθηναι. Hær. Fab. lib. 2. cap. 10. Opera, vol. 4. p. 224.

† Ελεγε και γαρ τον κυριον ημων Ιησυν χριστον, μητινα ὑποστασιν ουσιας ιδιαν κεκτησθαι, πριν η τοις καθ ημας ενδημειν· αλλ' ουδε θεοτητα ιδιαν εχειν, μονην δε πατρικην ὑποστασιν και θεοτητα εν τω επιδημησασαν πολιτευσασθαι. Hist. lib. 5. cap. 22. vol. 1. p. 371.

to the Father himself, or only to the divine ray, or logos, that was in Christ, does not appear. Perhaps it was the latter. On this subject Tertullian replies to them as follows. "Wherefore neither had the Father compassion for the Son. For so, thinking to avoid a direct blasphemy, they think it will be lessened in this manner; granting that the Father and Son are two persons, the Son suffering, and the Father sympathizing with him. But in this they are foolish; for what is *sympathizing*, but suffering with another *."

Notwithstanding this mode in which the unitarian doctrine was held by some philosophizing persons, it appears that they were considered as being mere unitarians, as much as the common people, to whom this mode

---

* Ergo nec compassus est pater filio; sic enim directam blasphemiam in patrem veriti, diminui eam hoc modo sperant, concedentes jam patrem et filium duos esse; si filius quidem patitur, pater vero compatitur. Stulti in hoc. Quid est enim compati, quam cum alio pati? Porro, si impassibilis pater, utique et incompassibilis. Aut si compassibilis utique passibilis. Nihil ei vel hoc timore tuo præstas. Times dicere passibilem, quem dicis compassibilem. Ad Praxeam, sect. 29. p. 518.

of explaining the doctrine muſt have been unintelligible; and all the more diſtinguiſhed unitarians of that age, whether they be ſaid to explain their ſentiments in this manner, or not, are repreſented as holding the ſame opinion, and the very ſame that was maintained by the Jews. Thus Sabellius, Marcellus, and Photinus, are all claſſed together by Chryſoſtom*; and inſtances frequently occur, in which all theſe are ſaid to hold the ſame doctrine with Artemon, Theodotus, and Paulus Samoſatenſis. That Sabellius in particular, though he is generally repreſented as a Patripaſſian, was neverthleſs a proper unitarian, who believed Chriſt to have no proper divinity of his own, is evident from the arguments with which his antagoniſts preſs him.—Thus Epiphanius, in anſwer to the Sabellians, ſays that " Jeſus came the Son of God " to the river Jordan †."

---

* Αλλ' ιδε παλιν επιπηδα Σαβελλιος και Μαρκελλ. και Φωτεινος. In Heb. Opera, vol. 10. p. 1763.

† Αρκεσυσιν αυτοις Σαβελλιανοις μεν μετα των αλλων μαρτυριων η μαρτυρια τυ Ιορδανυ, ως ηδη ειπον. υιος γαρ εν Ιορδανη αληθως παραγινεται. Ancoratus, ſect. 119. Opera, vol. 2. p. 121.

Whatever Sabellianism was, whether the more simple, or the more philosophical kind of unitarianism, it appears to have been very popular in Africa, and to have had many adherents among the bishops of that country. Athanasius makes heavy complaints on this subject, saying, as was quoted before, that Sabellianism prevailed so much there, that the Son of God was hardly preached in the churches.

The controversy with the philosophical unitarians took a turn considerably different from that with the simple unitarians, and unfortunately led the orthodox into an embarrassment and inconsistency, which became very apparent when the Arian controversy arose. And, indeed, the language that had been adopted as proper for the controversy with the philosophical unitarians, appears to have contributed very much to the rise of Arianism. For as these learned unitarians asserted that the Father, Son, and Spirit (meaning the *divinity* belonging to them) were *the same*, their adversaries had incautiously advanced, that they were *essentially* different, and that the Father and Son had

had even *different natures.* And so far were the orthodox, in this state of things, from asserting, as they did at the council of Nice, that the Son was *consubstantial* with the Father, that they were the first to assert the direct contrary, as they did in the condemnation of Paulus Samosatensis. Thus Basil says, " that they who condemned " him rejected the word consubstantial *."

But this language was retracted when Arius was to be condemned. So different a thing was the orthodoxy of the different periods. Optatus, and others, acknowledge that the famous term *consubstantial*, was first introduced in the Sabellian controversy, when it seems to have been used by the Sabellians, and disclaimed by the orthodox, whose object was to distinguish the members of the trinity, which the Sabellians were charged with confounding (Lib. 1. p. 8.) Origen, in answer to the Sabel-

---

* Και γαρ τω ονλι οι επι Παυλω τω Σαμοσαίει συνελθονίες, διαβαλον την λεξιν ως εκ ευσημον. Εφασαν γαρ εκεινοι την τε ομοεσια φωνην παριταν εννοιαν εσιας τε η των απ' αυλης, ως τε καλαμερισθεισαν την εσιαν παρεχειν τε ομοεσια την προσηγοριαν τοις εις α διηρεθη. Epist. 300. Opera, vol. 3. p. 292.

lians,

lians, shows, that in several places the Father and Christ are spoken of as different persons, especially when the Father is said to raise Christ from the dead *. I have observed that Origen expressly maintained that the Son had an *essence* different from that of the Father; and he makes it an objection to the unitarians, that they made the essence of both to be the same. "Because," says he, "Christ is called the true "light, and in the epistle of John God "is called light, some think that the es- "sence of the Son does not differ from "that of the Father †." On this account, among others, the orthodoxy of Origen was called in question by some after the Arian controversy; whereas it is very evident that

---

* Μετα δε τετω εκ ατοπον εςι τον ομολογεντα μηδεν δυνασθαι ποιειν εαν μη τι βλεπη τον πατερα ποιεντα κ᾽ λεγοντα οτι ο δε αν πατηρ ποιει ταυτα ομοιως κ᾽ ο υιος ποιει, τον νεκρον οπερ το σωμα ην ηγηγερκεναι, τε πατρος αυτο τετο χαριζομενε, ον προηγεμενως λεκτεον εγηγερκεναι χριςον εκ νεκρων. Comment. vol. 2. p. p. 187.

† Επει δε φως απαξαπλως ενταυθα μεν ο σωτηρ, εν δε τη καθολικη τε αυτε Ιωαννε επιςολη λεγεται ο θεος ειναι φως, ο μεν τις οιεται και εντευθεν κατασκευαζεσθαι η εσια μη διεςηκεναι τε υιε τον πατερα. Ibid. p. 70.

both

both his opinions, and his language, were the very same that were held by all the orthodox of his own age; and Athanasius and others made allowance for this, and apologized for him, as they also did for Dionysius of Alexandria, who is often called the Father of Arianism.

Though the orthodox found it convenient to change the use of this word *consubstantial* when the circumstances of things were changed, the unitarians did not; and therefore Marcellus and Eustathius of Antioch, his disciple, declared loudly for it, at the council of Nice, as Beausobre observes*.

There is another circumstance relating to this controversy that deserves to be particularly noticed; as it also shews what different ideas, and what different language, men will adopt in different situations. As the philosophical unitarians held that the Father, Son, and Spirit (meaning the divinity belonging to them) were the same, and alledged in

* Hist. de Manicheisme, vol. I. p. 542.

proof of this our Saviour saying *I and my Father are one*; the orthodox, in answer to them, said that the *one* was in the neuter gender, and therefore, that the unity between them was not an unity of *essence*, but only of *harmony*, and *affection*. Novatian says, that " because Christ says *they were* " *one*, in the neuter gender, let the heretics " understand that it signifies the concord " of society, not unity of person*." This is the very explanation of this text, that the unitarians after the council of Nice always gave, when the orthodox availed themselves of it, as a proof that the Father and the Son were one in *essence*, or were *consubstantial* to each other. Then nothing could be said too high of the divinity of the Son. But Novatian, who lived before the Arian controversy, says, " Most of the " heretics, moved with the greatness and

---

* Qui potuisset dicere, ego pater, si patrem se esse meminisset. Et quia dixit unum, intelligant hæretici quia non dixit unus. Unum enim neutraliter positum societatis concordiam, non unitatem personæ, sonat. Cap. 27, p. 99.

" truth

"truth of Christ's divinity, extend his
"honours beyond bounds, daring to call
"him not God the Son, but God the
"Father himself*." Thus the great object of the orthodox in the second century, was to make a God of Christ, but a far *inferior* God, and also a God *of*, or *out of God* the Father, lest he should be thought to be *another God*, and independent of the Father. On the other hand, the great object of the orthodoxy of a later period, was to exalt the Son to a perfect equality with the Father, so as to allow the Father no advantage but what was *nominal*, or respected mere *order*. Hence the difference of the language, and in the arguments of the two different periods. While the unitarians always considered the Father as the only true God, and Christ *a mere man*, the servant of God. And if the more philoso-

---

* Ut plerique hæreticorum, divinitatis ipsius magnitudine et veritate commoti, ultra modum extendentes honores ejus, ausi sint non filium, sed ipsum deum patrem promere vel putare. Cap. 23. p. 87.

phical among them ascribed any divinity to him, it was only the divinity of the Father, residing in him, and acting by him, and that only for a time; it being withdrawn from him again, when the purpose of its emission had been answered.

CHAPTER XVIII.

Of the Principles and Arguments of the ancient Unitarians.

I SHALL now proceed to give a distinct view of the principles of the ancient unitarians, and of the arguments by which they defended them; and I beg that my readers would compare them with the arguments of the trinitarians, of which an account has been given already.

SECTION I.

Their Zeal for the Divine Unity, and their Sense of the Word Logos.

ALL the denominations of unitarians, comprizing both the vulgar and the philosophical part of them, considered themselves as advocates for *the unity of God,* which they thought was infringed by their opponents.

opponents. Of this we have sufficient evidence in every period of their history; and thus much is acknowledged by all their adversaries. Whatever their mistakes were, it was owned that they were led into them by their dread of violating the first, and the greatest of all the principles of religion, viz. that of the proper *unity of the divine nature*. Sufficient evidence of this hath been given already; but to this view of their arguments, I shall prefix a few other passages of the Fathers, which likewise clearly prove it.

Origen evidently considered the unitarians as persons who really *dreaded* lest, by admitting Christ to be God, they should infringe upon the honour that was due to the Father only. "By these means," he says, "may be explained that which greatly "disturbs many persons, who plead a prin-"ciple of piety, and who fear to make "two Gods*." He afterwards recurs to the same subject, and introduces it as an

---

* Και το πολλυς φιλοθεως ειναι ευχομενυς ταρασσον, ευλαβομενυς δυο αναγορευσαι. Comment. in Johannem, Edit. Huetii, vol. 2. p. 46.

CHAP. XVIII. *of ancient Unitarians.* 401

objection of persons with whom he would not trifle, and whom he was far from charging with hypocrisy. "But since," says he, "it is probable that many may be "offended, because we say that one is the "true God, namely, the Father, and be- "sides this true God, there are many who "are made gods by participation; fearing "that the glory of him, who exceeds all "creatures, should be brought down to "that of others, who obtained the appella- "tion of Gods, &c.*" Origen, therefore, must have thought respectfully of those early unitarians, and have considered them as objecting to the doctrine of the divinity of Christ from the very best principles.

Novatian says, that "when they," the unitarians, "observe, that it is written there "is but one God, they think that they "can no otherwise maintain the truth of "this, than by asserting, either that Christ is a

* Αλλ' επει επι⊙ προσκοψειν τινας τοις ειρημενοις ενος μεν αληθινε θεε τε πατρος απαγγελλομενε, παρα δε τον αληθινον θεον θεε· πλειονων τη μετοχη τε θεε γινομενων, ευλαεομενες την τε πασαν κτισιν υπερεχοντος δοξαν εξισωσαι τοις λοιποις της θεος προσηγοριας τυγχανεσι, &c. Comment. in Johannem, Edit. Huetii, vol. 2. p. 46.

Vol. III.   D d   " mere

"mere man, or that he is God the Fa-
"ther *. Eusebius says, that "Marcellus
"wrote his book in order to assert the
"the unity of God †." He also says, that
"Marcellus gloried in acknowledging but
"one God ‡." Athanasius says, that "the
"followers of Marcellus and Photinus de-
"nied the pre-existence of Christ, and his
"divinity, and his everlasting kingdom,
"along with the Jews, on pretence of esta-
"blishing a monarchy §." "They so cor-
"rupt the sacred faith of the gospel," says
Hilary, "that from a profession of re-
"verence towards God, they denied the
"nativity of his only begotten Son, saying,

* Quia cum animadverterent scriptum esse quod unus sit deus, non aliter putaverant istam tenere se posse sententiam, nisi aut hominem tantum Christum, aut certe deum patrem putarent esse credendum. Cap. 30. p. 116.

† Τῦτο φησι πεποιηκεναι, δια το ενα γνωριζειν θεον. Ec. Theol. lib. 1. pref. p. 57.

‡ Αλλα και σεμνυνεῖαι αυχων ενα θεον ειδεναι. Ibid. cap. 17. p. 80.

§ Οι απο Μαρκελλυ κͺ Φωτεινυ των Αγκυρογαλατων, οι την προαιωνιον υπαρξιν τυ χριςυ, και την θεοτητα, κͺ την ατελευτητον αυτυ βασιλειαν ομοιως Ιυδαιοις αθετυσιν, επι προφασει τυ συνιςαςθαι δοκειν τη μοναρχια. De Synodis Armen. Opera, vol. 1. p. 898.

"that

CHAP. XVIII. *of ancient Unitarians.* 403

" that there is a protension, rather than
" a descent into man *." In this he alludes to the principles of the philosophical unitarians. Gregory Nazianzen, addressing the unitarians, calls them, by way of ridicule, φιλαγεννητοι, φιλαναρχοι, as pretending to a great zeal for the honour of the Father, as the unbegotten, and without origin †; and in another place he complains, that " the greatest obstacle to the
" reception of the truth, was the piety
" of his hearers ‡." He says they had zeal, but not according to knowledge, and therefore would be punished with few stripes §.

* Quidam ita evangelicæ fidei corrumpunt sacramentum, ut sub unius dei pia tantum professione nativitatem unigeniti dei abnegent: ut protensio sit potius in hominem quam descensio. Lib. I. p. 10.

† Προσερησομαι σε ολιγον φιλαγεννητε συ κ̓ φιλαναρχε. Or. 13. p. 209.

‡ Αλλ᾽ ὁτι και ο τοις αλλο τι διδασκειν υπισχνυμενοις ρᾳον ποιει τον λογον κ̓ ευπαραδεκτον, η των ακουοντων ευλαβεια, τετο ενταυθα η ζημια καθισται κ̓ ο κινδυνος. Or. I. p. 17.

§ Και τετο ετι λεγω, των μετριωτερων κ̓ ε πανῃ κακων το παθος, οι καν της αληθειας διαμαρτανωσιν, αλλα τω γε δι ευλαβειαν τετο πασχειν, κ̓ ζηλον μεν εχειν, αλλ᾽ ε κατ᾽ επιγνωσιν, τυχον εσονται των ε

D d 2 σφοδρα

There is something particularly striking in the account that Epiphanius gives of the manner in which Sabellians would accost men of plain understanding on the subject of the unity of God, and the usual effect of such zeal and good sense. " Well, my " friends," say they, " have we one God, or " three Gods ? and when a pious person, " and one who is not sufficiently upon " his guard, hears this, he is immediately " alarmed, and assents to his error, so as " to deny the Son, and the Holy Spirit *."

Cyril of Alexandria says, that " they " who acknowledged only one God, and " who denied that he had generated a Son " out of himself, pretended that it was from " a principle of piety †." Beausobre there-

σφοδρα καταχρινομενων, ουδε πολλας δερομενων, ως οι δια κακιαν κỳ πονηριαν, τυ δεσποτικυ θεληματος αποπιπτοντες. Or. 1. p. 18.

* Ειτα οταν συναντησωσι τισι των αφελεςατων, η ακεραιων, των μη τα σαφη των θειων γραφων γινωσκοντων, την πευσιν αυτοις υφηγυνται ταυτην. τι αν ειπωμεν, ω υιοι, ενα θεον εχομεν, η τρεις θευς; οταν δε ακυση ο εν ευλαβεια ων, κỳ μη τα τελεια της ασφαλειας επιςαμενΘ-, ευθυς τον νυν ταραχθεις, συνκαταθλιθεται τη εκεινων πλανη, κỳ ευρισκεται αρνυμενΘ- τον θεον, κỳ ευρισκεται αρνυμενΘ- το ειναι υιον κỳ το αγιον πνευμα. Hær. 62. Opera, vol. 1. p. 514.

† Ειτα τι φαιεν αν, οι τοις προς ημων αντιτιςαμενοι λογοις, κỳ υποπλατομενοι μεν την ευσεβειαν, δια γε τυ συνομολογειν ως ειη θεος,

CHAP. XVIII. *of ancient Unitarians* 405

therefore had reason to acknowledge that Sabellianism was innocent in its origin, and arose from the fear of making more gods than one *.

That the cause of the unitarians was considered as the same with that of the Jews, the great advocates of the divine unity appears from Chrysostom, who, speaking of the divinity of Christ, as proved from the Old Testament, says, that " if " any Jew, under the form of a christian, " lift up his head (I mean Paulus Samosa- " tensis) the same arguments may be used " against him;" and afterwards, " what " was said against the Jews, may be said to " those who have the same origin †." M. Caleca also makes Sabellianism to be the same thing with Judaism ‡.

εις τε κ̓ μονος· ὑμην ὅτι κ̓ γεγεννηκεν εξ ἑαυτȣ τον υιον. Contra Julianum, lib. 1. Juliani, Opera, vol. 2. p. 22.

* Histoire de Manicheisme, vol. 1. p. 535.

† Ει δε ἑτερος ἡμιν Ιȣδαιος ανακυπτει παλιν προσωπον χρισιανȣ περιφερων, Παυλος ὁ Σαμοσατευς, λεγω, δυναῖον μεν και προς τȣτον και απο της καινης λεγειν Δει δε τα αλλα απερ προς Ιȣδαιȣς ειρηται, και προς τȣς απο τȣτȣ ειπειν. In Ps. 109. Opera, vol. 3. p. 323.

‡ Ου τȣτο λεγω, ὅτι ὁ πατηρ εστι και υιος, και αγιον πνευμα· τȣ- το γαρ Ιȣδαικον εστι και δοξα τȣ Σαϐελως. Combefis Auctuarium, vol. 2. p. 203.

My readers will probably wiſh to know in what ſenſe the ancient unitarians underſtood the term *logos*, of which ſo many different opinions have been entertained by chriſtians; and on this head it is in my power to give them the moſt complete ſatisfaction. The *logos* has been ſo long conſidered by the generality of chriſtians as ſynonymous to *Chriſt*, that they think any other interpretation to be harſh and unnatural. Socinus himſelf, and many who are now called Socinians, conſidered it as meaning *the goſpel*, or the word of God, in its moſt literal ſenſe. But all the ancient unitarians, without exception, conſidered it as ſignifying that *word of God* by which the world was made, viz. the *power* of God, his eſſential operative attribute; and it will appear, that they were exceedingly ſurpriſed at hearing of any other interpretation of it. Now, conſidering that the common people, as well as the learned, among the unitarians, had this idea of it, it cannot but be concluded to have been the proper original ſenſe of the term, becauſe it was ſo underſtood by thoſe very perſons for whoſe use the gospel of John was written. This is an article of so much consequence, that I shall produce a considerable number of authorities for it; disposing of them pretty nearly according to the age of the writers from whom they are collected.

Hippolytus, writing against Noetus, says, "I shall be told, you tell me something strange, when you call the logos the Son *." In the larger exposition of faith ascribed to Gregory Thaumaturgus, it is said, "Some make the wisdom of God to resemble the wisdom of man, because he is wise, and his word to be like that word which is uttered, or conceived, in the mind, without any hypostasis †." "Some disciples of Paulus

---

* Αλλ' ερει μοι τις, ξενον μοι φερεις λογον λεγων υιον. Opera, p. 16.

† Non minus alieni sunt, qui trinitatem non secundum veritatem ex tribus personis confitentur, sed in unitate triplicatam secundum compositionem impie fingunt, et sapientiam in deo existimant esse sicut in homine sapientiam humanam, qua sapiens est: et verbum simile esse interpretantur verbo quod ore profertur, vel mente concipitur, nulla hypostasi. Opera, p. 16.

"Samosa-

"Samosatensis," says Athanasius, "distin-
"guish the logos from the Son, saying,
"that the Son is Christ, but the logos is
"another thing*." "Paulus Samosaten-
"sis," says Epiphanius, held that the logos
"of God, and his spirit, was always in
"God, as the logos of man is in man; and
"that the Son had no personal subsistence,
"which was also the doctrine of Sabellius,
"Novatus, Noetus, and others †." Hilary also says that "the word of God, according to the heretics, was the power
"of God ‡."

That this was the doctrine of Marcellus and Photinus, we have the clearest evidence,

---

* Τινες των απο τȣ Σαμοσαλεως, διαιρȣνίες τον λογον απο τȣ υιȣ, φασκȣσι τον μεν υιον ειναι τον χριϛον, τον δε λογον αλλον ειναι. Contra Arianos, Or. 5. Opera, vol. 1. p. 543.

† Εν Θεω δε αει ονία τον αυίȣ λογον, και το πνευμα αυίȣ, ωσπερ εν ανθρωπȣ καρδια ο ιδιΘ- λογΘ- . μη ειναι δε τον υιον τȣ Θεȣ ενυποϛαίον, αλλα εν αυίω Θεω . ωσπερ αμελει και ο ΣαϬελλιΘ-, και ο ΝαυαίΘ-, και ο ΝοηίΘ-, και αλλοι. Hær. 65. Opera, vol. 1. p. 608.

‡ Per quod etiam illud vitii adjungitur, ut deus verbum tanquam pars aliqua virtutum dei, quodam se tractu continuationis extendens hominem illum, qui a Maria esse cæpit habitaverit, et virtutibus divinæ operationis instruxerit; animæ tamen suæ motu naturaque viventem. Lib. 10. p. 258.

especially

CHAP. XVIII. *of ancient Unitarians.* 409

especially from Eusebius, who wrote against the former of them. "Marcellus," he says, "believed Christ to be the word of God, but a *mere word*, like that of man, and not a living and substantial son*." Again, he says, "Marcellus asserts, that the logos is not used by way of figure, though those who teach the contrary should burst with their lies, but simply and truly logos," or reason †. "Marcellus held that the logos was always united to, and connected with the Father ‡." He held that the "logos was in God, as his reason; that it was for a time out of God, and returned into him at the day of judgment, and was then united to him as it had been before §." Chrysostom

---

* Ψιλον γαρ, και τω ανθρωπειω λογω ομοιον, ουχι δε υιον αληθως ζωντα και υφεϛωτα, τον χριϛον ειναι ομολογειν εθελει. Contra Marcellum, lib. 1. p. 19.

† Ου καταχρηϛικως λογος ονομαϛθεις καν διαρραγοιεν οι ἑτεροδιδασκαλουντες ψευδομενοι, αλλα κυριως τε και αληθως υπαρχων λογος. Ibid. lib. 2. p. 40.

‡ Τουτον αυτον λογον εχειν εν εαυτω ενωμενον και συνημμενον αυτω φησιν. Ec. Theol. lib. 1. cap. 5. p. 63.

§ Τοσαυτα Μαρκελλος περι τε λογε ειπων, τε εν τω θεω, καθ' ο νουν ειναι τον λογικον ειναι, δεινη δυσχωρια περιπεπλακε, τολμησας εκ ἑαυτε

also says, that " Marcellus, Photinus, and
" Sophronius, say that the logos is an
" energy, and that this energy inhabits
" him who was the son of David, but is
" not a subsisting person *." Theophilact
repeats this in almost the same words, saying, " Marcellus of Galatia, Photinus, and
" Sophronius, said that the logos was the
" energy of God, and not a personal sub-
" sistence, and that it inhabited a descen-
" dant of David †." Epiphanius says, that
" Photinus asserted that the logos of God
" was from the beginning, but that it was
" not the Son of God ‡."

I shall add a few other testimonies from later writers. Cyril of Alexandria, writing

τȣ Θεȣ γεγονεναι τοδε φαναι τον εν αυτω λογον. και παλιν ενίος αυτȣ μετα τον καιρον της κρισεως· ιν ᾱλως ην εν τω Θεω ενωθεις αυτω, ωσπερ και προτερον ην. Ec. Theol. lib. 1. cap. 8. p. 113.

* Μαρκελλος και Φωτεινος, και Σωφρονιος, τον λογον ενεργειαν ειναι φασι, την δε ενεργειαν ταυτην ενοικησαι τω εκ σπερματος Δαϐ. δ, ȣκ ȣσιαν ενυποϛατον. In Phil. 2. Opera, vol. 10. p. 1239.

† Μαρκελλος ο Γαλατης, και Φωτεινος, και Σωφρονιος, ελεγον τον λογον τȣ Θεȣ ενεργειαν ειναι, ȣκ ȣσιαν ενυποϛατον· ταυτην δε ενοικησαι τον εκ σπερματος Δαϐιδ. In Phil. 2. Opera, vol. 2. p. 591.

‡ Και αυτος φημι ειναι τον λογον απ αρχης, αλλ' ȣχ υιον Θεȣ γεγεν-ημενον. Hær. 71. p. 831.

against

Chap. XVIII. *of ancient Unitarians.*

against Theodorus, who is said to have been the proper father of Nestorianism (which differed very little from the unitarian doctrine) evidently supposes that this was the received doctrine of the unitarians, when he says, " It is false to say that the word " of God has no substance. It is the " eructation of a foolish heart; For he " himself said to Moses, I am that I am, " and therefore they who think so we deem " most stupid *." Again, replying to those who said that the logos is *verbum insitum*, or the proper internal reason of the Father, " Why did not our Saviour say, I and the " word of my Father are one, and he that " sees me, sees the word of the Father." He adds, that " the logos, in the introduc- " tion to the gospel of John has the article " prefixed to it, which shews that it did

---

* Minime enim mentietur falsissimum esse sermonem, quod verbum quod ex deo apparuit, dicatur non habuisse substantiam: est enim stultissimi cordis eructatio. Nam ipse dicebat Mosi ego sum qui sum: quomodo autem unquam hoc quod vere est, in substantia per se non servari intelligitur? et propterea eos qui sic sentiunt, merito rudissimos esse definimus. Opera, vol. 2. p. 687.

" not

"not mean *reason* in general, but a particular specific logos *." I do not think it at all necessary to reply to the reasoning of Cyril in this place, I only quote him in order to ascertain what it was that the unitarians, his adversaries, thought on the subject.

The emperor Julian gives his testimony to the unitarians having supposed that by logos was intended the power of God, "Some of the impious," meaning the christians, he says, "say that Jesus Christ is one person, and he that is called the logos by John another †." He likewise says that "John does not mention the name of Jesus, or

---

* Præterea si unigenitus dei filius idcirco verbum est et vocatur, quoniam (ut ipsi dicunt) insitum patris verbum suscipiens, ad illud formatur: cur non dixit ad discipulos, ego et verbum patris unum sumus: et, qui me videt, is etiam verbum patris videt?——Ideo videmus filium hominis, articulo ad utrumque nomen præposito, salvatore nostro proferri, quando se solum ab infinita hominum multitudine velit significare. In John, cap. 4. Opera, vol. 1. p. 610.

† Και τοι δοκει τισι των δυσσεβων αλλον μεν Ιησυν ειναι χριστον, αλλον δε τον υπο Ιωαννυ κηρυτλομενον λογον. Cyril. Contra Jul. lib. 10. Opera, vol. 2. p. 333.

CHAP. XVIII. *of ancient Unitarians.* 413

" of Chrift, when he calls him God and
" logos *."

This ufe of the term *logos* or *word*, is common in the Old Teftament, as when the Pfalmift fays, *By the word of the Lord were the heavens made*, &c. and Macarius, having no view to this controverfy, fays, " The word of God is God, and the " word of the world is the world," and then fpeaks of the difference between the word of God and the word of the world, and between the children of God, and the children of the world †.

In this fenfe, according to Eufebius, the Jews always underftood the term *logos*. " If " any one," fays he, " fuppofe that the " Son is a mere *word*—that it is quiefcent " in the Father, when he is quiefcent, but " was active when he made the world, re-

---

* Ουδαμε δε αυτον ειε Ιησεν, ειε χριςον, αχρις ε Θεον και λογον αποκαλει. Cyril. Contra Jul. lib. 10. Opera, vol. 2. p. 327.

† Ο τε Θεε λογ⊙, Θεος εςι. και ο λογ⊙ τε κοσμε κοσμ⊙ εςι· πολλη δε διαφορα και μεσοτης τυγχανει, τε τε λογε τε Θεε, και τε λογε τε κοσμε, και των τεκνων τε Θεε, και των τεκνων τε κοσμε· εκαςον γαρ γεννημα τοις ιδιοις εοικε γονευσιν. Opera, p. 223.

" fembling

" fembling the logos of man, which is
" quiefcent when we are filent, but active
" when we fpeak; it is evident that he
" interprets as the Jews do, and according
" to human reafon, and that he denies the
" true Son of God *." He then adds what was quoted in this volume, p. 13. concerning the Jews acknowledging that God has a logos, but no Son.

* Ο δε ψιλον λογον ειναι τον υιον απολαμβανων, και μονον λογον ειναι μαρτυρομενος, κỳ πολλακις τετ' αυτο λεγων ως εδεν ετερον ην ο λογΘ-, ενδον μενων εν τω ησυχαζοντι τω πατρι, ενεργων τε εν τω ημετερω την κτισιν δημιεργειν· ομοιως τω ημετερω, εν σιοπωσι μεν ησυχαζοντι, εν δε φθεγγομενοις ενεργετιι, δηλον αι ειη Ιεδαικω τινι κỳ ανθρωπινω συντρεχων φρονηματι, τον δε αληθως υιον τε θεε αρνεμενΘ-. Contra Marcellum, lib. 1. p. 4.

SEC-

SECTION II.

Arguments of the ancient Unitarians from Reason.

HAVING stated what the principles of the ancient unitarians were, I shall in the next place, give a view of the *arguments* by which they defended them; and as some of these were drawn from the principles of reason, and others from the scriptures, I shall mention the former in the first place. But in this I need not insist upon their capital argument, viz. that the doctrine of the divinity of Christ and of the trinity, is an infringement of the great doctrine of natural and revealed religion, *the unity of God*. This has appeared sufficiently already. Also many of their other arguments have been mentioned in the replies of their trinitarian adversaries. I shall, therefore, only recite such others as have happened to occur separately.

That

That the ancient unitarians were much addicted to *reasoning*, and that they often disputed with great acuteness and subtility, so as to puzzle their opponents, may be inferred from what is said of them by Eusebius, viz. that " they neglected the " scriptures, and reasoned in syllogisms *." No doubt they did reason, and probably in the syllogistic form, as was the custom with logicians, and I doubt not very closely and justly; but it will be seen that they were far from neglecting the scriptures.

According to the most ancient doctrine of the generation of the Son, there was a time when the Father was simply *one*, and had not generated this Son. Upon this idea, Marcellus said that, " if it be a per-" fection in the Father to have a Son, he " was imperfect while he was without " one †."

---

* Ου τι αι θειαι λεγεσι γραφαι ζητουντες, αλλ᾽ οποιον σχημα συλλογισμε εις την της αθεοτητος ευρεθη συςασιν, φιλοπονως ασκουντες. Hist. lib. 8. cap. 28. p. 253.

† Ει γαρ αει τελειος ο θεος, και παρεςιν αυτω δυναμις τε πατερα αυτον ειναι, κỳ καλον αυτον ειναι πατερα τε τοιετε υιε, αναβαλλεται, κỳ εαυτον τε καλε ςηρισκει, και ως εςιν ειπειν, εξ ε δυναται πατηρ ειναι υιε. Contra Marcellum, lib. 1. p. 22.

To

CHAP. XVIII. *of ancient Unitarians.* 417

To the doctrine of divine generation in general, the objection was, that the divine essence must then be corporeal. "Marcellus said, that, if the Son be a *probole*," or production, "from the Father, and he be
" his offspring, like the offspring of other
" living creatures, both the being pro-
" ducing, and the being produced, must be
" corporeal *."

That the Son, who was generated from the Father, was allowed by those who first advanced that doctrine to be inferior to the Father, the most abundant proof has been given. Afterwards all this was retracted. But the unitarians retorted it upon them. " The enemies of truth," says Chrysostom,
" urge that, if the Son be equal to the
" Father, why did not the Father become
" incarnate? As it was the Son who took
" the form of a servant, is it not plain that
" he is inferior. But if on this account
" he took human nature, the Spirit, who,

‡ Ει γαρ προβολη εστιν ο υιος τε πατρος, και γεννα μεν εξ αυτε οποια τα των ζωων γεννηματα, αναγκη σωμα ειναι τον προβαλλοντα κ) τον προσεβλημενον. Contra Marcellum, lib. I. p. 22.

Vol. III.   E e   " they

"they say (though we do not acknowledge
"this) is inferior to the Son, should have
"been incarnate *."

The trinitarians, giving a reason for the mystery of the incarnation, held that the divinity gave a value to the sufferings of the human nature to which it was united. But the unitarians urged the absurdity of this; saying, according to Theodoret, "If a man "only suffered, it was a man that saved "us †." This is an argument to which the orthodox have always made very lame replies. They have never chose to say that the *deity* of Christ suffered, or that it partook of the sufferings of the human nature. Consequently, if it was only *man* that suffered, the satisfaction made by that suffering could only be finite; and in fact,

---

* Και γαρ και τ𐐌το περιφερ𐐌σιν οι της αληθειας εχθροι, λεγοντες; ὅτι ει ιϲος ην τω γεγεννηκοτι, τινος ενεκεν ο πατηρ 𐐌κ ανελαβε σαρκα, αλλ' υιος υπεδυ την τ𐐌 δ𐐌λ𐐌 μορφην; αρα 𐐌κ ευδηλον, ὅτι επειδη καταδεεϲτερος ην; και μην ει δια τ𐐌το την ἡμετεραν υπεδυ φυσιν, το πνευμα, ο φασιν αυτοι τ𐐌 υι𐐌 ελατίον ειναι (𐐌 γαρ αν ημεις ειποιμεν) εκεινο ϲαρκωθηναι εδει. Ser. 51. Opera, vol. 5. p. 697.

† Ανθρωπος εν ημιν παρεσχε την σωτηριαν. Dial. 3. Opera, vol 4. p. 116.

could

CHAP. XVIII. *of ancient Unitarians.* 419

could extend no farther than the sufferings of any other man.

Novatian says, in proof of the divinity of Christ, " if he be only a man, why is he every where invoked, since it is the nature not of man, but of God, to be present in every place *?" But whatever might be the case in the time of Novatian (when what he says could not be true of any besides the trinitarians) this certainly was not the practice even with *them* in the time of Origen, who flourished not more than twenty years before him. This has been shewn already, and therefore this universal practice might have been urged, and probably was urged, by the ancient unitarians, as an argument in their favour. According to Origen, the custom of christians was to pray to God through Christ †. And

* Si homo tantummodo Christus; quomodo abest ubique invocatus, cum hæc hominis natura non sit, sed dei, ut adesse omni loco possit? Cap. 14. p. 45.

† Θρησκευομεν εν τον πατερα της αληθειας, κỳ τον υιον την αληθειαν, ονια δυο τη υποτασει πραγμαία, εν δε τη ομονοια, κỳ τη συμφωνια, κỳ τη ταυτοτητι τε βελημαίος. Ad Celsum, lib. 8. p. 386.

Christ

Chrift was fuppofed to join in their prayers. "We are not to pray," fays he, "without our high-prieft *." In like manner, other faints were fuppofed, in the time of Origen, to bear their part in the prayers of the churches to which they had belonged, long before it was thought right to pray *to* them, and this was the natural progrefs of things with refpect to Chrift.

It has been feen how ftrenuoufly the ancient unitarians infifted upon the *antiquity* of their doctrine, and how far all the learned trinitarians conceded to them, by admitting that, in the time of the apoftles, the doctrine of the divinity of Chrift was not taught openly; becaufe the world was not then ready to receive it. It has alfo been feen that Bafil was charged with introducing *novelty* into his diocefe, efpecially in his form of doxology to the Holy Spirit; from which it is evident, that the unitarians of that age and country confidered his doctrine as having had fome other origin than either the fcriptures, or chrif-

* Αλλα μη χωρις τε αρχιερεως. De Oratione, p. 49.

tian

CHAP. XVIII. *of ancient Unitarians.* 421

tian antiquity; and one of them certainly thought very juftly of it, when he faid to Bafil, " I know nothing of your foreign " philofophy*." In that country, the authority of Gregory Thaumaturgus was very great, and it was appealed to both by Bafil and his adverfaries, who were perhaps better judges than himfelf, of what had been the cuftom before he came into the diocefe. In a letter to his clergy, he fays, " do not " defpife the hypoftafes, do not deny the " name of Chrift, or pervert the fayings of " Gregory †."

Gregory Nyffen fays, that he and his friends were charged with innovation when they taught the doctrine of three hypoftafes, of one goodnefs, one power, and one divinity ‡."

* Ου γαρ συνιημι υμων της αλλοκοτα σοφιας. De Sp. S. cap. 17. Opera, vol. 2. p. 330.

† Τας υποςασεις μη αθελειτε, το ονομα τα χριτα μη απαρνεισθε, τας τα Γρηγοριυ φονας μη παρεξηγεισθε. Epift. 63. Opera, vol. 3. p. 98.

‡ Αλλ' καινοδομιαν ημιν προφερασιν αιωσι το εγκλημα καθ' ημων συνιθεντες. τρεις υποςασεις ομολογαντων, μιαν αγαθοτητα, μιαν δυναμιν κ μιαν θεοτητα λεγειν ημας αιτιωνται. De Trinitate, vol. 2. p. 439.

E e 3   The

The apostles creed has been shewn to afford a strong argument for the antiquity and purity of the ancient unitarian doctrine. This argument was urged by Photinus, who, according to Ruffinus, pleaded that " the apostles creed, literally under-" stood, was in his favour*." Marcellus, in his epistle, quotes the whole of the apostles creed, and assents to it †.

The orthodox used to alledge the received mode of baptism as a proof of the divinity of Christ; but we learn from Basil, that the unitarians replied, that " baptiz-" ing in the name of the Spirit was no " proof of his godhead, because mention is " made of baptizing unto Moses‡."

---

* Fotinum vero hæreticum scio eatenus scripsisse, non ut rationem dictorum audientibus explanaret, sed ut simplicitur fideliterque dicta, ad argumentum sui dogmatis traheret. In Symbol. pref. p. 169.

† Epiphanii, Opera, vol. 1. p. 836.

‡ Αλλ' ᾖδε ει βαπτιζομεθα, φησιν, εις αυτο, ᾖδ' ἀῖω δικαιον μετα Θεᾳ τετάχθαι. κ᾿ γαρ, κ᾿ εις τον Μωσην τινες εβαπτισθησαν, εν τη νεφελη κ᾿ εν τη θαλασση. De Sp. S. cap. 14. Opera, vol. 2. p. 318.

SECTION III.

Arguments of the ancient Unitarians from the Scriptures.

THE great strong hold of the unitarians was the scriptures, and the plain literal sense of them. "They bawl out", says Basil, "with their proofs from scripture, "and make no account of the unwritten "traditions of the Fathers*." And Photinus, in his dispute with Basil, said that "he could prove his doctrine by a hundred "passages of scripture †." The orthodox in general, complained of the advantage which the unitarians had in appealing to the literal sense of the scripture. "If," says Gregory Nyssen, "a man rests in the

---

* Τας εκ των εγγραφων αποδειξεις επιδουναι, την αγραφον των πατερων μαρτυριαν ως ουδενος αξιαν αποπεμπομενοι. De Sp. S. cap. 10. Opera, vol. 2. p. 313.

† Και μετα καυχησεως περι της υποθεσεως εκατον μαρτυριας φερειν ο γενναδας επηγγειλατο. Epiphanius, Hær. 70. vol. 1. p. 829.

"bare

"bare letter, so far he judaizes in opinion, and has not learned that a christian is not the disciple of the letter, but of the Spirit, for the letter killeth, but the Spirit giveth life*."

It is to be observed, that by *judaizing*, was meant adopting the doctrine of the simple humanity of Christ. For the ancient unitarians were commonly compared by the orthodox to Jews, and the Arians to Gentiles, as worshippers of two gods; the Arian logos not being of the same substance with the Father; and therefore a maker of the world, or a God, quite distinct from him.

Gregory Nazianzen also represents the heretics as drawing many to them by their interpretation of the scriptures †.

---

* Ουκυν, ει ψιλω παραμενει τω γραμματι, η κατα τυτο το μερος Ιυδαιζει τη γνωμη, η υπω πεπαιδευται ότι υχι γραμματος ετι χριστιανος μαθητης, αλλα πνευματος. το γαρ γραμμα, φησιν, απεκτεινε, το δε πνευμα ζωοποιει. Contra Eunomium Oratio 16. Opera. vol. 2. p. 311.

† Τας δε παρα των θειων γραφων, ενστασεις τε η ανθιθεσεις αις οι τυ γραμματος ιερυσυλυι, η τον νυν των γεγραμμενων κλεπλοντες τας πολλας σφετεριζονται, η την οδον της αληθειας ταρασσυτι. Or. 36. Opera, p. 577.

With

CHAP. XVIII. *of ancient Unitarians.* 425

With respect to the Old Testament, it was the general complaint of the orthodox that the unitarians interpreted it as the Jews did, and proved the doctrine of the unity of God from it. I therefore do not need to mention many of their arguments. Justin Martyr pretended to prove from the appearance to Moses in the bush, that it was not Jehovah himself who spake to him, but Christ. But Marcellus argues from the same thing, in favour of his doctrine, probably considering the God that spake from the bush as the Supreme Being, who was self-existent, and had no rival; for Eusebius says, that "Marcellus argued from "*I am that I am*.*"

Of the unitarians alledging, Deut. vi. 6. *Hear O Israel the Lord thy God is one Lord,* and also, Isa. xli. 4. *I am the first and I am the last,* and *besides me there is no other* (a text almost as celebrated as that of Moses) I could produce numberless instances, and they are both generally alledged at the same time. Marcellus, after quoting the latter,

* Ec. Theol. lib. 2. cap. 19. p. 130.

says,

says, "There is therefore no younger God, "nor any other besides the God who is the "last, able to co-operate with God *."

It has been seen, that the trinitarians endeavoured to prove the divinity of Christ from the Old Testament. On the other hand, the unitarians were not wanting, on their part, to prove his simple humanity from it.

Theodotus urged, Deut. xviii. 13. *A prophet shall the Lord thy God raise up unto thee, of thy brethren like unto me* †. And certainly, if he was to be like Moses, he could not be God.

The unitarians argued from Pf. cx. *(Thou art a priest for ever after the order of Mel-*

---

* Εγω γαρ ειμι, φησι, θεος πρωτος, κ̓ εγω μετα ταυτα, κ̓ πλην εμε θεος έτερος εκ εστιν. ετε εν νεωτερος τις θεος εστιν, ετε αλλος τις μετα ταυτα θεος ων, θεω συνεργειν δυνατος ην. Eusebius Contra Marcellum, lib. 2. p. 41.

† Και παλιν δε ο αυτος Θεοδοτος φησι, κ̓ ο νομος περι αυτε εφη, Προφητην εκ των αδελφων υμων εγερει κυριος ως εμε· αυτε ακεσετε. Μωυσης δε ην ανθρωπος. ο δε εκ θεε εγειρομενος, φησι, χριστος ετος εκ ην θεος αλλα ανθρωπος· επειδη εξ αυτε ν ην, κ̓ Μωυσης ανθρωπος ην. Epiphanius, Hær. 54. Opera, vol. 1. p. 461.

chizedek)

CHAP. XVIII. *of ancient Unitarians.*

chizedek) *that Christ was* inferior to Melchizedek *.

Theodotus argued from If. liii. in which the Messiah is foretold as to be a *man of sorrows*, &c. †.

It is remarkable that the *wisdom*, of which Solomon gives a figurative description in the book of Proverbs, had been so long interpreted to mean *Christ*, that even Marcellus allowed it, and made use of it to prove, that Christ was a creature, as the Arians did, and thought that it referred to his human nature only ‡. A much better, and a more natural, interpretation is, that it has no reference to Christ at all.

* Και ως ειναι τ8ον 8 μονον δυναμιν τινα, αλλα κ, μειζοτερον τ8 χριςε φασκεσι, χριςον δε ηγεινται απλως εληλυθοια, κ, καταξιωθεντα της εκεινε ταξεως, δηθεν εκ ρητε τε ειρημενε, συ ει ιερευς εις τον αιωνα καια την ταξιν Μελχισεδεκ. ως ειναι, φησιν, αυτον ετι υποδεεςερον τε Μελχισεδεκ. Epiphan. Hær. 55. p. 468.

† Ειτα ο αυτος παλιν φησι Θεοδοτ@-, οτι κ, Εσαιας περι αυτε εφη, οτι ανθρωπος εςιν, 8τως ειπων, ανθρωπ@- ειδως φερειν μαλακιαν· κ, ειδομεν αυτον εν πληγη, κ, εν κακωσει κ, ητιμασθη, και 8κ ελογισθη. Ibid. Hær. 54. p. 466.

‡ Το τοινυν κεφαλαιον τ8τι της παροιμιας, 8 την αρχην της θεοτητ@-, ωσπερ αυτοι νομιζ8σι, τ8 σωτηρος ημων παραςησαι β8λομενον, κυριος εκτισε με, εφη, αλλα την δευτεραν καια σαρκα οικονομιαν. Euseb. con. Marcellum, lib. 2. p. 45.

Dr.

Dr. Lardner difcovers traces of Nazaræan, or Sabellian interpretations of fcripture in Eufebius, which he accounts for by fuppofing, that they were borrowed from fome other writer, and inferted into his own work, which, he fays, was a frequent method with chriftian commentators. He gives the following inftances:

"All the Father's grace was poured out upon the beloved, for it was the Father that fpake in him." Again, upon Pf. lxxii. "This righteoufnefs of the Father is given to the king's fon, of the feed of David, according to the flefh, in whom, as in a temple, dwelled the word, and wifdom, and righteoufnefs of God."

Once more, referring to Ifaiah lxi. 1. and Luke iv. 18. "fhewing," fays he, "that his was not a bodily anointing, like that of others, but that he was anointed with the fpirit of the Father's deity, and therefore called *Chrift* *."

---

* Επει δε τ8 αγαπηλ8 πασα η πατρικη εις αυτον εκενωθη χαρις· ην γαρ ο πατηρ λαλων εν υιω. Αυτη τοινυν η τ8 πατρος δικαιοσυνη τω υιω τ8 βασιλεως δεδοται, τω εκ σπερματος Δαυιδ κατα σαρκα. εν ω κατωκησεν ωσπερ ναω ο τ8 θε8 λογος, και η σοφια, και δικαιοσυνη. Διδασκων,

CHAP. XVIII. *of ancient Unitarians.* 429

Well might Gregory Nyssen, and others, complain of the advantage which the unitarians derived from the literal interpretation of the *New Testament*, which it is hardly possible to open without finding a decisive argument against the trinitarian system. I shall give some examples of the arguments which the ancient unitarians drew from it.

In proof of the proper unity of God, Marcellus argued from Mark xii. 28. *There is one God, and there is no other but he* *.

The inferiority of the Son to the Father, the unitarians proved from a variety of circumstances, one of which was, Christ being called a *servant*; and they chose to adhere to that language in speaking of Christ, that they might honour the Father. " On what

δασκω", τω δε πνευματι της πατρικης θεοτητ۞ κεχρισμενον, και δια τελο χριτον ανηγορευμενον. Credibility, vol. 8. p. 82.

* Αλλ' ο μεν γραμματευς, δια τε νομε θεοσεβειαν μεμαθηκεναι δοκων, επαινων το τε Σωτηρος ρητον φαινεται, ακεε Ισραηλ, λεγων, κυριο, ο θεος σε εις εςι · και ορκω καλως ειρησθαι πιςευομενον · επ αληθειας γαρ φησιν, ειπας, οτι εις εςιν ο θεος και εκ εςιν αλλος πλην αυτε. οι δε τα της νεας διαθηκης αυχεντες ειδεναι μυτηρια, ετοι και δευτερον αναπλατίειν θεον βελονται υποςασει και δυναμει χωριζομενον τε πατρς. Euseb. Ec. Theol. lib. 2. cap. 19. p. 131.

" account,"

"account," says Chrysostom, "do you call Christ a servant? That we may honour the Father. But the Son says, that all men may honour the Son, even as they honour the Father*."

The unitarians urged, that, as a servant, Christ was *sent* by the Father, being subject to his orders. This, they also said, was a proof that Christ was not omnipresent. It may be curious to see what Chrysostom said in answer to this argument. "To be sent of God," says he, "does not imply removal from place to place, but the manifestation of the œconomy. Concerning John the Baptist, who was of the earth, and who appeared upon the earth, the gospel says, There was a man sent from God †."

---

* Τινος δε ενεκεν αυτον υπυργον φατε· ινα τιμησωμεν τον πατερα. χ) μην ο υιος φησιν; ινα παντες τιμωσι τον υιον καθως τιμωσι τον πατερα. In Ps. Opera, vol 3. p. 121.

† Οτι το απεταλθαι παρα του θευ, υ την απο τοπων εις τοπυς μεταςασιν σημαινει αλλα της οικονομιας την φανερωσιν. Περι Ιωαννυ τυ βαπτιςου λεγει το ευαγγελιον τυ απο γης οντος, και απο γης φανερωθεντος. Εγενετο ανθρωπος απεςαλμενος παρα θευ. Ser. 5. Opera, vol. 6. p. 59.

CHAP. XVIII. *of ancient Unitarians.* 431

When the unitarians were urged with the Father and the Son being said to be *one*, they said that they were one by consent and harmony, and proved it from Christ's saying, that his disciples might be one with them, as they two were one*.

The reward that was given to Christ, on account of his services and sufferings, was alledged by the ancient unitarians as a proof of his having been employed by God as his servant, and that he had no dignity before. " The heretics," says Chrysostom, " urge " that Christ was advanced on account of " his sufferings. But he replies, that men- " tion is made by John of his dignity before " his suffering †." The unitarians likewise

---

* Quando igitur ad evertendam naturalem trinitatis identitatem, hunc locum in medium hæreticus affert, quemadmodum dicens, nos non identitate absoluta corporum, nec animarum alterius in alteram confusione unum sumus; sed affectu charitatis, animarumque ad servanda mandata dei consensu; sic et unum filius cum patre est. Cyril Alex. in Joan. lib. 11. p. 987.

† Διο και ο θεος αυτον υπερυψωσε· δια το παθος, ως μισθον τε παθους δεδωκως αυτω την υψωσιν. Παυλος λεγεις, αιρετικε και εσ̇κει αυτω ονομα υπερ παν ονομα. Ινα εν τω ονοματι, Ιησυ παν γονυ καμψη, επυρανιων, και επιγειων, και καταχθονιων. Ορας φησι, μετα τον ςαυρον υψωθη, ορας, φησι, μετα το παθος μισθον ελαβε την υψωσις.

urged the Father raising the Son from the dead *.

The gospels were thought to furnish the strongest arguments for the simple humanity of Christ; and this was urged with the more force, as it was acknowledged by the orthodox, that the three first gospels did not teach his divinity. But the ancient unitarians brought as many arguments from the gospel of John, as from any of the others.

We learn from Epiphanius, that Theodotus urged, Luke i. 35. *The spirit of the Lord shall come upon thee;* arguing that he did not enter into her, as the orthodox supposed †; and, John viii. 40. *Ye seek to kill me, a* MAN *who told you the truth* ‡. Austin says, that the Sabellians

σιν. Ει τοινυν μετα τον ςαυρον υψωθη, ως υμεις φατε, δια τι ο βαπτιςης Ιωαννης προ τε παθες, προ τε ςαυρου ελεγεν. Ser. 4. Opera, vol. 6. p. 33.

* Αλλ' επιπηδωσιν οι αιρετικοι λεγοντες, ιδε ο πατηρ εγειρει τον υιον. Chrysostom in Gal. 1. Opera, vol. 10. p. 965.

† Ειτα, φησι, και το ευαγγελιον εφη τη Μαρια, πνευμα κυριε επελευσεται επι σε, και εκ ειπε πνευμα κυριε γεννηθεται εν σοι. Hær. 54. Opera, vol. 1. p. 465.

‡ Και οι απ' αυτε συναχθεντες Θεοδοτιανοι, ψιλον ανθρωπον φασκοντες ειναι τον χριστον, και εκ σπερματος ανδρος γεγενησθαι. ειτα εις κακην εαυτων απολογιαν οταπερ χρησιμα ευρεν, εχ αγιως οιομενω,
αλλα

CHAP. XVIII. *of ancient Unitarians.* 433

urged, John vii. 6. *My doctrine is not mine* *. Basil's enemies quoted against him John vi. 57. *I live by the Father* †.

It is remarkable enough, that both Chrysostom and Theophylact blame Paulus Samosatensis for making a pause before the words, *Marvel not at this,* John v. 27. as if they would connect them with the account of God's giving all judgment to the Son ‡. For all

αλλα προφασει της εαυτε παρεκτροπης ταυτα εαυτω επισωρευων συνηγαγεν. ὁτι φησιν, ὁ κυριος εφη· νυν δε ζητειτε με αποκτειναι ανθρωπον, ος την αληθειαν υμιν λελαληκα. ορας φησιν, ὁτι ανθρωπος εστιν. Hær. 54. Opera, vol. 1. p. 463.

* Utique si tua doctrina non est tua, O domine, cujus est nisi alius sit cujus sit? Quod dixisti, Sabelliani non intelligunt: non enim trinitatem viderunt, sed sui cordis errorem secuti sunt. Nos cultores trinitatis et unitatis patris et filii et spiritus sancti, et unius dei, intelligimus de doctrina Christi, quomodo non est ejus. In John, Tr. 29. cap. 7. Opera, vol. 9 p. 246.

† Τα δε ρηματα της θειας γραφης, απερ λαμβανοντες οι αντικειμενοι και διαστρεφοντες προς την οικειαν συνειδησιν εις καθαιρεσιν της δοξης τε μονογενες ημιν προσφερουσιν, εως εξετασομεν, και το δυνατον ημιν αναπτυσσοντες αυτα. και πρωτον ημιν προτιθεσθω το, εγω ζω δια τον πατερα. τετο γαρ εστιν εν των βελων των εις ερανον πεμπομενων υπο των ασεβων αυτω κεχρημενων. Epist. 141. Opera, vol. 3. p. 166.

‡ Χρη δε γινωσκειν ὁτι Παυλος ὁ Σαμοσατευς ψιλον ανθρωπον δογματιζων τον κυριον εως ανεγινωσκε τετο το χωριον, και εξεσιαν εδωκεν αυτω

Vol. III.   F f

our printed bibles are now divided, as Paulus Samosatensis and his followers had pointed the passage; and the punctuation received by Chrysostom and Theophylact is followed by no person.

Epiphanius says that Theodotus argued from Acts ii. 22. where Peter calls Christ *a man approved of God**. And indeed it was acknowledged by the orthodox, that, in all the period to which the history of Luke extends, the apostles did not openly preach such offensive doctrines as those of the pre-existence and divinity of Christ.

The unitarians found a variety of solid arguments in the *apostolical epistles*. There is hardly any text of which the trinitarians avail themselves more than Phil. ii. 6. *Who being in the form of God, thought it no robbery to be equal to God.* But even this text the ancient unitarians thought favourable to themselves. Epiphanius says, the here-

αυίω και κρισιν ποιειν ότι υιος ανθρωπε εςιν. ενίαυθα δε ριζων, απ αλλης αρχης ανεγινωσκε το, μη θαυμαζηίε τδίε. In John. cap. 5. vol. 1. p. 632. See Chrysostom, vol. 8. p. 201.

* Αλλα, φησιν, ειπον οι αποςολοι, ανδρα αποδεδειγμενον εις υμας σημειοις η τερασι η εκ ειπον θεον αποδεδειγμενον. Hær. 54. Opera, vol. 1. p. 467.

tics

CHAP. XVIII. *of ancient Unitarians.* 435

tics avail themselves of this text, "as if it meant that Christ would not by robbery make himself equal to God*." i. e. it would have been robbery if he had done so. Chrysostom also says, that the Arians prove that Christ is not God from this text, saying, that Christ being in the form of God, did not seize upon an equality with God; ουκ ηρπασε †?

Lardner observes that Origen understood this text as expressive of the humanity of Christ ‡, and that it seems to have been so understood in an epistle from the churches of Vienna and Lyons, they supposing the apostle to have meant that to be *equal*, or *like to* God, Christ did not think a thing to be catched at §.

Theophylact, commenting on Eph. iv. 6. *One God, and Father of all, who is above all,*

---

* Ου γαρ ειπεν, ουκ ηθελησε γενεσθαι ισος θεω δι αρπαγμα. αλλ' ουχ αρπαγμον ηγησατο ειναι ισα θεω, το θεον ειναι φυσει, ὁτι ην. Ancoratus, sect. 45. Opera, vol. 2. p. 50.

† Αλλα τις ο σοφος αυτων λογος, ἡ μην τουναντιον δεικνυσι, φησι. ειπε γαρ ὁτι εν μορφη θεου υπαρχων, ουχ ηρπασε το ειναι ισα θεω. ἡ μην ει ην θεος, πως ειχεν αρπασαι. In Phil. 2. Opera, vol. 10. p. 1240.

‡ Credibility, vol. 3. p. 399. § Ibid. vol. 1. p. 339.

and through all, and in you all, observes that the heretics thought that the preposition διa (*through*) was peculiar to the Son, and εν (*in*) to the Spirit; both implying inferiority; whereas he says they are now both applied to the Father *."

In Coll. i. 15. Christ is called the *first born of every creature*. On this Marcellus said, " How could he who existed always " be the first-born of any thing; but *the* " *first new man*, in whom God would that " all things should be collected; the holy " scriptures calling him the first-born of " the creation †." Cyril of Alexandria, also says, " They continually urge the more " simple with the word *first-born* ‡."

---

* Σημειωσαι δε οτι οι μεν αιρετικοι την, δια, προθεσιν αποκληρυσι τω υιω, κỳ την, εν, τω πνευματι, ως ελαττωσιν εισαγυσαν. νυν δε τω πατρι ευρισκονται προσκειμεναι. εκ αρα ελαττωσεως. Vol. 2. p. 533.

† Πως γαρ δυνατον, τον αει οντα, πρωτοτοκον ειναι τινος, αλλα τον πρωτον καινον ανθρωπον, εις ον τα παντα ανακεφαλαιωσασθαι εβυληθη ο θεος. τυτον αι θειαι γραφαι πρωτοτοκον πασης ονομαζυσι κτισεως. Euseb. contra Marcellum, lib. 2. p. 44.

‡ Semper insipienter dicunt nomen primogenitus simplicioribus objicientes. De Trinitate, lib. 4. Opera, vol. 2. p. 415.

But the two decisive texts in proof of the unity of God, and the proper humanity of Christ, in this epistle, are the following: Eph. iv. 5. *One Lord, one faith, one baptism, one God and Father of all, who is above all, and through all, and in you all*; which was urged, as Eusebius informs us, by Marcellus*; and 1 Tim. ii. 5. *There is one God, and one mediator between God and man, the man Christ Jesus*; which was pleaded by the same †. This was also alledged by Photinus ‡.

* Και παλιν ειναι τον πατερα [και] τον υιον επιδειξαι πειρωμενος ἑτω γραφει· αυτος γαρ ομολογει λεγων, εν εμοι ο πατηρ, καγω εν τω πατρι· ὁτι δε τᾳτο ᾳχ απλως ᾳδε ασκοπως ειρηκε, δηλον [αν] και αφ' ἑτερας αποτολικης ρησεως. εις γαρ ο, ειπων, κυριος, μια πιστις, εν βαπτισμα, εις θεος εφη, ᾗ πατηρ, ο επι παντων ᾗ δια παντων, ᾗ εν πασιν Ec. Theol. lib. 2. cap. 19. p. 131.

* Νυν αυτον συκοφαντει, ως ψιλον ανθρωπον λεγοντα ειναι τον χριστον, προφανως καταψευδομενος, εν τε οις ειρηκε, ᾗ εν οις εξης επαγει αυθις περι αυτα λεγων· αλλ' ο προειρημενος, βραχεα των αγιων προφητων φρονησας, ως απορρητον τινα ᾗ λανθανεσαν τε αποτολα θεολογιαν εξηγαμενος, εις θεος εφη, εις ᾗ μεσιτης θεα ᾗ ανθρωπων, ανθρωπος Ιησας χριστος. Euseb. Con. Marcellum, lib. 1. p. 28.

† Hoc si timemus, deleamus in apostolo quod dictum est: mediator dei et hominum homo Christus Jesus, quia ad authoritatem hæresis suæ Photinus hoc utitur: et non legatur a nobis, quia ab illo male intelligatur. Hil. Ad Arianos, Opera, p. 392.

If my readers only compare these unitarian interpretations of scripture with those made by the trinitarians, in a former part of the work, he must be sensible, without any assistance from me, how infinitely more natural these are than those. The wonder is, that any other sense should ever have been put upon them. The history, however, that I have given of the rise of the doctrine of the trinity, solves this difficulty, and shows the necessity the trinitarians were under of wresting the scriptures so miserably as they did.

Παλιν δε προφασιζεται λεγων, ὁτι εφη περι αυτε ὁ αποστολος, ὁτι μεσιτης θεε κ᾽ ανθρωπων χριςος Ιησες. Epiphanius, Hær. 54. Opera, vol. 1. p. 467.

CHAP.

CHAPTER XIX.

Of the Practice of the Unitarians with respect to Baptism.

THE form of baptism, supposed to be prescribed in the gospel of Matthew, viz. *in the name of the Father, the Son, and the Holy Spirit,* and the *trine immersion,* which was used along with it, contributed very much to establish the doctrine of the trinity. It was natural enough, therefore, for the unitarians to oppose this superstition by discontinuing the practice; though it is probable that the custom itself was an innovation. That it was not in use from the beginning, is pretty evident from there being no trace of it in the New Testament, though we are not able to say at what time it began. However, that many persons did not baptize in this manner, before, as well as after, the council of Nice, is evident from the decrees of that council, and other proceedings

ceedings of a similar nature; and this was the foundation of the different treatment of those who were called heretics, when they returned into the bosom of the church. For if they had been baptized in the usual form, their baptism was deemed to be *valid*, how heretical soever the church had been in which they had received it; but if they had not been baptized in that particular form, it was decreed that they should be rebaptized.

In what manner the unitarians, who disapproved of the common form, *did* baptize their catechumens, does not clearly appear. But it should seem that some of them baptized *in the name of Christ only*, and others *into the death of Christ*, which they probably adopted from that expression of the apostle Paul. It appears from Basil, that " some held that it was sufficient to " baptize in the name of Christ*." And the canons which are ascribed to the apostles ordered that " if any bishop did " not use trine immersion, but baptized

---

* Προς τες λεγοντας εξαρκειν κ; μονον το εις τον κυριον βαπλισμα. De Sp. S. cap. 12. Opera, vol. 2. p. 315.

" only

"only into the death of Christ, he should be deposed *."

The Eunomians, Theodoret says, baptized in this form, and also did not immerse the whole body, but only applied the water to certain parts of it †.

According to Athanasius, all the unitarians did not object to the common form of baptism; for, he says, both the Manicheans and Paulus Samosatensis baptized in the common form ‡. But they must in general have disliked that form; because it was decreed at the council of Nice, that the Paulianists, returning to the church, should be rebaptized §. Austin also says, that "the

---

* Ει τις επισκοπος, η πρεσβυτερος μη τρια βαπτισματα μιας μυήσεως επιτελεσει, αλλα εν βαπτισμα εις τον θανατον τε κυρια διδομενον, καθαιρεισθω. Zonaras, p. 26. Canon 50.

† Μη χρηναι λεγων τρις καταδυειν τον βαπτιζομενον, μη δε ποιεισθαι την της τριαδος επικλησιν. αλλ᾽ απαξ βαπτιζειν εις τον θανατον τε χριστε. κỳ βαπτιζοντες δε μεχρι των τερνων τω υδατι δευσι, τοις δε αλλοις μοριοις τε σωματος ως εναγεσι προσφερειν το υδωρ απαγορευουσιν. Hær. Fab. lib. 4. Opera, vol. 4. p. 356. Ed Halæ.

‡ Ουτω Μανιχαιοι κỳ Φρυγες κỳ οι τε Σαμοσαιεως μαθηται, τα ονοματα λεγοντες, ουδεν ηττον εισιν αιρετικοι. Contra Arianos, Or. 3. Opera, vol. 1. p. 413.

§ Περι των Παυλιανισαντων ειτα προσφυγοντων τη καθολικη εκκλησια ορος εκτεθειται αναβαπτιζεσθαι αυτες εξαπαντος. Canon 19. Zonaras, p. 64.

"Paulians

"Paulians were ordered to be rebaptized by the council of Nice; from which," he says, " it is evident, that they did not observe the rule of baptism, which many heretics, though they left the catholic church, did *." Pope Innocent also would not receive the Paulianists without baptizing, " because they did not baptize in the name of the Father, the Son, and the Spirit, as the Novatians did †."

* Istos sane Paulianos baptizandos esse in ecclesia catholica Nicæno concilio constitutum est. Unde credendum est eos regulam baptismatis non tenere, quam secum multi hæretici cum de catholica discederent abstulerunt, eamque custodiunt. Catalogus Hær. Opera, vol. 6. p. 30.

† Unde prædictus papa Innocentius, cum de duabus hæresibus Paulianistis videlicet, et Novatianistis communiter disputaret, cur a Paulianistis venientes baptizandos esse decerneret, a Novatianis autem funditus prohiberet, causam his reddidit verbis, dicens: quia Paulianistæ, inquit, in nomine patris, et filii, et spiritus sancti minime baptizantur, nec apud istos, videlicet Novatianos, de unitate patris et filii, et spiritus sancti quæstio aliquando mota est. Damiani Epist. cap. 23. Bib. pat. App. p. 634.

Paulianistæ in nomine patris et filii et spiritus sancti minime baptizabant. At Novatiani iisdem nominibus tremendis vinerandisque baptizant, nec apud ipsos de unitate potestatis divinæ, hoc est et patris, et filii, et spiritus sancti, aliquando quæstio commota est. Epist. P. Innocentie ad Macedoniæ Episcopos, Apud Binnii Concilia, vol. 1. p. 620.

At a council held at Carthage, in 419, the Paulianists were ordered to be rebaptized*. And at the council of Constantinople, the Montanists, Eunomians, and Sabellians, were all ordered, after much preparation, in which exorcism was not omitted, to be rebaptized when they returned to the catholic church†. This seems to show, that the unitarians in general, and also the most zealous Arians, refused to make use of the common form of baptism; and it is probable that they continued to do so till a very late period, if, indeed, they ever dropped it at all. For Damascenus, who wrote in the eighth cen-

* De Paulianistis refugientibus ad ecclesiam catholicam definitio prolata est rebaptizare omnino. Binnii Concilia, vol. 1. p. 726.

† Ευνομιανως μεν]οι τας εις μιαν καταδυσιν βαπ]ιζομενας, και Μον]ανιτας τας εν]αυθα λεγομενας Φρυγας, και Σαβελλιανας τας μιοπα]οριαν διδασκον]ας, και ε]ερα τινα χαλεπα ποιαν]ας, και τας αλλας πασας αιρεσεις (επειδη πολλοι εισιν εν]αυθα, μαλιτα δι απο της Γαλα]ων χωρας ερχομενοι) παν]ας τας υπ αυ]ων θελον]ας προτιθεσθαι, τη ορθοδοξια ως Ελληνας δεχομεθα, και την πρω]ην ημεραν ποιαμεν αυ]ας χριτιανας, την δε δευ]εραν κα]ηχαμενας, ει]α τη τρι]η εξορκιζομεν αυ]ας με]α τα εμφυσαν τρι]ον εις το προσωπον και εις τα ω]α, και α]ως κα]ηχαμεν αυ]ας, και ποιαμεν χρονιζειν εις την εκκλησιαν, και ακροασθαι των γραφα και το]ε αυ]ας βαπ]ιζομεν... Canon 7. Zonaras, p. 77.

tury, says, that " they who had not been baptized into the holy trinity, ought to be re-baptized.*." It is to be hoped, that the unitarians of the present age will imitate their predecessors, by baptizing, as the apostles did, in *the name of Christ* only, without the invocation of the Father, Son, and Holy Ghost, or expressing what they apprehend to be the real meaning of that phraseology.

* At qui in sanctam trinitatem minime baptizati sunt, hi denuo baptizentur necesse est. Orthod. Fid. lib. 3. cap. 10. p. 446.

END OF THE THIRD VOLUME.

www.ingramcontent.com/pod-product-compliance
Lightning Source LLC
Chambersburg PA
CBHW022134300426
44115CB00006B/176